P9-BYL-826

# contemporary newspaper design

## a structural approach

**mario r. garcia**
*Syracuse University*
*S. I. Newhouse School of Public Communications*

prentice-hall, inc., englewood cliffs, n.j. 07632

*Library of Congress Cataloging in Publication Data*

GARCIA, MARIO R
    Contemporary newspaper design.

    Bibliography: p.
    Includes index.
    1. Newspaper layout and typography.  I. Title.
Z253.G27     686.2'24    80-24936
ISBN 0-13-170381-1 (case)
ISBN 0-13-170373-0 (pbk.)

*To my wife Maria*

© 1981 by Prentice-Hall, Inc., Englewood Cliffs, N.J. 07632

All rights reserved. No part of this book
may be reproduced in any form or
by any means without permission in writing
from the publisher.

Printed in the United States of America

10  9  8  7  6  5

Editorial/production supervision by Virginia Rubens
Design by Mario R. Garcia, Virginia Rubens and Maureen Olsen
Page layout by Gail Cocker
Art production by Bob Verbeek, Debbie Watson, and Bruce Kenselaar
Cover design by Mario R. Garcia, assisted by Randy Stano, Assistant Art Director, Kansas City
    *Star and Times*
Manufacturing buyer: Harry P. Baisley

PRENTICE-HALL INTERNATIONAL, INC., *London*
PRENTICE-HALL OF AUSTRALIA PTY. LIMITED, *Sydney*
PRENTICE-HALL OF CANADA, LTD., *Toronto*
PRENTICE-HALL OF INDIA PRIVATE LIMITED, *New Delhi*
PRENTICE-HALL OF JAPAN, INC., *Tokyo*
PRENTICE-HALL OF SOUTHEAST ASIA PTE. LTD., *Singapore*
WHITEHALL BOOKS LIMITED, WELLINGTON, *New Zealand*

# contents

**1**

## design alone won't do it *18*

**2**

## redefining the role of the newspaper: three challenges *25*

**3**

## the front page *32*

**20 design and the new technology 226**

A book often involves contributions from many individuals. Such is the case with *Contemporary Newspaper Design: A Structural Approach.* I have been fortunate enough to receive suggestions, ideas, sample pages, and encouragement from many men and women who share an interest in newspapers and who think that newspapers should be attractive and readable.

First, I am most grateful to my good friends Professor Barbara Garfunkel and Dr. Arthur M. Sanderson for reading the manuscript and offering valuable suggestions.

For their continued support during the planning and research stages of the manuscript, I would like to express sincere thanks to my colleagues at the S.I. Newhouse School of Public Communications, Syracuse University: Dean Henry F. Schulte, Dr. Maxwell McCombs, Samuel V. Kennedy III and C. Marshall Matlock.

Special thanks to Joseph Ungaro, of the Rockland-Westchester Newspapers, for his willingness to share timely information concerning the new technology; to Wallace Allen, associate editor of the *Minneapolis Tribune;* and to Frank Ariss, of Ariss & Eaton Design Corporation of Minneapolis, for allowing me to spend time with them while researching Chapter 19.

To the many who contributed materials for illustration and to all who had encouraging words for the project, I am grateful:

- James N. Allison Jr., *Midland* (Texas) *Reporter Telegram*
- N. Christian Anderson, *Seattle Times*
- Paul Back, *Newsday*
- John Bodette, *St. Cloud Daily Times*
- Les Bridges, *Chicago Tribune*
- John E. A. Brooks, *Toronto Star*
- Vic Cantone, *Editor & Publisher*
- Michael Carroll, *Minneapolis Tribune*

- Jim Clark, Orlando *Sentinel*
- Richard Curtis, *Baltimore News American*
- Michael J. Davies, *Kansas City Star and Times*
- Geoffrey Edwards, Journal Newspapers (Washington, D.C.)
- David Eisele, *North County News* (Yorktown, N.Y.)
- Roger Fidler, Knight-Ridder Newspapers
- Edward M. Gottschall, International Typeface Corporation
- Gus Hartoonian, *Chicago Tribune*
- Larry Hale, American Press Institute
- Robert Healy, *Boston Globe*
- Frank Hoy, Arizona State University
- Stephen Kent, *Yakima* (Washington) *Herald-Republic*
- Michael Killelea, *Boston Herald American*
- Howard Kleinberg, *Miami News*
- Robert Lockwood, *Allentown Morning Call*
- Drake Mabry, *Des Moines Tribune*
- Mal Malette, American Press Institute
- Richard Manville, Brown Newspapers (Baldwinsville, N.Y.)
- Robert Mellis, *Miami Herald*
- JoAnne O'Doherty, *Suffolk County* (N.Y.) *News*
- Peter Palazzo, Palazzo and Associates, New York
- James F. Paschal, University of Oklahoma
- W. Frank Peters, *St. Petersburg Times*
- Frank Quine, American Press Institute
- Phillip Ritzenburg, *New York Daily News*
- Stephen Rogers, *Syracuse Post-Standard*
- Jerry Ryan, *Louisville Courier-Journal*
- Janet Sanford, American Press Institute
- Lou Silverstein, *New York Times*
- Harry L. Sonnebord, *Milwaukee Sentinel*
- Carol Sutton, *Louisville Courier-Journal and Times*
- Carl A. Veno, *Free Press* (Quakertown, Pa.)
- Barney Waters, *Today* (Cocoa, Fl.)
- Ben Van Zante, West High School, Iowa City, Iowa

I was fortunate to work with illustrators like Greg Daily and Michael Freed, who paid attention to every detail as they prepared the many sketches throughout the book; photographers John H. Scott and William Thompson were most helpful and so were Darryl Grandy, of Syracuse Lithographing, whose task was to reduce hundreds of newspaper tearsheets to the size in which you see them in this book, and Randy Stano, my graduate assistant, who contributed ideas for the cover design. This project would never have been possible without the encouragement and continued support of my Prentice-Hall editor, William Oliver, and Lisa Femmel, of Prentice-Hall's College Division. My personal thanks also to Virginia Rubens, who served as production editor. Finally, thanks to my patient and devoted family, including my sons Mario and Brian, whose help with filing and categorizing illustrations is greatly appreciated.

Mario R. Garcia
Syracuse, New York

introduction

The look of American newspapers is rapidly changing. Better packaging, more white space, new typefaces, larger photographs, more organized positioning of advertising, and a new surge of graphic creativity are all part of this new look.

Editors are making a conscious attempt to create a timely, relevant, and visually attractive package for the day's news. In many newsrooms across the nation there is a graphics editor whose task it is to coordinate the way words and other visual images will combine to make the message clearer and more attractive. These graphics editors are no longer isolated as part of the advertising art staff, or labeled as ''art people.'' Instead, the graphics editor is an integral part of the day-to-day operation of the newsroom, a sort of translator of news messages into visual statements. Some call these new arrivals in the newsroom *graphic journalists*. The demand for journalists who have training in basic journalistic skills combined with design skills—typographic training, the ability to organize disconnected statements to make them look unified and easy to read—has never been greater, and it is likely to increase within the next ten years.

The decade of the 1970s marked the beginning of new interest in newspaper design—an interest which spread across the newsrooms of newspapers of all sizes. This new interest in newspaper design has manifested itself in different ways, mostly through the growing number of dailies and weeklies which have changed their appearance, but also through the participation of news personnel in seminars and workshops to make them more graphically aware. At the American Press Institute in Reston, Virginia, at least two newspaper design seminars are held yearly, and officials there report that the waiting list for prospective participants always includes more members than can be accommodated. The American Newspaper Publishers Association (ANPA) devoted a segment of its 1979 convention to newspaper design. Two of the ANPA *Research Bulletins* in 1980 dealt with design and its effects on readership. And to make things more official, a group of practicing graphic journalists, led by Roger Fidler of the Knight-Ridder Newspapers, Robert Lockwood of the *Allentown* (Pa.) *Morning Call,* and Richard Curtis of the *Baltimore News American,* started the Society of Newspaper Designers in 1979. The group publishes the *Journal of Newspaper Design.* Fidler also edits *Newspaper Design Notebook,* a slick publication and useful guide for newspaper editors and designers that presents visual case studies of redesigned newspapers.

These manifestations of recent interest in newspaper design should not obscure the fact that many newspaper editors have always shown tremendous concern for the visual aspects of their products. What working newspaper editor with years of experience has not been exposed to the theories of Professor Edmund Arnold, a pioneer in the field and one of the strongest advocates of functional and attractive newspaper makeup? Arnold unquestionably paved the way for the changes in graphics that newspapers are experiencing today.

During the 1960s newspapers started to experiment more with typography and design, aided perhaps by the use of cold type and the overall graphics awareness of that decade. Peter Palazzo, of Palazzo and Associates, redesigned the now defunct *New York Herald-World Tribune* in the early 1960s, providing readers of that newspaper wtih memorable visual design during the last two years that it circulated. Unfortunately, Palazzo's graphic ideas could not save a newspaper that had lost many of its readers and, some say, its soul. Palazzo's pages show what must have been considered

Notice the distinctive and elegant look of these four section openers for a Sunday edition of the *Herald-World Tribune,* 1963. The organization, use of white space, large photographs, art, and overall graphic impact must have been considered avant-garde in the 1960s. (Courtesy of Peter Palazzo.)

an avant-garde style for that time: abundant white space (probably a sinful practice by 1960 standards), large photographs, ragged type, departmentalization of content, and a sense of continuity and sequence. Take an issue of the *Herald-World Tribune* of the early 1960s, cover the date and the name, and it could pass for a stylish publication of today. What Palazzo did was to apply the format, design, and graphic strategies of magazines to a large daily newspaper—nothing new by today's standards, but probably a historic accomplishment for Palazzo then.

With the 1970s came greater awareness of graphics among newspaper readers and the need for those in charge of publishing newspapers to produce more graphically attractive pages. Newspapers like *Newsday,* the *Louisville Courier-Journal, Today* (Cocoa, Florida), the *Christian Science Monitor,* and the *Minneapolis Tribune,* among others, experimented with new styles, smaller headlines, larger photographs, and more departmentalization of content. By the mid-1970s newspapers everywhere had given new meaning to the familiar word *style* or, better yet, had added *graphic style* to their publications. Just as editors have always been concerned with appropriate and consistent writing style, they have now become aware of the need to preserve a sense of graphic continuity and sequence throughout the newspaper.

Even the *New York Times,* characterized by a usually gray and congested front page, started to make changes, moving to a six-column format and creating some of the most innovative and beautifully designed inside sections of any newspaper in the country.

Sections such as the ones displayed here and in the following pages are part of what has brought graphic design to the forefront in American newspapers. As readers acquire new and more diversified lifestyles, newspapers are forced to seek means to cater to special audiences whose interests range from fashion to leisure to sports to food. Even the smallest dailies have incorporated weekly sections as part of their standard fare. At the *Chicago Tribune,* editors refer to this change as the *sectional revolution,* and it is taking place not only in the Sunday editions but also in the dailies. These special sections demand the greatest talents and skills in terms of typography and design as well as content.

Many newspapers have created graphically appealing sections on a regular basis without altering the appearance of the news sections, as did the *Dallas Morning News,* a newspaper with a rather conservatively designed front section but with one of the most dazzling fashion sections in the country—and a weekly one at that. ''Fashion!Dallas'' appears every Wednesday with a colorful front page, emphasizing photos and art, and innovative inside pages that blend advertising and editorial content in an appealing and effective manner. ''The design is the key to the success of 'Fashion!Dallas,' '' says editor Ellen Kampinsky. ''We try to package a lot of information, photos and art, while making every page stand out graphically. It is no easy task.''

The 1970s provided an impetus for improved newspaper design—but one that was usually more realistic for large dailies or newspapers with trained designers as part of their staffs. This is likely to change in the future, as smaller dailies and weeklies begin to discover the beneficial effects of design on their publications.

One of the first newspapers to undergo a redesign in 1980 was the *St. Cloud Daily Times,* with a circulation of approximately 29,000 and a devoted staff whose commitment to change made it possible to undergo a major redesign. The staff of the *Times* had moved to a new building in the late 1970s, had acquired the latest computer technology, and was eager and talented enough to carry out the changes. But there was a lot of tradition to uphold, as well as the usual cases of isolated cold feet among editors who did not want to change too much too soon.

The result? A redesign that changed the newspaper typographically but maintained 40 percent of what the St. Cloud readers had grown accustomed to: lots of front-page stories, a familiar eagle as part of the nameplate, and a sense of community journalism. The redesign of the *Times* brought with it a reevaluation of content. New sections were added for ''Food/Consumer,'' ''Business/Farm,'' and ''Bulletin Board.''

For the newspaper's Sunday supplements, Palazzo experimented with type and art. (Courtesy of Peter Palazzo.)

Front pages of the *New York Times* from 1864 and 1980 show that although the six-column format is nothing new to that newspaper, today's front page is more graphic and appealing.

"All the News That's Fit to Print"

# The New York Times

**CITY EDITION**

Metropolitan area weather: Variable cloudiness today, tonight, tomorrow. Temperature range: today 28-41; yesterday 25-40. Details on page B15.

VOL.CXXIX .... No. 44,493 — Copyright © 1980 The New York Times — NEW YORK, THURSDAY, FEBRUARY 14, 1980 — 25 CENTS

## CARTER BACKS AN IRAN COMMISSION AS STEP TOWARD FREEING CAPTIVES; CAUTIONS ON 'EXCESSIVE OPTIMISM'

### BANI-SADR CITES PLAN

Says Khomeini Approves a Secret Formula for the Hostages' Release

By Reuters

TEHERAN, Iran, Feb. 13 — President Abolhassan Bani-Sadr said today that Ayatollah Ruhollah Khomeini had approved a secret plan for the release of the 50 Americans held hostage since Nov. 4.

Mr. Bani-Sadr spoke in a French radio interview after the governing Revolutionary Council, which he heads, reported that Iran had received new proposals for a possible solution but refused to disclose what they were or where they had originated. These developments came before President Carter's news conference in Washington.

While details were being withheld by both President Bani-Sadr and the council, Iranian officials expressed new confidence that the crisis with the United States over the occupation of the American Embassy was moving toward resolution.

**Council Aide Favors Early Solution**

The Revolutionary Council's secretary, Ayatollah Mohammed Beheshti, who previously had taken a hard line on the hostage issue, said at a news conference that Iran's leaders wanted to resolve the crisis "as soon as possible."

He said he thought a settlement could be reached by the time of the elections for a new Iranian Parliament, scheduled to be held March 14. A week ago he said such a development was out of the question.

Similarly, Iran's chief delegate to the United Nations, Mansour Farhang, said today in Geneva that he expected diplomatic moves initiated by Secretary General Kurt Waldheim to lead to the release of the hostages. Mr. Farhang said that an international commission proposed by Mr. Waldheim to investigate Iranian grievances over the rule of the deposed Shah was about to be formed.

A spokesman for the Islamic militants who hold the hostages said, meanwhile, that they would not believe that Aytatollah Khomeini had approved a plan to release the captives until the revolutionary leader personally announced it publicly. The militants have said repeatedly, how-

Continued on Page A17, Column 2

Associated Press

President Carter answering reporter's question at his news conference

### 'SOME POSITIVE SIGNS'

At News Session He Hints Approval of 'Carefully Designed' Inquiry

By HEDRICK SMITH
Special to The New York Times

WASHINGTON, Feb. 13 — President Carter tonight signaled his approval of a "carefully defined" international commission of inquiry into Iranian grievances as a step toward freeing the American hostages held in Teheran for 102 days.

In his first news conference in 11 weeks, the President said he had noted

*Transcript of news session, page A16.*

"some positive signs" recently from Iran, where the new President, Abolhassan Bani-Sadr, has been making proposals for a compromise. But Mr. Carter cautioned against "excessive optimism," and other Administration officials said there was not agreement yet on a formula for releasing the hostages.

Since mid-November, he said, the United States has been discussing the idea of a commission with the Iranians through Kurt Waldheim, the United Nations Secretary General. "No stone has been left unturned," he said.

**'Step Toward Resolution'**

"Recently there have been some positive signs, although experience has taught us to guard against excessive optimism," Mr. Carter declared in an opening statement. "We would support steps by the United Nations that would lead to the release of the hostages if the steps are consistent with our goals and our essential international principles. An appropriate commission with a carefully defined purpose would be a step toward resolution of this crisis."

The Administration has previously refrained from publicly endorsing such an idea, which has become a central element in compromise proposals put forward by Mr. Bani-Sadr. Diplomats at the United Nations have said that until very recently the Americans have conveyed the impression that such a commission could be established only after the 50 American hostages were released.

The President charged that Senator Edward M. Kennedy had exceeded "bounds of both propriety and accuracy" in suggesting recently that he had originated the idea of an investigative commission to break the Iranian deadlock.

**'No Aversion to Campaign'**

Speaking sternly and mounting his most forceful criticism of Mr. Kennedy in the campaign so far, Mr. Carter declared that he had "no aversion to a campaign" but that Senator Kennedy's comments had not been accurate and had been "very damaging to our country."

When asked to respond to Mr. Kennedy's criticism that he had had the idea of

Continued on Page A16, Column 4

UNITED STATES

Associated Press

The United States team in Olympic Stadium at opening of 1980 Winter Games

### Winter Games Under Way In Show of Color and Pomp

By RED SMITH
Special to The New York Times

LAKE PLACID, N.Y., Feb. 13 — With a blaze of color and some hopeful rhetoric, the XIII Olympic Winter Games opened formally today on Lake Placid's snowy horse-show grounds.

After weeks of debate over the location of next summer's Games, which are scheduled for Moscow, after lawsuits involving the flag, the anthem and the emblem to be used by Taiwan, the athletes from 37 nations assembled before a near-capacity crowd of 23,000.

Transportation problems left 1,000 spectators stranded at Whiteface Mountain, about 10 miles away. [Page B17.]

Those who made it to the ceremonies heard Vice President Mondale deliver the traditional pronouncement: "In the name of the President of the United States and the people of the United States, I am happy to declare open the XIII Winter Olympic Games."

The Taiwan delegation, denied the right to appear as the Republic of China, did not participate.

Governor Carey welcomed participants and visitors with the hope that there might be "contests without conflict."

The Rev. J. Bernard Fell, head of the Lake Placid Olympic Organizing Committee, spoke of this village's pride in bringing back the carnival that was staged here in 1932, and added, "We shall be prouder still if we can say that what we did here contributed to the preservation of the Olympic Games."

Lord Killanin of Ireland, president of the International Olympic Committee, made no allusion to the controversies that some have said might spell the end of the Olympic movement. Topcoated but hatless under gray skies, he spoke briefly in introducing Mr. Mondale.

Bundled against a stiff wind that tore

Continued on Page B21, Column 3

### Egypt Says It Is Training Afghans To Fight Soviet-Supported Regime

By CHRISTOPHER S. WREN
Special to The New York Times

CAIRO, Feb. 13 — Some Moslem rebels from Afghanistan are receiving military training in Egypt and will be armed and sent to their homeland to fight against the Soviet-backed Government, Egypt's Minister of Defense said today.

Lieut. Gen. Kamal Hassan Ali, asked at a news conference whether Egypt was providing assistance to Afghan rebels, replied tersely: "It is training some of them to some extent."

He would not say how many Afghans were in Egypt, at what sites they were being trained or what they were being trained to do. But he confirmed that some training camps were in operation. Asked later whether the guerrillas would return to Afghanistan with weapons from Egypt, he replied, "Yes."

The Defense Minister's remarks provided the first confirmation that Egypt had followed up on an offer early last month to help Afghan rebels against the Soviet forces in Afghanistan.

Monsour Hassan, Minister of State for Information, reported early in January that the Political Bureau of President Anwar el-Sadat's National Democratic Party had recommended training Afghans. General Ali alluded to the offer in subsequent interviews.

Egypt's decision to help the Afghan guerrillas is consistent with Mr. Sadat's strong view that the Soviet Union is trying to encircle Egypt and other Arab states and that they must join together to resist the Russians.

Mr. Sadat has responded to the Soviet military intervention in Afghanistan by ordering Moscow to cut its diplomatic staff in Cairo sharply and by expelling the last Soviet civilian technicians.

General Ali, echoing President Sadat's concern in a speech to the Foreign Press Association in Cairo, defended Egypt's request for advanced American arms.

"It is about time to look around us to see the dangers around the area," the De-

Continued on Page A18, Column 1

### FRAUD BY TEACHERS FOUND IN NEW YORK

Gold Says 11 Faked Studies to Get Raises — Sees Wide Abuses

By MARCIA CHAMBERS

The Brooklyn District Attorney charged yesterday that in an investigation of 40 schools in the Bronx and Brooklyn, his office had found that 11 public school teachers forged or falsified training course records to obtain promotions and salary increases. Six other teachers, he said, engaged in serious misconduct or improprieties.

But the District Attorney, Eugene Gold, said that he would not prosecute any of the teachers because school records of "in-service" courses — those administered to teachers by the central Board of Education — were either in a state of disarray, missing or inadequately prepared. In addition to problems with evidence, he said that to file criminal charges against the 17 teachers would be unfair.

They should not be "singled out for committing acts which were rampant throughout the entire New York City school system," the prosecutor said.

Mr. Gold's comments were made in an interview and in a 38-page report that he released at a news conference in his office. The report was based on a nearly

Continued on Page B6, Column 1

Associated Press

Part of battalion of 1,800 U.S. marines bound for the Indian Ocean arriving at naval base at Subic Bay, the Philippines

### Jerseyan Is Deported as Alien, Jailed, Then Freed

By JOSH BARBANEL
Special to The New York Times

NEWARK, Feb. 13 — A United States citizen was detained as an illegal alien in San Juan, P.R., deported to Guatemala and then imprisoned while relatives frantically sought to convince immigration officials that they had deported a native-born American.

The citizen, Norberto Gautier, came home tonight.

State Department officials and representatives of the Immigration and Naturalization Service have refused to provide any details on Mr. Gautier's case. But relatives told of officials who dismissed all documentation, including birth certificates, marriage certificates and baptismal papers, as possible forgeries, while decisions were made on the basis of a consular officer's determination that Mr. Gautier had a Guatemalan accent.

"It appears to be an instance of gross misconduct," said Mr. Gautier's attorney, Jeffrey Fogel, of the Urban Legal Clinic of Rutgers University Law School.

According to relatives, Mr. Gautier's troubles began when he was about to board American Airlines Flight 694 from San Juan to Newark on Jan. 29. He was on his way to his home in Lodi, N.J., after a four-month visit with a brother in Guayanilla, P.R., and had only $8 and his Social Security card in his pocket. Mr. Gautier, who is 42 years old and an unemployed laborer, has lived in the metropolitan area since 1954.

After checking in his suitcase, he said, he was stopped by a uniformed Immigration and Naturalization Service official, who asserted that he was a Guatemalan. Though Mr. Gautier showed his Social Security card and said he was born in Puerto Rico, he was taken to an immigration detention facility in San Juan where

Continued on Page B2, Column 3

"Corrine W. Will you marry me?" Mike S. —Advt.

### Recovery of Art by F.B.I. in 1978 Was Test of 'Abscam' Technique

By GRACE GLUECK

The Arab cover story used by the Federal Bureau of Investigation in its political corruption inquiry was first tested with the successful recovery in 1978 of two 17th-century paintings stolen 14 years ago from a New York art dealer. But the thieves were never brought to trial, apparently because investigators were afraid that it would expose the larger operation that has come to be known as Abscam, for Arab scam.

An account of the links between the corruption inquiry and the earlier operation has emerged from court documents and from interviews with lawyers and others connected with the case.

The paintings, an oil sketch by Peter Paul Rubens and a portrait by Gerard Terborch, were valued at $150,000 each. They disappeared from a Santini Brothers van carrying the household effects of Lawrence A. Fleischman, director of the Kennedy Galleries in New York, when he moved from Michigan in 1966.

*Representative John M. Murphy says happenstance led him to a house used by Federal agents in an undercover investigation. Page B13.*

On Feb. 17, 1978, F.B.I. agents, acting on a tip from an informer, met two men from upstate New York, Dominic Casareale and Arthur Palmer, at Kobelt Airport near Peekskill. Apparently, one of the agents posed as an Arab sheik willing to buy stolen art and, according to an F.B.I. complaint filed in Federal District Court, the agents negotiated with the two men for the sale of the two paintings.

The paintings were found in a Ford van

Continued on Page B10, Column 1

### INSIDE

**P.B.A. Rejects Shotgun Plan**

Delegates of the Patrolmen's Benevolent Association rejected an arrangement to keep one-man radio cars if they were equipped with shotguns. Page B3.

**Chrysler May Not Seek Loan**

Chairman Lee A. Iacocca of the Chrysler Corporation said that because of bank help, the company might not need emergency public financing. Page D1.


| | | | |
|---|---|---|---|
| Around Nation | A20 | Music | C17,C19 |
| Books | C24 | Notes on People | B6 |
| Bridge | C19 | Obituaries | B14,B16 |
| Business Day | D1-15 | Op-Ed | A27 |
| Crossword | C24 | Shipping | B15 |
| Dance | C18,C21 | Sound | C14 |
| Editorials | A26 | Sports | B17-23 |
| Going Out Guide | C14 | Theaters | C19,C23 |
| Home Section | C1-15 | TV/Radio | C24,C27 |
| Man in the News | B13 | U.N. Events | A2 |
| Movies | C21 | Weather | B15 |

News Summary and Index, Page B1


The front page of today's *New York Times* shows more use of photography, fewer stories and an overall organized appearance.

weather sailing
ques, P. 10

U.S. wins
8 of 11
matches
on final day
to capture
Ryder Cup,
17-11,
P. 8

**GOLF**

**FOOTBALL SCOREBOARD**

| Cowboys 24, Bears 20 |
| Steelers 24, Cardinals 21 |
| Broncos 20, Falcons 17 |
| Browns 13, Colts 10 |
| Buccaneers 21, Packers 10 |
| Dolphins 27, Vikings 12 |

Details, P. 5

# SportsMonday

The New York Times

Copyright © 1979 The New York Times    MONDAY, SEPTEMBER 17, 1979    C1

## Expos Regain First

By THOMAS ROGERS

The largest crowd ever to attend a baseball game in Canada, 59,282, jammed Olympic Stadium in Montreal yesterday and saw the Expos move into first place by one percentage point in the National League East.

The big crowd was rewarded for its loyalty. After the Cardinals had won the first game, 4-1, the Expos rallied to win the second, 5-1, in 10 innings and move past the Pittsburgh Pirates.

Montreal opened the day half a game behind the Pirates, who lost to the Mets, 5-0. The Expos proved they were contenders by battling back in the second game. The triumph was their 18th in the last 21 games.

The Expos, who lead the Pirates, 90-4 to 90-5, play Pittsburgh at Montreal tonight and tomorrow night. They play two games in doubleheaders at Shea Stadium against the Mets on Wednesday and Thursday, while the Pirates are in Philadelphia.

In the Western Division race, the Cincinnati Reds opened some ground on the second-place Houston Astros. The Reds, who topped the Dodgers, 3-0, in Los Angeles, hold a 2½-game edge over

Continued on Page C2

Kevin Long of Jets bursting through Lion defense for first down yesterday. Long scored three times in Jet victory.

*The New York Times/Barton Silverman*

## Jets, Behind Todd, Rout Lions, 31-10

By GERALD ESKENAZI

Suddenly, in less than three hours yesterday, the Shea Stadium fans began to love the Jets and Richard Todd again.

And, more important to the future of the team, the Jets renewed their confidence in themselves, posting a 31-10 triumph over the Detroit Lions.

It was a game with many small personal battles that did not always show on the field. In the morning, for instance, Walt Michaels, the Jets coach, decided to bench his starting right linebacker, Bob Martin, because of some complaints Martin made about the team to a newsman last week.

"I wanted to make sure we had the most cheerful people playing," Michaels explained later. "You know what made me happy when I played? I went on the field, and I struck at everything."

Michaels's displeasure with Martin was such that the coach even created a risky situation, replacing Martin with Mark Merrill, a second-year man who had never played outside linebacker. The rest of the linebacking corps included Greg Buttle on the left side, and Buttle had lost 13 pounds during the previous five days because of food poisoning. The middle linebacker was a rookie, Stan Blinka.

Whatever the problems with inexperience, though, the Jet defense was equal to them, limiting the Lions to only 33 yards rushing and 231 in all.

All of Todd's problems also came before the game. He had made a bet with Michaels that the boos would outnumber the cheers when his name was announced, and he was right. Last week, he replaced Matt Robinson in what turned out to be the Jets' worst loss in their 20 years, the 56-3 trouncing by the New England Patriots.

But the Lions, led by Jeff Komlo, a rookie quarterback, are not the Patriots, a fact realized by the bettors, who had made the Jets a 6½-point choice for yesterday's game.

Todd was powerfully confident in directing the New Yorkers after the debacle of the week before. He connected on almost everything he threw, hitting on 9 of 13 attempts for an impressive total of 208 yards. Six of those passes, for 177 yards, were caught by Wesley Walker, who was in the surprising position of being covered man to man. Walker averaged virtually 30 yards a catch, a week after having

Continued on Page C4

Anderson on Jets' controversy, P. 4

## The Bear Keeps Rolling With the Tide

*Paul (Bear) Bryant, the Alabama football coach, has termed himself "a tired old man," but he denies that he is planning retirement. Bryant said last night that he had no inclination to step down from his Alabama coaching post, contrary to published reports. — Jan. 26, 1964*

By MALCOLM MORAN

TUSCALOOSA, Ala. —

**H**E is up every morning at 5 o'clock, preparing for the morning meetings with his staff, planning for another national championship. He is up in his tower every afternoon, overlooking the practice fields, sending instructions, praise and criticism through a bullhorn just when his players start to think that the old man cannot possibly notice everything. He wears his hound's-tooth hat on the sideline on Saturday afternoons, a color-coordinated coach surrounded by assistants in plain red-and-white outfits. He calls and visits a younger group of teen-agers each year, and tries to convince them that they would be wise to go to the University of Alabama and become part of the Crimson Tide.

At the age of 66, Bear Bryant rolls on. He has gone from the days before two-platoon football to a dropback-and-pass offense to a washbone, changing a little here and borrowing a little there whenever necessary. He has won 285 games as a head coach in more than 34 years at four bigtime universities — Maryland, Kentucky, Texas A & M and Alabama — and unless he suddenly becomes ill or the entire freshman class flunks out, he will pass Amos Alonzo Stagg's record of 314 victories.

His teams have won or shared five national

Continued on Page C7

**ARTS/ENTERTAINMENT:** Utah Symphony in a New Home C13/Books: Intellectuals of Vienna C17

"SportsMonday," the *Times'* special section on sports, displays large photographs, a visual index at the top of the page and special effects, as for horizontal package at bottom of page.

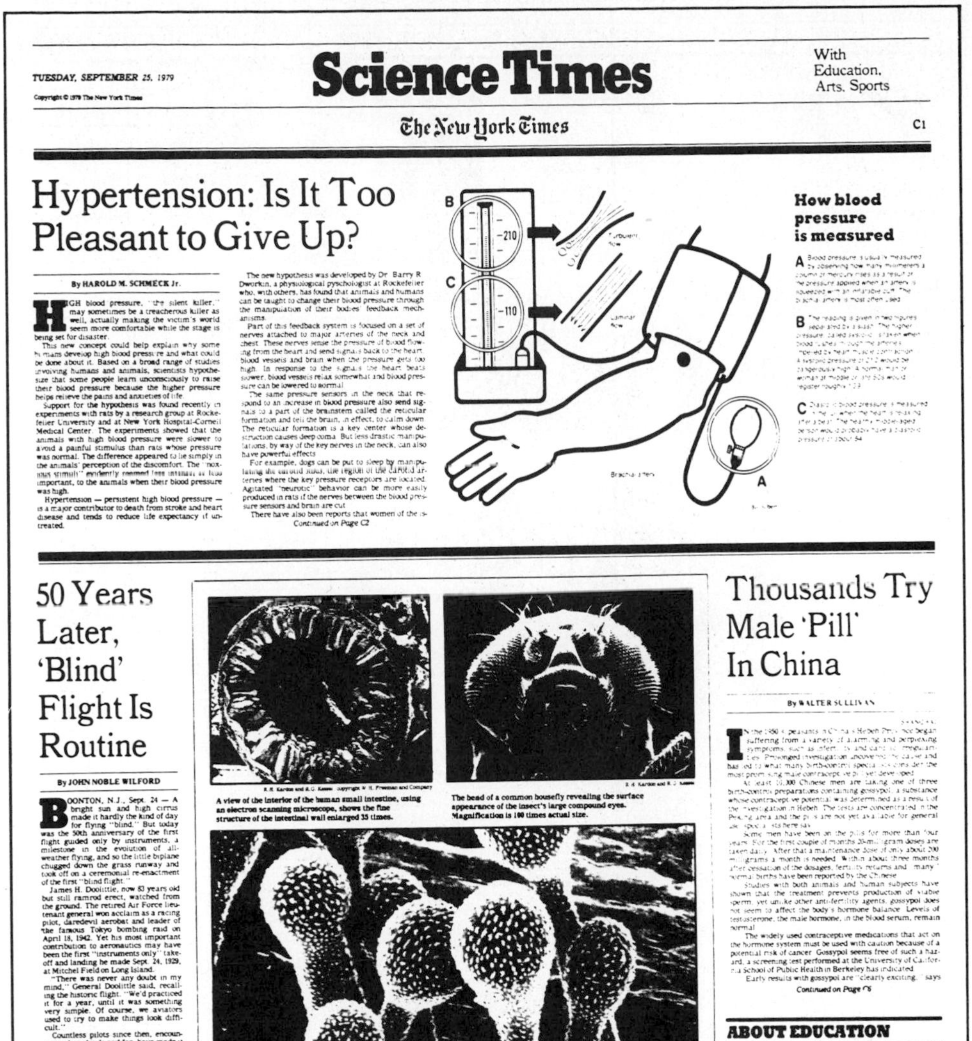

TUESDAY, SEPTEMBER 25, 1979
Copyright © 1979 The New York Times

# Science Times

The New York Times

With
Education,
Arts, Sports

C1

## Hypertension: Is It Too Pleasant to Give Up?

By HAROLD M. SCHMECK Jr.

HIGH blood pressure, "the silent killer," may sometimes be a treacherous killer as well, actually making the victim's world seem more comfortable while the stage is being set for disaster.

This new concept could help explain why some humans develop high blood pressure and what could be done about it. Based on a broad range of studies involving humans and animals, scientists hypothesize that some people learn unconsciously to raise their blood pressure because the higher pressure helps relieve the pains and anxieties of life.

Support for the hypothesis was found recently in experiments with rats by a research group at Rockefeller University and at New York Hospital-Cornell Medical Center. The experiments showed that the animals with high blood pressure were slower to avoid a painful stimulus than rats whose pressure was normal. The difference appeared to be simply in the animals' perception of the discomfort. The noxious stimuli evidently seemed less intense, or less important, to the animals when their blood pressure was high.

Hypertension — persistent high blood pressure — is a major contributor to death from stroke and heart disease and tends to reduce life expectancy if untreated.

The new hypothesis was developed by Dr. Barry R. Dworkin, a physiological psychologist at Rockefeller who, with others, has found that animals and humans can be taught to change their blood pressure through the manipulation of their bodies' feedback mechanisms.

Part of this feedback system is focused on a set of nerves attached to major arteries of the neck and chest. These nerves sense the pressure of blood flowing from the heart and send signals back to the heart, blood vessels and brain when the pressure gets too high. In response to the signals the heart beats slower, blood vessels relax somewhat and blood pressure can be lowered to normal.

The same pressure sensors on the neck that respond to an increase in blood pressure also send signals to a part of the brainstem called the reticular formation and tell the brain, in effect, to calm down. The reticular formation is a key center whose destruction causes deep coma. But less drastic manipulations, by way of the key nerves in the neck, can also have powerful effects.

For example, dogs can be put to sleep by manipulating the carotid sinus, the region of the carotid arteries where the key pressure receptors are located. Agitated "neurotic" behavior can be more easily produced in rats if the nerves between the blood pressure sensors and brain are cut.

There have also been reports that women of the is

*Continued on Page C2*

### How blood pressure is measured

A Blood pressure is usually measured by observing how many millimeters a column of mercury rises as a result of the pressure applied when an artery is squeezed with an inflatable cuff. The brachial artery is most often used.

B The reading is given in two figures — above and below a slash. The higher pressure, called systolic, is seen when blood rushes through the arteries, especially the heart muscle's contraction. A second pressure of 120 would be dangerously high. A normal mid-life figure is 140/90 or 150/95.

C Diastolic blood pressure is measured in the space when the heart is resting after a beat. The healthy middle-aged person would probably have a diastolic pressure of about 94.

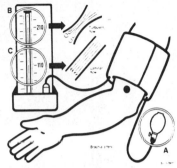

## 50 Years Later, 'Blind' Flight Is Routine

By JOHN NOBLE WILFORD

BOONTON, N.J., Sept. 24 — A bright sun and high cirrus made it hardly the kind of day for flying "blind." But today was the 50th anniversary of the first flight guided only by instruments, a milestone in the evolution of all-weather flying, and so the little biplane chugged down the grass runway and took off on a ceremonial re-enactment of the first "blind flight."

James H. Doolittle, now 83 years old but still ramrod erect, watched from the ground. The retired Air Force lieutenant general who made the first instrument flight, daredevil aerobat and leader of the famous Tokyo bombing raid of April 18, 1942. Yet his most important contribution to aeronautics may have been the first "instruments only" takeoff and landing he made Sept. 24, 1929, at Mitchel Field on Long Island.

"There was never any doubt in my mind," General Doolittle said, recalling the historic flight. "We'd practiced it for a year, until it was something very simple. Of course, we aviators used to try to make things look difficult."

Countless pilots since then, encountering low clouds and fog, have made it through because of instrument landings of the type pioneered by General Doolittle. All commercial airliners make radio instrument landings routinely, and in the near future more sophisticated microwave scanning systems will be bringing in the planes and the space shuttle, America's next-generation space transportation system.

General Doolittle made his flight in a Consolidated NY-2 training plane whose hooded rear cockpit was "carefully sealed to keep out all light" and prevent the pilot from seeing where he was. Among the few displays on the cockpit panel were a new and more sensitive altimeter, a newly invented artificial horizon and another indicator consisting of a pair of vibrating reeds connected to the radio receiver. If the plane drifted to the right of a radio beacon at the airport, the left reed vibrated more vigorously. If the plane was on course, both reeds vibrated on the same frequency.

Following these few instrument cues, General Doolittle, an Army lieutenant at the time, flew the biplane over a 15-mile course that included several sharp turns and found his way back to an accurate touchdown. Another pilot, Benjamin S. Kelsey, sat in the forward cockpit as a safety precaution, but he always held his hands up to show that he was not helping control the plane.

A shopping center stands on old Mitchel Field and so the re-enactment flight was made here at the landing field of Aircraft Radio and Control Corporation.

*Continued on Page C3*

A view of the interior of the human small intestine, using an electron scanning microscope, shows the fine structure of the intestinal wall enlarged 35 times.

The head of a common housefly revealing the surface appearance of the insect's large compound eyes. Magnification is 100 times actual size.

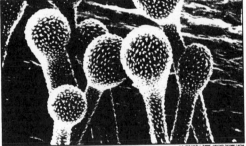

Hairlike structures on the petal of a snapdragon, enlarged 200 times

## New Revelations of Microscope Research

THE pictures seem to take the viewer into an alien world — nightmare dragons staring with huge, unnatural eyes above cruel fangs and hairy forelaws, forests of unearthly, bulb-headed trees sprouting from mossy dunes, thickets of twisted tubes and stalks that look like nothing at all familiar to humans, strange caves and canyons inhabited by floating spheres whose surfaces are covered with tendrils.

But the world of these pictures is actually all around us — and inside us — mostly invisible except through a triumph of modern science called the scanning electron microscope.

The microscopes give a startling three-dimensional view of things that often look flat with sparse surface detail when examined using other techniques. A depth of focus that is 300 times greater than that of the light microscope gives a surprising beauty to some of the scanning electron microscope pictures, but the devices also provide a wealth of valuable information.

Scanning electron microscopes, in wide use for little more than a decade, are being employed more and more to diagnose disease, help solve crime, detect tiny flaws in vital materials and, in general, to give humans a more realistic view than they have ever had of things

that are far too small to be seen with the unaided eye.

New advances in scanning electron microscopy have made it possible to pinpoint the location of traces of metallic elements in human tissues, for example. Pathologists have used pictures made with the microscopes for such purposes as matching a suspect's teeth with a bite that figured importantly in a rape case.

Agricultural scientists have used the microscopes to view in exquisite detail the interaction of microbes in the soil with the root hairs of plants and shrubs. One such type of cooperative interaction is a key factor in putting biologically useable

*Continued on Page C2*

## Thousands Try Male 'Pill' In China

By WALTER SULLIVAN

IN the 1960's peasants in China's Hebei Province began suffering from a variety of alarming and perplexing symptoms, such as illness, numbness, impotence. Prolonged investigation uncovered the cause and had to do with what many birth-control specialists consider the most promising male contraceptive in years, yet to be tested.

At least 10,000 Chinese men are taking one of three birth-control preparations containing gossypol, a substance whose contraceptive potential was determined as a result of the investigation in Hebei. The tests are concentrated in the Peking area and the pills are not yet available for general use. Since it is here that they have been taken by men for more than four years. For the first couple of months 20-milligram doses are taken daily. After that a maintenance dose of only about 200 milligrams a month is needed. Within about three months after cessation of the dosages, fertility returns and many normal births have been reported to the Chinese.

Studies with both animals and human subjects have shown that the treatment prevents production of viable sperm, yet unlike other anti-fertility agents, gossypol does not seem to affect the body's hormone balance. Levels of testosterone, the male hormone, in the blood serum, remain normal.

The widely used contraceptive medications that act on the hormone system must be used with caution because of a potential risk of cancer. Gossypol seems free of such a hazard, a screening test performed at the University of California School of Public Health at Berkeley has indicated.

Early results with gossypol are "clearly exciting," says

*Continued on Page C6*

### ABOUT EDUCATION

## Specialists Leery Of Math 'Reforms'

By FRED M. HECHINGER

MATHEMATICIANS and educators warned last week that reports of students declining performance in mathematics may touch off "reforms" that will make the problem worse. In interviews, they expressed the view that pressures to increase classroom drill and prepare students for minimum competency tests will further erode students' capacity to use mathematics to solve problems.

"It is simply anyone to move back to the old drill," said John G. Kemeny, president of Dartmouth College and a prominent mathematician. "The skills that are least needed are computational skills."

Current reforms, he added, are going in the opposite direction of what is called for, largely because people, remembering their own schooling, think that the way they learned math must have signaled the good old days. Actually, Mr. Kemeny said, from the mathematics point of view, they were "the bad old days."

News of the decline, by 1 percent for 9-year-olds, 2 percent for 13-year-olds and 4 percent for 17-year-olds, since the last similar survey five years ago, came with publication of the National Assessment of Educational Progress by the Federal Government's National Institute of Education. The tests, administered at regular intervals in a variety of sub-

*Continued on Page C5*

**BOOKS:** Ralph G. Martin's biography of the fabulous newswoman Cissy Patterson, page 9

**ARTS:** An art critic ponders legends that simply aren't so and the origins of misinformation that seems to get perpetuated, page 19

Combining illustrations and photographs has become a graphic trademark for the *New York Times'* special sections, as showcased through this "Science Times" page.

Large initials are used at the beginning of every article; art and photography are combined to create visual interest; an index guides the reader through this opening page of "The Living Section," one of the most popular of the *Times'* special sections.

## Bringing A Mansion Back to Life

By MICHAEL deCOURCY HINDS

ONE expects to see Lurch, dusty with cobwebs, loom out of trap door. Or to hear Morticia, the scary witch, scolding her demonic children about possessing each other. By ghoulish coincidence, 54 West Market Street in Rhinebeck, N.Y., is nearly a replica of the Victorian mansion that the cartoonist Charles Addams drew for his monstrous family in The New Yorker and that was later adapted for the television series, "The Addams Family."

Though Addams Family fans will always be on the lookout for Lurch and Gomez, who liked to pour boiling oil on merry visitors, the house has never been haunted. Actually, this fine example of Second Empire Victorian architecture is now being stripped of cobwebs, peeling paint and 30 years of neglect and is being completely restored, as well as made energy-efficient, by a pair of Manhattan doctors.

"Never in my wildest dreams did I think we'd find anyone who would take such an interest in the Charles Addams House," said Madeleine Post, president of Hudson River Heritage Inc., a nonprofit preservation group in Rhinebeck, N.Y., that had "put the house up for adoption" last spring. The turreted mansion, surrounded by withering elms, has been known locally as the Charles Addams House, she said, "for as long as I can remember."

The woebegone condition of the house didn't bother Dr. Antout Parisi, a Manhattan surgeon, and his wife, Dr. Drulla Parisi, an internist, who had admired the property for many years. They leaped at the chance to buy it from the preservation group for $56,500, on condition that they restore it and maintain the integrity of its Victorian architecture.

"I certainly approve of them fixing it up and making it livable," Mr. Addams said when notified that his "dream house" had been sold. Although he admitted to some qualms about the restoration ruining certain "dusty, fly-blown" aspects of the house, the cartoonist didn't think the renovation would diminish the building's innate spookiness. "I like the way it's so stark and gaunt, looming up off the barren hill."

Although the house is very similar to those in Mr. Addams's cartoons, it wasn't his inspiration. "I only saw the house five years ago," said Mr. Addams, who lives in Manhattan. "I was struck by it. I thought, that's my family's house, that's what I've been drawing all these years."

But Mr. Addams, an active advocate of historic preservation, is glad that the house is being rescued. "In a few years, we wouldn't have been able to give it away," Mrs. Post said. "There was a terrible leak in the roof and it could have collapsed and destroyed the house," she explained, adding that the house, designed by the architect G.B. Croff around 1875, is "one of the most outstanding examples of Victorian architecture in the country."

Although the house has never been abandoned, if has

Continued on Page C9

The cupola of a 20-room Victorian mansion in Rhinebeck, N.Y., known locally as the 'Charles Addams House.' It is being restored and made energy-efficient after years of neglect.

---

# The New York Times
## THE
# Home
### SECTION

THURSDAY, FEBRUARY 14, 1980

## The Basically Black Room

By SUZANNE SLESIN

COZY. That's what Eric Bernard calls his shiny, decidedly hard-edged, all-black apartment. A lot of people would disagree. Mr. Bernard has talked to many of them. "People think black is depressing," the 38-year-old interior designer said. "They're wrong. Black is serene, relaxing, dramatic, a perfect background."

Like many other contemporary designers, Mr. Bernard favors a monochromatic scheme. He has done beige apartments, is just finishing an all-white residence and "went through an entire gray period." But now, joining other enthusiasts of black interiors, he is committed to the esthetic of all-black rooms.

There have, of course, been black rooms before. In the 1920's and 30's, during the glamorous Art Deco period, a black marble bathroom was synonymous with luxury. In the 1970's, minimalists championed the starkness of the black-floored, white-walled room and recently, with surfaces lacquered in blazing, matte, theatrical finishes, black has revived the all-black room.

"I've been trying to sell black for years," said Mr. Bernard, whose work, by his own admission, has gotten progressively darker and darker. When the time came for the designer to renovate a floor in the 100-year-old brownstone in which he lived, he decided to go all out for a black scheme.

In his small, 12-by 15-foot bedroom,

Continued on Page C9

---

## Bye-Bye, Valentine: Only the Fit Survive

By GEORGIA DULLEA

THE following individuals will receive less than their usual ration of Valentines today: Melissa, who smokes Vicereos Extra Longs; Roger, who weighs 20 pounds more than he should and who saves phooey to the Scarsdale Diet, and Daphne, who remained abed in the morning as her lover ran through Central Park.

These are no longer lovable. On this Valentine's Day, dear hearts, it is well to remember that the constraints to love have less to do with breeding or religion or socio-economic ethnic characteristics than with the physical fitness of the beloved.

Which is why lovers like Melissa and Roger and Daphne, who did nothing all year to improve their bodies while their mates grew thinner and firmer and fitter by the hour may wind up without much in the way of hearts and flowers today.

Melissa once had a live-in Valentine named Barney, who shared her addiction to nicotine. They smoked up a storm, Melissa and Barney. One day Barney read an advertisement in the newspaper: You Will Stop Smoking on Oct. 26. Obedient, he turned himself in to Smokenders. After Oct. 26, things were no longer the same between Melissa and Barney.

It was not that Barney preached or nagged as reformed smokers are wont to do when their loved ones refuse to forsake the weed. Nor did he cough and fan the air at the first whiff of smoke. Rather, Barney bought himself a gas mask that he wore at all times in the apartment. This produced a strain on their relationship.

Declaring, "I cannot make love to a masked man," Melissa took to reading thrillers in bed and chain-smoking Viceroys Extra Longs. One night she looked up to find that Barney's mask was no longer on the pillow beside her.

Roger and Olga met at a party. Having searched in vain for a woman who was not on a diet, the overweight Roger was instantly smitten with the equally overweight Olga when she returned his gaze over a wheel of cheese.

"You are the most desirable woman here," he said, placing an extravagant smear of paté on her waiting plate. "All the others are eating crudités.

"I cannot bear to be in the same room with so many raw vegetables," she said. "Take me to the nearest Italian restaurant."

The minute Olga picked up her fork, Roger was filled with a desire to dine forever at her table. She ate steadily and wholeheartedly, pausing only to praise the sauce on the fettucine and the texture of the cheesecake. If the cuisine court of the dishes was a matter of any concern to Olga, she did not confide as much to Roger who professed marriage before the cappuccino was cold.

Roger sensed that the honeymoon was over when he found Olga weeping on the bathroom scale. Olga had gained 23 pounds since the wedding. From that day on she ate nothing but grapefruit, every time she took a bite she put her spoon down for 30 minutes. Then she wrote about it in her diet journal. Then she talked about it with her group. Soon Olga was as thin and frantic as all the other women Roger had ever known.

One morning he found a note on the kitchen counter: "Dear Roger: I am leaving you because you abuse food. Have a nice day. Olga."

Daphne and Jonathan were guilty of the sin of sloth. Their idea of exercise was twirling the television dial. They had flaccid muscles, weak hearts and cellulite to beat

Continued on Page C9

---

Vertical placement is the dominant element in the "Home" section opener. The section's name appears set in square serif, reversed against photograph. An index at bottom right of page guides the reader through inside content.

The *Times'* "Weekend" section is highlighted by large photograph at top of page, which protrudes dramatically into folio lines at top. Art and photo combine to give emphasis to bottom of page.

"Fashion!Dallas," the weekly section published by the *Dallas Morning News,* displays large photos and art, plenty of copy, inside pages that blend advertising and editorial content, and graphic appeal throughout.

Front pages show comparison of the *St. Cloud Daily Times* before and after its redesign. The *Times* was probably the first small daily to undergo a complete redesign in the 1980s.

Bostonians have learned to rely on "Calendar," the weekly entertainment section of the *Boston Globe,* as their guide to restaurants, events, movies, and concerts. The twenty-four-page tab is well designed and easy to follow.

The Sunday front page and Metro page from the *Baltimore News American* show the effective blend of bold and light typefaces, large photos, and structural design created by Richard Curtis.

---

**Baltimore Clippers: Newest game in town. Sports, 3E.**

# The Sunday News American

FINAL
★★

Baltimore, Maryland     Sunday, November 25, 1979     60 Cents

## Three weeks ago, life in the U.S. changed

Television has brought the shocking reality of the embattled U.S. Embassy in Tehran into the living rooms of the American people. Their outcry has been restrained, but they are seething beneath the surface. Meanwhile the history of oil and politics is being rewritten.

Don Oberdorfer
Washington Post News Service

### Analysis

WASHINGTON — Three weeks after the seizure of the U.S. Embassy by Iranian militants, there is growing evidence the long-running crisis may be one of those rare international "hinge events" that change the way people think and governments act, therefore altering the course of history.

The American government, beset by the draining demands of day-to-day maneuvers, is just beginning to look beyond the tactical situation to the broader repercussions. It is increasingly clear, even in the first phase of studies the State Department recently ordered, that the post-crisis world will be different than the world of three weeks ago, regardless of the final outcome.

Two international events of the past dozen years, in the view of this reporter, bear a close resemblance in the powerful tremors and upheavals they generated.

About five years apart, these events were the 1968 Tet offensive by the Communist forces in Vietnam, which changed the minds of Americans about the Indochina war and was the turning point of U.S. involvement in faraway military conflict, and the 1973 Middle East War and oil embargo, which changed the terms of trade in the world and inaugurated the age of Arab oil power.

As another potential hinge event, the U.S.-Iranian clash of 1979 may resemble Tet more than the oil embargo because its most direct effects are on the minds of people rather than material commodities. But the world's petroleum supply, as well, is ultimately at risk.

Like Tet, a near-simultaneous television coverage via satellite of an invaded U.S. Embassy in Tehran brought shocking symbols as well as substance into the living rooms of the American people. Unlike Tet, the immediate public and political outcry has been held in check by concern while fierce emotions continue to seethe just beneath the surface.

As did the Tet offensive of January

See HINGE, 13A

---

## The bugeye Jenny Norman

### Family boating tradition ending as a master finishes a classic

By Larry Lewis
News American Staff

LLOYDS — James B. Richardson's arms and legs tremble under the weight of the long, 2-inch-thick plank he is straining to hold against the uncompleted belly of the classic-design "bugeye," Jenny Norman. He is wiry and determined, but the years have outlasted his strength. Still, he refuses to back off for a rest until the massive board is fitted properly and clamped to the unfinished boat.

When he stands to straighten his hat, he is breathing heavily.

Ahead now are hours of swinging a large hammer, using it like a croquet mallet, thrusting upward with it to anchor the plank permanently in place.

"It makes me ache to think about being under her," he says, "and to his brother Bill who is helping him and half to the loblolly pines around his boat shed in this community of farms and fields just west of Cambridge. The comment is made softly, as though his voice, too, is resting. "It's hard on old people."

There is an air of ending here. In some sense, the importance of a final chapter has attached itself to the scene in the open shed with the corrugated metal roof on the edge of LeCompte's Creek. It is here that the sharply rounded form of the bugeye, a nearly forgotten ancestor of the water industry, is taking shape.

Jim Richardson, two weeks short of his 73rd birthday, is building his last boat, and this one is for himself. "I'll finish her if the good Lord gives me time," says the Seventh Day Adventist who is so devoted to his faith he spent six years helping to build his congregation's church.

He will name her after a memory held by another boatbuilding Richardson.

"Jenny Norman had been a girlfriend of my father's. I only saw her once, when I was a little tyke. When I was older, I asked my father about her. He didn't answer me. A little while later, I heard him say to himself, 'She would have been

a joy to live with.' I'm naming my bugeye the Jenny Norman because she'll be a joy to live with."

When she task is done and the Jenny Norman is pushed onto the nearby arm of the Choptank River, an emptiness will settle on this 90-acre neck of land where the Chesapeake's sailing fleet has been replenished and repaired for at least three generations of Richardsons.

There will be one more spot of stillness in the Dorchester County marshes that once teemed with English outcasts — people who came to this country to pull their livings from the rivers and creeks of a new land or build the boats that

carried the watermen to the oyster bars and crabbing grounds.

"I don't blame people for giving up on boatbuilding," Richardson says. "You stay killed half the time."

When he lifts his left trouser leg to make his point, he bares bruises and knots from knee to ankle.

"That's just from this week. The big scars on the lower part of my leg are from when I set myself afire a couple of years ago. I was welding, I guess a spark went into my pants cuff where there were shavings, and I had to jump into the water at the railway slip where we put

boats over to get the flames out."

Richardson has built a worldwide reputation from his home off the beaten path along Route 343, a large house that sits in a compound where 11 families of his relatives still live in stone and log houses they built themselves. The two or three visitors a week who drive or sail up to his front door might be arriving from the Bahamas, the West Coast or overseas.

"I sent a set of skipjack plans to Germany not long ago, and I had one fellow write me from Tanzania. Most of the time they just want information."

See BOATS, 13A

THE LAST BOAT: Jim Richardson, nearly 73, works on the Jenny Norman. He explains, "I don't want to be called a legend. It makes me feel strange."

---

## Khomeini says Carter is using 'jungle law'

News American Wire Services

TEHRAN, Iran — The 49 Americans being held hostage by radical Islamic students at the U.S. Embassy here ended their third week in captivity Saturday with no sign of a relaxation of tensions that could lead to their release.

Ayatollah Ruhollah Khomeini, in a new attack on the United States Saturday, accused President Carter of using "medieval logic and jungle law" in his demands for release of the hostages. He also accused the United States "and its corrupt colony Israel" of attempting to "take over" the Great Mosque in Mecca.

In a message broadcast to 80 Arab liberation movements with headquarters in Algiers, the 79-year-old religious leader said U.S. threats of military intervention were the hostages to be harmed, amounted to "the law of the jungle" that ignored "all humanitarian and international values."

Khomeini said one of Carter's gravest mistakes is not to understand the depth of the Islamic movement." He called on "Moslems of the world" to "rise up and defend your countries and Islam."

Carter met for more than three hours with his chief military advisers Saturday and while Iran was discussed, a spokesman said the "primary focus" was on the fiscal 1981 defense budget.

See IRAN, 13A

---

## Mine sweepers reported ready for Mideast

Newsday News Service

WASHINGTON — The U.S. Navy has ordered that additional mine-sweeping equipment be in working order and ready for transport to the Mideast by today, according to informed military sources.

The order indicates the type of contingency planning now under way in the Pentagon, in case President Carter decides to resort to military action because of the taking of American hostages in Iran. But the Navy move does not mean Carter plans to impose a naval blockade of Iran's oil shipments, the sources said.

If it is used, the mine-sweeping equipment could be employed either to clear the way for such a blockade or to keep the Persian Gulf free if mines have been placed in the area by the Iranian navy, according to the sources.

Pentagon spokesman Thomas Ross said he would not comment on any contingency plans and would neither confirm nor deny that the mine-sweeping equipment had been ordered. White House officials would only repeat statements made earlier last week that, in essence, the United States was not ruling out a military response in case any of the 49 remaining American hostages in the U.S. Embassy in Tehran are harmed.

U.S. officials continued to say they are pursuing a diplomatic solution to the situation.

---

## Are presidents of local unions paid too much?

By Joe Calderone
News American Staff

Al Akman carries a long title after his name — president of Baltimore's Retail Store Employees Union Local 692 and vice president of United Food and Commercial Workers.

With that title last year with a reported gross salary of $75,433. With allowances and expenses included, he drew $110,203.

Helen Peck also is a member of the union. As a cashier at Giant Food, she makes $6.39 an hour, or $17,451 a year if she's allowed to work full-time, which she said she isn't.

Peck doesn't approve of the huge gap between her salary and that of her union president.

"I think it's awful," Peck said. "He stands up there in his $300 suits and sells us out. He makes way too much for what he does."

For union leaders like Akman, the paychecks they take home can be a delicate issue.

Although they function as executives looking after the interests of thousands of people and requiring sophisticated skills, union officials also are responsible to a large membership sensitive to differences in pay and status, a membership with the power to replace local presidents who might be "out of touch."

According to a survey by The News American, there is sometimes a considerable — and an Akman's case, occasionally vast — distance between the average pay of union members in Baltimore and the salary of their elected union leaders.

But in some cases, the survey also shows, local union leaders are paid no more than what their members receive through collective bargaining agreements.

Sometimes, union officials say, they actually make less money than their members because they miss opportunities for promotion and overtime work.

Union leaders are paid with dues deducted automatically from each member's paycheck. Interviews with union members show that although most know how much they pay weekly in dues, they do not know the salaries of their union leaders.

The survey was based on records on file with the U.S. Department of Labor in Washington, D.C., and included the leaders of the largest and most powerful unions in Baltimore. About 100 locals were included in the study.

Local unions are required to file annual reports on the finances of their organizations, including the salaries of officers.

See SALARIES, 12A

---

## INSIDE SUNDAY

### Restore those floors

Is it time to give your hardwood floors a new life? Can you do it yourself or do you need a professional? What kind of sander should you use? A complete do-it-yourself guide, see Home, 1G.

### Rock 'n' roll is here to stay

Rock is no longer Elvis Presley and Chuck Berry of the '50s or the message-bearer of the '60s' counterculture. As the '70s end, rock 'n' roll is a dominant force in popular entertainment, vying with television and movies as America's primary leisure outlet. Showplace, 1H.

### Change in a Catholic parish

St. Stephen's is a microcosm of the Catholic Church. And members are facing a crisis: Do they follow their conscience as their priests often recommend or do they hold fast to church doctrine? It's a modern dilemma for the church. Page 12A.

William Randolph Hearst Jr.
Editor in chief, The Hearst Newspapers

### Editor's report

Iran: A religious war. Page 17A.

### Index

9 sections Vol. 2U/-No. 98

| | |
|---|---|
| Abby / 4B | Jackpot Puzzle / 10D |
| Books / 8H | Letters / 8H |
| Bridge / 8H | Lively Arts / 8H |
| Classified / 11D | Lottery / 11E |
| Crosswords / 8H | Main Line / 7B |
| Decorating / 2G | Movies / 3H |
| Drama / 7X | Music / 8H |
| Editorials / 18A | Outdoors / 9E |
| Financial / 6D | Radio / 10H |
| Fashion / 8B | People / 4H |
| Food / 1G | Sports / 1E |
| Hobbies / 8B | Sylvia's Scene / 3B |
| Horoscope / 18E | Travel / 11B |

### Showers

Chance of showers today with highs in mid 60s. Details, 2A.

# Metro

## Patriot
### Arbutus bar owner pushes his brand of Americanism

Columnist
**Tom Coakley**

Al Flora, Arbutus bar owner and consummate defender of America, the flag and Spiro Agnew, thinks those Marine guards who left their 49 fellow hostages behind in the U.S. Embassy in Tehran last week really blew it.

"Those Marines who were released," said Al in his husky, ex-fighter voice, "whether they be black or white or pink or yellow, they could have gone down in history by saying: 'If we all can't go, we're staying.'

"This is the true American way in which I believe," Al said. He didn't shout as he sat in his small paneled office. He simply spoke earnestly, almost sadly about this state of affairs.

Now Al never fought in World War II. He worked on ships for Bethlehem Steel at Key Highway. His jaw had been broken twice in the ring, and it was infected so he couldn't get into the service.

And Al Flora, he of the gray hair and the long, chiseled Italian face, would be the first to admit that it's easy for him to sit in his bar office and say what the Marines should have done, to sit amid the pictures of his family and the framed plaques of Spiro Agnew letters and second-guess grevmes over in Iran.

But Al thinks he knows about Americanism. It was Al, after all, who put up those billboards around these parts a few years back that told a beleaguered Agnew to "Keep Punchin."

And it was one of Al's barmaids who refused to serve two long-hairs years back (4 steel. ice might sdd, that it moderately mellowed Al Flora might be less quick to condone these days, although to Al, a gentleman is still a gentleman.)

Al grew up hard in Wilkes Barre, Pa., hustling since he was 9 when his coal worker father died, leaving him with an immigrant mother who spoke no English.

At Al he's success. Just take a look at the bar with the naked water bearer fountain in the center, the long, red curtains on the wall, the embossed mirrors, the nice-looking barmaids, Frankie Sinatra on the jukebox.

So Al appreciates America, and what he sees going on around the world bothers him a lot.

"To me it's very disgusting. The spirit of America doesn't seem to be there anymore.

"What really bothers me is we bring so many aliens into this country to educate them in our system and our ways, and all they do is ridicule us and burn the flag," Al said.

To Al, the flag means life itself and the future of America. "It means," said Al, "the future of my grandchildren."

He will tell you that when students took over the embassy in Tehran that "it reminded me of Pearl Harbor. They snuck in there, and from what I understand it's a declaration of war. If we let them get away with it, then other countries will do the same thing. This thing is going to mushroom."

Al thinks President Carter is doing the best he can. But if Al had his way, he'd do what he thinks Agnew might do as president. Give those students an ultimatum to free the hostages in 24 hours or else.

"Then," said Al, offering the or else, "I'd bring the fleet in there or drop the Marines in there. But we got to make a stand. We can't get pushed around.

"I saw the news. Those guys are tied up. Christ Almighty, those guys aren't criminals. I mean we don't even treat murderers like that over here."

Anyway, Al said, those students won't kill the Americans.

"Hey, if I'm going to do it, I do it. If a guy's going to do something, he's not going to advertise it. He's going to do it."

Even if it came to sacrifice and Al Flora was trapped in that embassy, he'd sacrifice. Or so he says.

"At least I would know within myself that I served a purpose, that I was dying for a cause."

But Al thinks the Iran situation won't come to tragedy and that it may, in fact, be a blessing in disguise.

"The average customer is very much irritated. So maybe we'll get our spirit back."

He senses the anger in the middle-class, conservative, sports-minded clientele patronizing his bar — the guys who buy his beer and whiskey with money made selling insurance or working in the factory.

"Even the young ones. These kids, I'll tell you, they'd be ready to fight tomorrow for what's happening over there."

So Al Flora thinks America should take a stand, although he's willing to admit there are other viewpoints about the world.

"Maybe if I had a degree out of Harvard, I'd talk different. But my way of life comes from the street. You push me, I'll push you back."

THE HARD LINE: Bar owner Al Flora says he knows the "true American way."

## He's the right man at the right time for Christ's Church

His name — the Rev. Dr. Winthrop Brainerd — and his title — the rector of Christ's Episcopal Church, are as imposing as his own Gothic Revival edifice, a Mount Vernon landmark at St. Paul and Chase streets.

Since his arrival here in March 1977, this Episcopal priest has made a distinct impression on the Mount Vernon neighborhood, where his portly figure and clipped, slightly British accent are familiar.

**Neighborhood WATCH**
By Jacques Kelly

Not so on Brainerd's first Sunday at Christ's. That day, there were but 42 souls scattered in its forest of oak pews. Today, there probably will be 100 or more — a rate of growth that is one sign that this neighborhood is well on its way back, both physically and spiritually.

"I see Christ's as a neighborhood church. There are some very loyal members who will make the long trek in each Sunday, but many of our members are within walking distance," he said.

More than one neighbor has remarked about Brainerd's presence in the community. His strolls around the neighborhood, marketing at a local gourmet shop or attendance at a Walters Art Gallery opening, have all been locally noted.

His face — with its warm smile and neatly groomed beard — has made a few rogues refer to him as Friar Tuck. But in conversation, which he constantly accompanies with a cigarette, Brainerd's perfect diction, friendly formality and equality refined manners reveal him to be of the ecclesiastic manner born.

"We don't take ourselves seriously here. We take what we do seriously, though," he said.

The good rector arrived in Baltimore after being the assistant to the Episcopal bishop of Lexington, Ky. At the time, Victor Frenkil was just completing the renovation of the Hotel Belvedere, another Mount Vernon landmark that was undergoing the same transition as Christ's Church.

One of Brainerd's first actions was to have a number of small posters printed with a celestial-looking angel saying, "You haven't been to Christ's Church."

The police gave permission to post the sheets. However, Mount Vernon preservationists didn't like the idea of them going up all over the historic district where signs are supposed to be kept to a minimum. Earlier this month, he presided over the naming of a short alley (at Preston Street) as Christ's Church Alley.

About 20 members of the "blue-rinse mafia," the little old ladies who rattled around the then-increasingly empty pews, became exercised when their new rector arrived and switched to St. David's in Roland Park or St. John's Huntingdon. Other members arched their eyebrows when the new rector restored an apostrophe and letter "s" to the church's name, making it Christ's Church (the original way it appeared on the institution's charter) instead of the familiar Christ Church.

He was immediately denounced — in some quarters at least — as being "Roman and popish."

What he does frankly denounce is what he refers to as "high Protestantism." He is a strict adherent to the Anglican tradition and avoids "eccentricity" in liturgy. But he is a person of decided convictions who wants to rebuild one of the city's oldest congregations.

In the 19th century, Mount Vernon almost had a church on every corner. Christ's Church, the second oldest Episcopal congregation in the city, moved to its present location in 1870 and immediately began an ambitious building program, as evidenced in its stone belfry, nave and parish hall.

As the neighborhood with Baltimore's wealthiest residents, the church fared well as long as the wealthy lived downtown. But as early as 1924, Christ's Church saw its constituency leave the Upstairs-Downstairs world of four-story St. Paul Street townhouses for countrified homes in the northern suburbs.

Brainerd, born in Montreal and educated in Canada, spent 10 years in England. He was ordained, "with the best Anglican credentials" in the Tudor-era St. Peter ad Vincula (St. Peter in Chains) chapel in the Tower of London. He subsequently served as a rector in Labrador.

"From his first days here, he set out to administer Christ's Church in an organized manner. He spends much of his workday at a large desk in the church basement, with his late afternoons devoted to visiting the sick. Yet, as he notes crisply, 'I don't have the time to be an illtrained social worker.'

Nevertheless, he sees such topics as prison reform, hunger in Baltimore and rent control as valuable topics for a Lenten discussion series. Other downtown clerics, he said, disagree "because it might offend members of their congregations."

But Brainerd is not worried.

FORCE IN THE COMMUNITY: Dr. Winthrop Brainerd came at the right time for the Mount Vernon area.

tion to the neighborhood. As a result, the church donates its facilities to a number of groups, including the Maryland Writers Council and the New Theater Festival.

## Local beer
### Like gasoline and food, the price heads upward

By Joe Nawrozki
News American Staff

The price of beer at local taverns has been going the way of gasoline and groceries — up.

Depending on where you drink, a bottle or can of premium beer like Budweiser or Miller can cost from 75 cents to $1, with popular local beer like Pabst or National running up to 75 cents.

Some local bars have raised their beer prices a nickel in the last few weeks.

"I sell some mixed drinks cheaper than the cost of most bottle beer," said Patrick Flanagan, co-owner of the Gandy Dancer on McHenry Street.

At the Irish Pub, 200 block of W. Chase St., the patrons aren't happy about the higher prices.

"They definitely don't like the increases in price, but they wind up paying anyway," explained Diane MacDonald, a barmaid.

"Gradually, I think beer is losing its reputation as the poor man's drink," said an official with Winner Distributing Co., the local firm that handles the Budweiser account.

James Murphy, manager for Terminal Distributing Co. Inc., which handles Pabst in the metropolitan area, said his company is trying to hold out raising prices, "but who knows how long we'll be successful?"

Robert Kroeger, president of Zamoski Beverage Co., was not available to comment on why brands like Schlitz, Old Milwaukee and Schlitz Light (Schlitz is one of the most popular sellers in Baltimore) continue to rise gradually in price.

The cost of beer starts with the hops and grain stored in silos of the Midwest, officials said. Then the grain is sold, processed in breweries like the local Carling National brewery, and delivered by distributors.

"The cost is passed on like anything else," one Winner spokesman said.

He added: "The wholesaler has complaints about union contracts, delivery costs, gasoline . . . The tavern owners have their legitimate gripes . . . The beer-drinker is the one who can't pass it along to anyone."

A woman at the Wigwam Bar, 1700 block of N. Charles St., said premium brew at her establishment sells for 80 cents a bottle.

"Sure, some complain, but let 'em pay my rent," she huffed.

A can of Miller or Bud costs 75 cents at the Buzz On In, 3000 block of Belair Road.

"A lot of our regulars drink draught beer," said a barmaid named Shirley. "But we get no complaints . . . It's not that quick a rise in price."

Area package goods stores also have increased beer prices, a case selling for an average of 40 cents more.

"The price hikes aren't affecting what we sell," said Joseph Kaufman, manager of Crosstown Liquors, a busy outlet at Belair Road and Erdman Avenue.

"A case of Bud is $7.05 now because we stocked a lot before Thanksgiving," he said. "But next month, when we have to reorder, it will jump to $7.45 a case. But it doesn't seem to matter. We sold over 300 cases the last two days," he said.

Abe Blidn, co-owner of the Midway Liquors on Pulaski Highway near Joppatowne, said, "Beer has been going up since it was invented, so why all the fuss? Why don't people complain about the cost of soda water, the most expensive beverage concocted by modern man?

"I really don't think it will matter how much the price of beer goes up. People will always drink it," he said.

## City policeman, 2 others wounded in shooting

By Cecily Deegan
News American Staff

A Baltimore city policeman was shot and wounded in the stomach — but saved from serious injury by his bullet-proof vest — after responding to a shooting late Saturday at a bar in the 2100 block of W. North Ave., near Coppin State College.

Two other men, who apparently were fighting inside the P&M Bar, were wounded and treated at local hospitals. Police said that they had not determined how the two men were shot, but that at least one was shot before the police officer arrived.

The police officer, who has a beat in the area of the bar, was identified as William Surratt, 41.

He was listed late Saturday in good condition at Mercy Hospital where he was treated for a laceration wound to the lower left abdomen. Police said that the bullet striking Surratt went underneath his rib cage but that he was saved from further injuries by his bullet-proof vest.

Police said Surratt was responding to what he said he thought were gunshots in the bar at about 9:30 p.m.

When Surratt arrived on foot, he attempted to accost one suspect who was leaving the bar.

Police said Surratt went up to one man as the man was leaving the bar and the suspect turned and shot Surratt with one shot from a .38-caliber Smith & Wesson revolver on the southside of West North Avenue about 25 feet from the bar, according Maj. Harry C. Allender, commander of Northwestern District.

Allender said that he was unsure how the other two men were shot, but that Surratt fired twice after he was shot.

One of the shooting victims was identified late Saturday as Carlie Fortune, 39, no address available, who was taken to Provident Hospital with multiple gunshot wounds and was in surgery late Saturday. He was listed in poor condition.

The other victim was identified as Ira Nelson, 25, no address available, who was taken to Lutheran Hospital with gunshot wounds of the right buttocks and listed in satisfactory condition.

## Court appeal readied to block PCB transfer

United Press International

ANNAPOLIS — When the U.S. Coast Guard applies for a permit to dispose 30,000 gallons of hazardous wastes from Sharptown, Wicomico County, to an Anne Arundel County warehouse, county officials hope to be a step ahead.

Richard Bayne, an aide to Anne Arundel County Executive Robert Pascal, has said Pascal will ask for a permanent injunction in Circuit Court against the transfer as soon as the Coast Guard applies for a permit to move the chemicals.

The wastes include polychlorinated biphenyl, or PCB. The proposed move would be from an abandoned tank farm in Sharptown to the U.S. General Services Administration depot in Curtis Bay.

Bayne said a hearing set for Friday on the county's request was canceled but should be rescheduled within two weeks. The Coast Guard plans to move the chemicals Dec. 15.

Judge Bruce C. Williams earlier this month granted a temporary injunction against the transfer.

Bayne said the county is trying to prevent the storage of chemicals at Curtis Bay, which straddles the border between the county and Baltimore, because "it is a very populated area."

"There are tributaries that run through there," Bayne said, alluding to possible contamination of nearby waterways.

He also said the county contends the chemicals would not be stored properly at Curtis Bay.

The controversy has triggered a review of hazardous waste-disposal sites in Maryland. State officials have no firm figures, but shipping manifests reviewed by The Baltimore Sun show that 86 percent of the 166,537 tons of hazardous materials transported to the state between January and September have been stored at three Anne Arundel County sites.

They are the Browning-Ferris Industries landfill near Annapolis, a Crownsville landfill and a Chessie System dump on Marley Neck.

The remaining 23,070 tons were taken to a Browning-Ferris landfill in Baltimore County, to Baltimore city, to a Kent County landfill and the Physicians Memorial Hospital in LaPlata.

---

This "Metro" page from the *Baltimore News American* displays modular placement of copy and contrast of horizontal and vertical photographs.

"Unconventional" best describes the front page from the *Boston Herald American*. This page is used for the July 4 edition. The treatment, designed by Michael Killelea, is definitely magazine-oriented.

Inside front pages from the *Washington Star* display excellent organization; good use of photos, art, and white space; and overall graphic impact. Notice that each section sig (logotype) uses a different typeface, a radical departure from the usual practice of maintaining typographic consistency for standing sigs.

The *Washington Star*'s "Calendar" page combines photos, art and type to give readers a thorough report of events in the capital area. Creative use of photography gives this page instant visual appeal.

The fashion page of the *Washington Star* emphasizes photo over type. White space cushions section's title at top of page. The use of a novelty typeface for headlines adds to the attractiveness and organization of the page.

The Washington Star
WEDNESDAY, OCTOBER 3, 1979

This is Star... FASHION

# Fall Coating

**By Eleni**
*Washington Star Fashion Editor*

This is one year when you are going to have to make up to a coat. Not for years have there been such colorful goings-on in coatdom. And not for years have there been so many coat styles from which to choose in every conceivable texture, tone and trim style.

Beauty houses, who work in colors at least a year and sometimes two in advance, know the impact color has on our lives. And they are not concerned with the face

Continued on Page Four

A boxy coat in ruby red with padded shoulders, $170, by Luba with leg-o-mutton sleeves at Ann Taylor. Her saucer hat, $45, and slate gray shoulder bag, $75, at Ann Taylor.

Photograph by John Bowden
Star Fashion Photographer
Coordinated by Madeleine Hurvell

## INSIDE FASHION

### CREATIVE DRESSING

Emily Scheuer, aka Emily Malino, is interior designer, syndicated columnist, mother, modern dancer. And wife of Rep. James Scheuer. Her basic rule of dress for all these roles: Form must follow function. Page Two.

### MEN'S FASHION

The Earl of Chesterfield and Baron Raglan, British peers nonpareil, are no longer swaggering about, but their topcoats are. In a matter of speaking, so to speak. Anyhow, some styles neither die nor fade away. Page Six.

### MODEL APPROACH

Betsy Farley's been driving trucks all over town. Also in a manner of speaking. Her eyes are the ones that have been peering over an advertisement for this very section. And quite beautiful eyes they are. Page Seven.

Many newspapers have used graphic design strategies to create a sense of visual identity for their pages. The *Baltimore News American,* under the direction of its graphics editor, Richard Curtis, has come out with an innovative blend of type, art, and photos that gives it a modern look. The *Boston Herald American* has turned its front page to very creative cover approaches designed by Michael Killelea. Both newspapers compete with larger and more traditionally designed newspapers, as does the

The *Lion,* the student newspaper at Lyons Township High School in LaGrange, Illinois, underwent extensive design changes in 1980. This front page shows a featurized approach, with photos and art, use of white space, a new and distinctive nameplate, and economical use of space. John Wheeler is the faculty adviser to the *Lion's* staff.

*Washington Star* in the nation's capital. The *Star* started making drastic changes in its graphic appearance, especially in its inside sections, which adopted magazine design effectively.

Interest in newspaper design has extended beyond the world of professional newspapers. Such student newspapers as the *Oklahoma Daily* (University of Oklahoma), *Minnesota Daily* (University of Minnesota), *Kentucky Kernel* (University of Kentucky), *Falcon Times* (Miami-Dade Community College, North Campus), and *High Point* (Cuyahoga Community College, Eastern Campus, Cleveland, Ohio) underwent extensive redesigns during the late 1970s.

High school newspapers, too, have received the impact of new ideas in newspaper design. The *Lion* (Lyons Township High School, La Grange, Illinois), *West Side Story* (West High School, Iowa City, Iowa), the *Lance* (Westside High School, Omaha, Nebraska), and the *Observer* (Winston Churchill High School, Potomac, Maryland) are displaying new looks.

The 1970s gave graphics a high degree of tolerance in the newsroom. The 1980s should provide that much-needed element of acceptance. It is my hope that this book will contribute toward that goal while showing that the design of newspaper pages can be one of the most interesting and creative aspects of newspaper production.

Mario R. Garcia
Syracuse, New York

**design alone won't do it**

## THINK GRAPHICS

A textbook devoted to design should include a reminder to editors and publishers that graphic design alone is not an instant cure for many of the problems that have caused decreasing newspaper circulations in the 1970s. Survival is more likely to result from a change in the attitude of editors and publishers about the role of the newspaper. Words to this effect have been echoed recently in gatherings of professional newspaper groups. John Brooks, executive managing editor of the *Toronto Star*, summarized it best when he explained that

> Too many newsrooms prefer to function in a vacuum, providing what they think is news and insisting that if the promotion people can't sell it, that is their problem.

Joseph Ungaro, vice-president and executive editor of the Westchester-Rockland Newspapers, agrees that editors need a change of attitude:

> Newspapers must stop thinking that it isn't news until we print it. The electronic medium can beat our fastest press on any story, and newspapers must offer the reader something that television and radio cannot.

Not only do editors need to change their attitudes about the concept of news as applied to the newspaper; they also need to gain a greater sense of graphic awareness. Those editors who contend that if the copy is superior and urgent it will command readership no matter how it is presented must reconsider their position.

18

We are fortunate to live in the midst of an unparalled graphic explosion that affects many of our daily activities. Billboards, television programs, movies, magazines, mail advertising, product packaging, company logos, airline tickets, menus, and even birth certificates and personal checks presently show a more visually appealing use of graphics.

Newspapers can be no exception. Wrapping the day's news in a dull package will only serve to alienate prospective newspaper readers. Anyone who served his apprenticeship on a newspaper years ago can remember an aggressive city editor shouting, "Think news." Today's successful city editor has added two other words to his command: "Think graphics."

To think graphically means to invite the reader into each page with attractive, provocative, and orderly use of photos, typography, and illustrations. Most importantly, it means to re-create a sense of graphic identity and consistency through every page of the newspaper every day. But a word of caution is in order here, as suggested by the title of this chapter: Graphic change alone will not save a newspaper, unless it is accompanied by relevant and contemporary thinking in terms of editorial content.

At least two significant publications, the *New York Herald-World Tribune* and the *Chicago Daily News*, made a last-minute effort to pull the graphics "rabbit" out of the hat when everything else pointed to failure. Attractive packaging of the news did not save either newspaper from folding. Peter Palazzo, a New York-based free-lance designer who was involved in redesigning both newspapers, laments that the editors and publishers acted too late to avert the unavoidable downfall.

In the case of the *Herald-World Tribune*, which folded in 1966, Palazzo introduced an avant-garde approach to newspaper design by creating pages with posterlike appeal, use of special typographical devices, large and dramatically cropped photographs, and a complete abandonment of the traditional newspaper look that was common in the early 1960s.

For the *Daily News'* redesign Palazzo utilized the packaging approach, combining extreme vertical and horizontal modules, a colorful front-page index, and generous use of color throughout. The 102-year-old newspaper folded in 1978 after it had lost touch with the majority of Chicago's potential readers, especially the young. A 1976 research study of the *Daily News* revealed that the newspaper was not "youthful," 52 being the average age of its readers.

Newspaper necrologists have said that this was the typical case of a newspaper that died because its rejuvenated graphic presentation came too late to perform a circulation miracle.

Fortunately, success stories of newspapers whose graphic face-lifts have helped boost circulation are numerous. At the *New York Times,* for example, the inception of four modernly designed weekly sections has increased sales by 35,000 copies a day.

## CHANGING ATTITUDE

Earlier in this chapter we referred to the need for editors and publishers to change their attitude about the daily product they create. Part of this change must include a realistic appraisal of newspaper readers today, most of whom are better educated, more sophisticated, more active, and more mobile than their counterparts twenty-five years ago.

Also, there must be a redefinition of what the term *news* should convey for today's newspaper reader. The sense of urgency and immediacy that once characterized the American newspaper has disappeared in many large cities. Although some editors do present scoops, the majority do not assume that their newspaper will be first to get the information to the reader.

This 1963 front page from the *Herald-World Tribune* reflects the avant-garde look that designer Peter Palazzo brought to this newspaper.
(Courtesy of Peter Palazzo's personal collection.)

During its last year of operation, the *Chicago Daily News* sported a modern look, with plenty of color, vertical and horizontal modules, and other elements of the "daily news magazine" concept.
(Courtesy of Peter Palazzo.)

The role of the newspaper of the 1980s should be to pick up where television leaves off. One plausible alternative is the *daily magazine concept*, which trades the news peg for a featurized angle. Newspapers that capitalize on this approach also gear their coverage toward a more consumer-oriented form of reporting, giving their readers stories that deal with such subjects as how to invest wisely; how to shop for everything from pets to plants; where to go for good food and entertainment, medical assistance, and legal counseling; and recipes for everyday survival in a diversity of areas, ranging from marriage and divorce to child rearing and body language.

It is not unusual nowadays to pick up a copy of the *New York Times* and find ample space devoted to lengthy articles on termite detection, the selection of wicker furniture, or the proper care of begonias.

The daily magazine concept, already implemented by such dailies as the *Washington Star*, the *Boston Herald American*, and the *Des Moines Tribune*, among others, is an outgrowth of the recent increase in magazine readership. Drake Mabry, managing editor of the *Des Moines Tribune*, finds nothing new in bringing a highly featurized approach to the daily newspaper:

> Sunday papers for years have recognized the need for this type of specialized editing and perhaps it is time daily newspaper editors realize that what we should be publishing is really a Sunday paper every day.

The *Tribune* has been applying the concept successfully, relying on backgrounders, analysis, depth features, good art, and graphics. This content is organized into a familiar package which allows the busy reader to find his favorite items quickly.

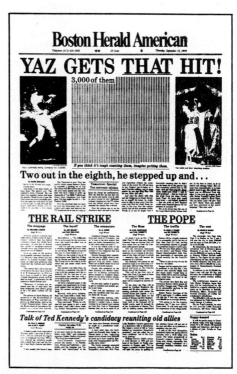

Graphic surgery for the *Boston Herald American* included a total redesign, creating rectangular blocks and generally a tidier newspaper. The approach to the front page is unconventional, emphasizing feature material while packaging the news as attractively and functionally as possible.

The *New York Times'* new sections—"Home," "Weekend," and "Living"—feature large photographs, heavy column rules, and recipes for everything from duck *à l'orange* to successful gardening and weekend entertainment.

The *Miami News* calls itself the newspaper for television viewers. This new format emphasizes a conventional and quick-reading approach to the day's news. Notice the use of rules and the neatly arranged packaging of news and photographs.

Mabry believes that this is probably the only successful way to produce an afternoon newspaper since, as he puts it, there isn't a whole lot of what editors like to call "hard news" between 8:00 a.m. and 1:00 p.m., which is the customary coverage time of afternoon newspapers.

Part of the *Des Moines Tribune*'s new format includes a weekly entertainment guide called "Datebook" and a tightly packed tabloid covering survival material: where to buy the best pizza in town, a guide to going places, interesting places to visit in one day, television schedules, and five ways to beat boredom. Essentially, this is the kind of bonus material that readers always expected as part of their Sunday newspaper fare. Today the feature banquet must be served daily.

Not only do readers want their features throughout the entire newspaper, but also they expect a greater dose of light and amusing items on page one.

At the *Milwaukee Sentinel*, a regular page one feature entitled "Good Morning!" triggered such favorable reader response that what initially was to be a short "brightener" on the front page has now resulted in a four-page entertainment section, which includes comics, radio and television listings, and syndicated columnists. Harry L. Sonneborn, executive editor of the *Sentinel*, describes the history of "Good Morning!":

> During the newsprint crunch of a few years ago we had to cut back on what we thought was less than essential content, as did many other newspapers. We dropped temporarily such columnists as Earl Wilson and found quickly that readers were very disturbed not to have this kind of light reading.

The front page from the *Des Moines Tribune* displays a strong vertical package for an inside index, some spot news, a depth feature on metaphysics (with local emphasis), and an illustrated teaser (bottom of page) on a continuing controversy over public television in Des Moines.

Magazine inserts such as "Datebook," the weekly weekend guide published by the *Des Moines Tribune*, were once a luxury readers expected as part of their Sunday newspapers. Today readers are treated to such bonus offerings during weekdays. Eventually, afternoon newspapers will be forced to publish daily bonus sections.

Readers of the *Milwaukee Sentinel* wake up to this "Good Morning!" section. Columnists, television listings, comics, and local features are the main fare, all positioned in the same areas every day for quick indexing.

The popularity of individual participation sports has led to these sections. "Your Sports" appears in the *Milwaukee Sentinel,* concentrating on such sports as body building and water skiing. Notice "What's Happening," a feature with information on bowling, camping, and even billiards. "P/S" (People/Sports) is the *Miami News'* version of the same concept.

Traditionally a women's page, this new section entitled "You" aims at general readership through a personalized approach to such topics as fashion, decoration, and books. Notice the horizontal modules, liberal use of white space, and simplicity of design.

The tone of the complaints went something like this: "I can't face the grim news of the world in the morning without the lighter features to get the day started more gently."

This theme was repeated by so many readers that the idea of "Good Morning!" began to take shape. . . . Readers are delighted!

The *Sentinel* has also created a new section entitled "You," where personality profiles are the main element. This section brings general readership to what had previously been the women's pages. Even when the subject is women's fashions, a general readership is gained through the emphasis on people. A four-column format gives this section an easy-to-read and attractive appearance. The success of these sections has led to the creation of "Your Sports," which provides coverage of individual participation in sports such as jogging, skiing, biking, golfing, fishing, and rowing.

## CONTENT RELEVANCY

In a sense, the progressive newspaper editor analyzes the trends of our times as much as he does the day's news. In his perception and treatment of newspaper content, today's editor must be a combination of the sociologist, who constantly seeks ways to classify groups and studies the changing roles of individuals in society, and the psychologist, who delves into the motives of human behavior.

He or she must understand readers' preferences and interests, what radio stations readers prefer and why, what churches they attend or why they don't attend, what schools they send their children to, and how involved they are in school decision-making processes. Awareness of societal trends affects the very fiber of the newspaper's day-to-day coverage: Why do so many marriages fail, what are the special problems faced by single parents, what impact does terminal illness have in the lives of victim and relatives, what is society doing about the high cost of dying (and living)?

Relevant newspapers result when editors possess the highest degree of concern and knowledge about everything that happens around them. Most importantly, editors must perceive modern styles of living without abandoning the more traditional values to which so many readers still adhere. Coverage of the modern woman, who may or may not wish to marry and become a mother, can be balanced by profiling the high number of women who hold to the more traditional interests of family life, motherhood and such.

Newspapers must cater to the preferences and interests of all potential readers. Doing so today is not easy, because the trends and lifestyles are highly diversified. One way to accomplish this difficult, but possible, task is through the guidance and direction of editors who are aware of modern trends.

Basically, this is the best reason we can use to support our earlier statement that graphics alone will not perform the miracle of increasing circulation. After all, the *Wall Street Journal* is not the most visually exciting newspaper published today, but its circulation continues to increase.

Improvement in content and emphasis on clear writing and editing, combined with effective graphic innovation, should be present before some of the magic becomes evident in the circulation ledgers. The two areas of content and design must be rejuvenated simultaneously. Redesigning a newspaper may prove useless unless the editors and publishers have also analyzed their product, paying particular attention to the sociological and psychological components that make up their present and potential audience.

*Potential* is a word to consider carefully, because many editors fail to make a serious effort to attract the countless readers who do not read newspapers. Unfortunately for those of us interested in newspapers, these nonreaders survive rather well without exposure to our products. They are the ones who literally broke the newspaper habit years ago or who grew up without exposure to adults who read newspapers. However, re-creating the newspaper habit should be one of the urgent priorities for the editors of American newspapers.

Who is the newspaper nonreader? If you are thinking of the very young, the elderly, the poor, the uneducated and unsophisticated, the findings of a 1977 study conducted by Paula M. Poindexter for the American Newspaper Publishers Association will change your mind.

Ms. Poindexter conducted personal interviews of 5,000 randomly selected adults in nine northwestern cities and identified 510 persons who said they never or seldom read a daily newspaper. The most common reasons given by those who did not read a newspaper ranged from lack of time to lack of interest to use of another medium.

The study reveals that middle-aged, middle- and upper-income and well-educated persons are among the nonreaders, and it recommends trying to attract this group.

A quality newspaper may be the only way to attract some of these nonreaders. John Brooks of the *Toronto Star* uses five words to describe what this quality newspaper should be like: (1) readable, (2) relevant, (3) topical, (4) urgent, and (5) exciting.

Twenty-five years ago this five-word evaluative criterion would have placed *urgent* as the first priority, and the term *relevant* would not have appeared on the list at all. More editors should be thinking of the logic behind these five words and the order in which Brooks has placed them.

PASS IT...IT'LL MAKE YOU FEEL BETTER.

GULLIBLE'S TRAVELS

These cartoons by Vic Cantone, of *Editor & Publisher,* illustrate the artist's view of newspapers at the end of the 1970s.
(Courtesy of *Editor & Publisher.*)

# 2 redefining the role of the newspaper: three challenges

Any discussion of contemporary newspaper design must be contained within the framework of three important challenges facing the industry:

1. Accepting the emergence of television as a far-reaching medium for news and entertainment.
2. Satisfying the informational needs of a greater number of readers who have moved to the suburbs and created "news microcosms" within the large metropolitan areas.
3. Developing content relevant to the changing lifestyles of young readers and reestablishing the newspaper habit among the large number of nonreaders.

## CHALLENGE #1—TELEVISION

In a sense, television has been a blessing for American newspapers. The threat of television has created a sense of introspection in many editors and publishers, which will inevitably result in better newspapers. That is, television has forced newspapers to change in order to survive. Frank A. Bennack, Jr., executive vice-president of Hearst Corporation, has stated that "never in my twenty-five years in this business have newspaper executives been as introspective about the product as they are today, and that is healthy."

Newspaper editors should be willing to accept the presence of television as a challenge, not a deterrent, and the most creative will try to provide what television does not.

25

An analysis of both television and newspapers inevitably puts newspapers at a disadvantage, mainly because of the desirable qualities of television as a medium. A comparative study conducted by Bradley S. Greenberg and Michael E. Roloff of the Department of Communications at Michigan State University indicates that the pre-digested and prepackaged quality of television news makes it easier to absorb than print news. The authors state that large segments of the American population that are "functionally illiterate" are not so frustrated when they *watch* news. "It does not require such mental effort on their part and is not a reminder of their personal inadequacy to deal well with reading material."

The report suggests that editors could implement similar changes in format and content with innovative typographical design, editorial use of color photographs, catchier headlines, and a "visual grabber." Realistically, editors should avoid competing in vain with television; instead, they should derive ideas from that medium that can be successfully adapted and translated to newspapers.

For example, one of television's most desirable qualities, as stated by the Greenberg-Roloff study, is that the audience may absorb its information painlessly. Newspaper editors may begin by striving, within the limitations imposed by the medium, to create well-designed pages that will require little effort from the reader. Continuity and sequence (to be discussed in detail in Chapter 6) should become the basic pattern of content organization: a place for every item and an item in every place, with the reader knowing where to find the place and the item every day. News digests and brief columns should be available for readers who are too busy to read longer pieces, and page-one indexes should be graphically displayed to provide quick reference to inside content. (Television news shows also include "top of the news" indexes at the beginning of the newscast.)

One newspaper that has succeeded through organization of content is the *Louisville Times,* a pioneer in progressive ideas to improve quality. Its front page is used as a window to the inside for the reader who wants more than a summary. The *Times'* front page also accommodates the relaxed reader, who plans to sit down to enjoy his newspaper leisurely, as others enjoy the evening news show on television.

At least one newspaper has stopped competing with television, proclaiming itself "the newspaper for television viewers." The *Miami News* not only changed its format to a completely modular approach but also boiled down much of its national and international wire copy to short items and covered them with informal brief headlines. Any extra space gained by the shorter wire copy was devoted to more personal coverage of local news. Larger and more dramatically cropped photography was moved to page one.

An increasing number of newspaper editors now turn to television to borrow display ideas for their pages. The news graphics director of one of the major television networks says he is convinced that some of the exciting graphic ideas utilized by the *New York Times* as part of its splashy new sections, "Home," "Living," and "Weekend," are carry-overs from television graphics.

Drawing graphic inspiration from other media is nothing new. Newspapers during the last few years have been influenced by the nation's best-designed magazines. *Life*, for example, pioneered in the use of large and dramatically cropped photographs, which are now common to newspaper front pages; other graphic ideas successfully transferred from magazines to newspapers include the use of unjustified or ragged body type, sans serif display type, wider columns, story packaging, and double-page spreads.

Television graphics borrows a sense of typographical organization and design appeal from the print media. Indeed, it is possible to transfer workable ideas from one medium to the other, and since neither medium is likely to eliminate the other in the race for audience preference, it seems reasonable for newspaper and television to engage in a mutual exchange of working ideas. For newspaper editors, this should be one of the three major challenges they will face in the next decade.

Few newspapers use the large headline banner to "shout" at a prospective reader passing by a newspaper stand, but television graphics capitalizes on the old technique in an effort to call attention to a given news item. (Courtesy of ABC News Inc.)

## CHALLENGE #2—THE SUBURBAN READER

Attracting the high number of readers who have moved from the inner city to the suburbs is an interesting but puzzling situation to many editors and publishers.

As the suburbs become news centers within the larger coverage area of the metropolitan cities, the needs of suburban readers parallel those of small-town residents. When the *Miami Herald* inaugurated its "Neighbors" section, it came as a surprise to many that one of the new supplement's most prominent sections was the classic police blotter. True, police blotters have always been a part of small-town weeklies; even today many community newspapers capitalize on the minute-to-minute routine calls that pour into police offices. The *Herald's* police blotter signifies more than a listing of seemingly inconsequential occurrences, however. It points out the need for a return to a more personalized type of reporting. Graphically, the *Herald's* police blotter is presented in an easy-to-read, well-packaged page with large type and effective use of white space, as designed by Robert Mellis.

It may seem a contradiction that this form of turn-of-the-century reporting may be enjoying a return. After all, we are constantly reminded that today's reader is more sophisticated, better educated, and more demanding. However, suburbanites find themselves at the crossroads of a double life. They work in the inner city and continue to enjoy the culture and entertainment available there, but they go home in the evenings to the more limited and familiar surroundings of the suburbs where they encounter a greater sense of personal identity. An advertising research executive describes the situation as controversial since it places the reader in the midst of a contradiction of "cosmopolitanism versus parochialism," a contradiction which has led to a host of suburban weeklies and zoned editions.

A newspaper survival study directed by Ben Bagdikian, entitled "Report of an Exaggerated Death: Daily Newspapers that Failed, 1961–1970," has revealed that the lowest number of failures were among newspapers published in the suburbs. In many cases, success has required a redefinition of local news. To suburbanites who read newspapers, local news is limited to what happens in their vicinity. With few exceptions, they have little concern with what is happening at City Hall downtown. Leo Bogart, general manager of the Newspaper Advertising Bureau, in an address to members of the American Society of Newspaper Editors, pointed out that readers in the suburbs are also unconcerned with what happens in all the little towns and municipalities of their metropolitan region.

As long as there are many readers in the suburbs, newspapers will have to seek alternatives that will make their products vital outside the inner city. Already, many metropolitan dailies are utilizing marketing and advertising strategies to attract strong readership in the suburbs, where fast-developing suburban dailies and weeklies are beginning to flourish.

Perhaps one of the most successful suburban publishers is Geoffrey Edwards, general manager of the Journal Newspapers, a group of five suburban biweeklies in the Washington, D.C., area. The Journal group has a weekly circulation of 110,000, which prompts its staffers to describe their product as the "third newspaper" in the nation's capital.

The five weeklies are the *Alexandria* (Va.) *Journal-Standard*, *Fairfax Journal*, *Arlington Journal*, *Montgomery Journal*, and *Prince George's Journal*. Edwards is confident that his newspapers are as "newsy" as any metropolitan newspaper, but strictly on a local level. The main thrust of their coverage is "intense coverage of people and what they're doing in each of our circulation areas."

Columnist James Reston's analysis of the suburban reader is worth remembering: "People followed the complexities of the world for a long time very, very carefully. Then Korea, the cold war and Vietnam broke their heart. They began to turn it off and try to think about life in human dimensions rather than world abstractions. . . . People began reading avidly family, school and church news—almost anything that has to do

The *Miami Herald* reaches suburban readers through this "Neighbors" section; notice the police blotter.

with local taxes, local zoning, pollution, anything that has to do with the atmosphere of local life.''

Edwards explains that his five newspapers adhere to the sense of community identification described by Reston:

> The Journal Papers mirror on the community level what the metropolitan dailies cover on the national scale. Journal sports pages, for example, are as professional as the [Washington] *Post* and the [Washington] *Star*. The big difference is that the names are those of the boy next door and the neighbor across the street; people you know—the little leaguers, the high school coach assessing the team's chances and the supermarket manager's daughter, who just won the playground tennis trophy.

These five suburban newspapers, operated by Journal Newspapers Inc. in the Washington, D.C. area, devote most of their coverage to local news of the suburbs, with heavy emphasis on people and what they are doing.

Alert editors in large and small dailies have begun to pay attention to the suburbs by servicing them with various alternatives. Zoned editions have been implemented by several major newspapers, including the *New York Times*, which now publishes regional sections as additions to the Sunday paper. One, the *Westchester Weekly*, serves primarily the county north of New York City. The other, the *Connecticut Weekly*, circulates predominantly in Fairfield County. The two suburbs involved represent highly competitive markets for the *Times*. The zoned editions of the *Times* follow the same attractive, six-column format used in the *Times'* special sections. A large photograph dominates the section's front page, usually accompanying a lead feature piece—such as the one illustrated here on hang-gliding students at a local workshop. The front page usually does not include more than three articles plus a short index. A reduced version of the *Times'* nameplate at the top of the page is teamed with a prominently displayed *Westchester Weekly* positioned on a slant at the upper left-hand corner.

This "Westchester Weekly" edition of the *New York Times* represents an attempt to capture the attention of suburban readers in a highly competitive market. Notice the six-column format, use of a large photograph as a center of visual impact, and the front section index.

## CHALLENGE #3—ATTRACTING YOUNG READERS

We have already cited the interruption of the newspaper habit and attributed part of its cause to the far-reaching effects of television. However, there is another reason for readership decline: for many years, newspapers have overlooked young adults.

Now, fortunately, the pendulum is swinging in a different direction. The word is out among publishers and editors: Survival means re-creating the newspaper habit among the young.

One of the most successful attempts is the Newspaper in Education program, which brings the newspaper to the classroom and makes it appealing to young readers. The objective of this program is to accustom students to the standard newspaper fare so that they will be more likely to want it in later years. As the editor of a large daily described it: "Every teacher in the NIE program is a ready-made missionary for us."

Relevant coverage constitutes the first step in capturing the attention of young readers, although attractive graphics make the initial contact between newspaper and young reader easier. Of course, the age range quoted under the "young" category varies, depending upon what study one refers to and in what publication. For purposes of clarification in this text, let's establish a fourteen-to-thirty range, ample enough to accommodate potential readers still in high school as well as the large segment of young adults who have finished high school and even college without becoming newspaper readers.

Editors who neglect young readers justify their position by saying that young people simply do not read. Bill Stegall, circulation director of the *San Jose Mercury and News*, feels differently, insisting that what young people are not reading is newspapers:

> Loss of readership is occurring because newspapers have failed, particularly with the younger groups, to maintain essentiality to keep pace with our marketing techniques.

Large dailies have never before made such tremendous effort to attract the young as they do today. In Canada, the *Toronto Star* is using what its executive managing editor describes as "aggressive, flamboyant and all-pervasive" merchandising of the newspaper. A current survey in Canada shows that young people respond to the hard sell, straight from the shoulder and in their language. John Brooks of the *Star* also points out what we already know about the purchasing power of the young.

They (young people) like participation, the vicarious living manifest in
their heroes, personal gratification. They love to hear about themselves.
The now generation? It's the me generation. And rich. My allowance used
to clink in my pocket. Today's allowance rustles.

Brooks wonders if newspaper promotional programs are really pitching to the affluent
lifestyle of the young and if editorial content is gripping the young reader.

The answer to those questions is a positive *yes* from the marketing and editorial
personnel of the *Chicago Tribune*. The *Tribune*'s efforts to gain young readers is seen
in a three-page magazine promotional ad presenting "eight ways the *Chicago
Tribune* goes after the young reader." The ad includes eight miniature front pages of
the *Tribune*'s daily special sections. "Ask any good newspaper person about those
precious young readers, and you're apt to get a similar appraisal," the ad reads. "They
are smarter, more aware, than the generations that have gone before."

What these smarter and more aware young readers want, more than hard news, is
a heavy dose of features on things to do, places to go, consumer awareness, sports
(especially participation activities), and generous entertainment sections.

Two Pennsylvania newspapers have taken note of these areas, with marked
success. The *Allentown Morning Call* followed this prescription and revamped its
regular Saturday edition from a standard-size newspaper to a tabloid called *Weekender*.

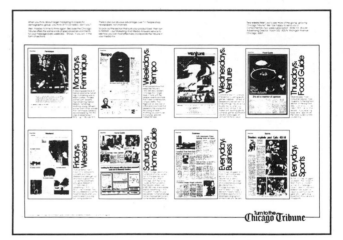

This promotional ad was used by the *Chicago Tribune* to advertise
its efforts in the battle to gain young readers.
(Courtesy of *The Chicago Tribune,* Marketing Department.)

This "Weekender" section aims at a young
readership, and the results have been
successful in terms of circulation for the
*Allentown Morning Call.* The front page serves
as an index to inside content; the back page
packs in information in an easy-to-read style.

This "Lifestyles" section of the *Free Press* (Quakertown, Pennsylvania) follows a four-column format. Notice the dominance of illustrations on the page, wider columns, white space, and large body type. The entire page is packaged as a unit, part of a new look to attract a new audience of young readers. (Courtesy of *The Free Press*.)

Reaching potential audiences begins at an early stage for the *Louisville Times*. This "Jelly Bean Journal" appears every Saturday and aims at the youngest possible readership. (Courtesy of *The Louisville Times*.)

Also, the *Free Press* in Quakertown, Pennsylvania was redesigned with young people as a primary target. Features such as a plant column, movie and record reviews, and health advice, and an overall news magazine approach have worked circulatory magic for the *Free Press*.

Reestablishing the newspaper habit begins with introducing very young readers to what the newspaper has to offer. The *Louisville Times* publishes a Saturday four-page tab section entitled "Jelly Bean Journal" as part of its other special Saturday offerings, "Scene" and "TV Scene." The "Journal," an easy-to-read four-column tabloid-sized section, uses large type and plenty of illustrations and represents a positive step in meeting the third important challenge of the next decade. To paraphrase the *Chicago Tribune's* promotional ad, the challenge should be that of understanding and responding with intelligence to the needs of a newspaper's present and potential audience.

To the challenges outlined here—facing television competition, capturing the attention of the suburban reader, and attracting young readership—we may add two other important realities:

1. The fight against the clock for a piece of the reader's twenty-four-hour day.
2. The realization that the only newspapers that are "gasping for air" are those whose editors continue to publish news as they did in the early 1950s.

We can't think of a more exciting period to be involved with newspaper work, particularly with its editing and designing aspects.

3

the front page

Every editor who plans a front page probably sticks to his own list of rules for design. However, regardless of how old that list may be, at least two basic ideas should stand out:

1. The front page continues to play a key role as the showcase for the newspaper and its contents.
2. The front page is analogous to an artist's mosaic in that it must be visually appealing to create an overall attractive effect. Unlike a mosaic, however, page one must communicate a series of messages that may or may not have any relationship to one another. The manner in which each message is presented must instantly convey its significance to the reader.

## PAGE ALIGNMENT

Page-one design often involves a basic choice between vertical and horizontal alignment for headlines and copy. Ideally, this choice should be made on the basis of what will make an individual group of articles and photos look better and read faster, as opposed to preconceived ideas concerning vertical and horizontal placement on a page. (Later chapters will show why certain specific situations call for horizontal emphasis and why other situations suggest vertical placement.)

The two concepts of page alignment are important and deserve careful consideration, not only for the design of page one but for other pages as well.

## Horizontal Placement

When horizontal placement developed in the post-World War II years, it represented a radical departure from the all-vertical page design cultivated by most newspapers. The new style capitalized on multicolumn headlines and horizontal movement across the page. Although horizontal headlines had become a part of page one as early as 1864, when last-minute breaking stories about the Civil War prompted the *New York Times'* editors to carry banner headlines across the top of the page, this early horizontal emphasis stopped with the headline. Body copy usually ran straight down the page. Editors recognized the impact of horizontal placement for headlines, but it would be many years before they applied the same concept to the placement of copy throughout the page for multicolumn display.

## Vertical Placement

In its most classic style, a front page used long vertical columns to illustrate the day's news. As a result, we tend to relate vertical design to elegance and dignity. These, however, are not built-in characteristics of vertical placement. More often, excessive use of long vertical columns, especially in broadsheets, leads to *tombstoning*, that is, gray masses of type and overall dullness. Vertical placement can work well only when surrounded by white space, simple design, easy-to-read headlines, and adequate column width.

This front page highlights three top stories by placing them side by side. Notice how two of the stories carry multicolumn headlines but force the reader to go down a narrow column. The story in the middle seems lost, overpowered by its more dominant adjoining headlines. The same design would look better with wider columns, no column rules between columns, and one lead story as opposed to three competing for the reader's attention. The *Gazette's* front page is newsy and economical.

The *Times* also highlights three top stories on this front page, but they are easier to read than those in the previous illustration, in part because of the wider columns in the six-column format. The three-column photograph creates interest and alleviates the possible typographical congestion at the top of the page. As in the case of the *Schenectady Gazette,* dropping the column rules would make this vertical page more appealing and easier on the eyes.

The *Sun* also displays three lead stories in vertical fashion at the top of page one, but how much easier this page is on the reader. Notice how those two-pica spaces without column rules help the page by adding white space. The designer here has been careful to place graphic elements between the headlines, thus avoiding unnecessary tombstoning. In addition, the page typifies the compromise between vertical and horizontal placement that usually leads to attractive pages.

Some of the best-designed newspapers are experimenting with vertical placement to create attractive and easy-to-read pages. The nature of many lengthy articles, especially those published in inside sections, gives vertical placement an edge over the more attractive but less economical horizontal treatment. One daily newspaper that is capitalizing on vertical placement for its new format is the *Des Moines* (Iowa) *Register*, which has adopted a classic turn-of-the-century front page with one-column headlines, no visible lead element on the page, and discreet use of photography. What is different about the *Register's* new vertical front page is its most generous use of white space, which makes the long masses of gray more palatable.

## THE NEW FRONT PAGE

The front page of today is best described as *individualized*. It adapts not only to the individual needs of the day's news and photographic content but also to the needs of the readership it serves. A sampling of a hundred front pages, stylistically miles apart, shows that all of them carry out that purpose effectively. Before we classify front pages according to design and content, let us analyze some trends that may be helpful to those students of newspaper typography who like to keep a handy list of rules. What are the general trends applicable to today's front page?

1. The front page includes items that are more significantly personal or local. And not all the items appearing on page one will be hard news as we usually know the term; rating high for front page space are articles related to consumer affairs, alternate lifestyles, and the quality of life in a particular city or suburb within the newspaper's readership.

2. Fewer national and international wire stories appear on page one, especially in small dailies. Locally produced copy and photos dominate. One newspaper, the *Free Press* (Quakertown, Pennsylvania), has moved national and international news to section three.

3. Photographic dominance on the page is evident through the use of larger and dramatically cropped photos. Technological advances, such as the invention of plastic engravings and lighter press plates, combined with the widespread use of offset printing, provide excellent clarity and sharpness of details in the reproduction of photographs. Photographers realize that newspapers can now make good use of photos, and as a result, even the traditional head shots, once relegated to "thumbnail" status, have emerged as potentially desirable graphic elements on the page.

Editors are giving more prominence to photos, paying attention to the positioning of individual photos on the page and cropping them carefully. Photo pages have become part of the newspaper's standard fare. Many newspapers, such as the *Yakima* (Wash.) *Herald-Republic*, use large photos as lead elements on the page to lure the readers, while maintaining a high story count.

4. A news summary and/or index box is part of the regular front page fare. Indexes not only provide an organized summary of inside contents but also serve as effective graphic tools to break the monotony of the page.

5. The front page is not stationary. Its appearance should vary from day to day so that the habitual reader will immediately notice a sense of freshness and vitality which will tell him he is not looking at yesterday's newspaper. Editors who design a front page every day risk the dangers of falling into a graphic pattern. Many editors unconsciously develop a preference for a certain graphic approach and constantly force it upon the page, regardless of how suitable it may be for a given situation. Continuity and sequence on page one should be derived from such standing features as the nameplate and the index or summary box, but not at the expense of varied design. The

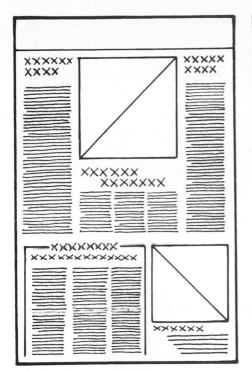

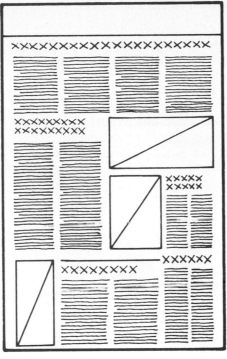

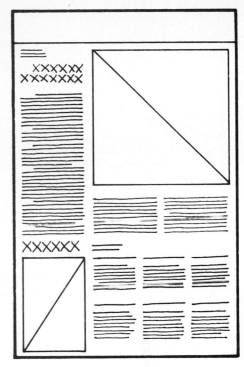

**U-shape design**         **C-shape**         **L-shape**

diagrams above illustrate many design possibilities for placing elements on the page. Notice how in all cases copy and photos alternate to create ''letter'' forms.

6. Typographically, front pages today show greater utilization of clean, easy-to-read sans serif headline typefaces. More pronounced use of contrasting bold and light typefaces within the same page are also evident, along with attractive design for nameplates and standing features. Balance and contrast are achieved through the striking contrast of bold and light typefaces, more so than through the customary interaction of roman and italic combinations. Many newspapers have abandoned the use of italic headlines altogether. (Chapter 5 deals with the typography of today's newspaper.)

7. Graphically, the new front page capitalizes on a simpler and more elegant design through the use of wider columns.

8. The front page of today appears vibrant and immediate, but the headlines no longer shout at the reader. Photographs are now doing most of the shouting. The smaller headlines, greater use of vertical column alignment, and generally fewer stories re-create the placid magazine look as the graphic framework for the day's news.

Richard Thien, managing editor of the Springfield, Missouri *Leader and Press*, says that editors should think about the page when they are putting it together, making it a design, not a scrambled exhibit with seven, nine, or eleven stories. ''Some things have gone the way of the green eyeshade, and they are a Page 1 that looks like the window of a True Value Hardware Store and that big grabber headline that shouts so loud, it blinds you,'' Thien says.

9. Overall, the front pages show more artistic and creative uses of graphics as functional tools to communicate the day's news.

10. More than ever before, today's front page represents the promise of better things to come. Some newspapers highlight front-page material on inside pages. For example, the *Providence Journal* labels page three ''The Second Front Page.'' The *Des Moines Register* calls it ''The Third Page'' and gives it all the standard front-page treatment.

## FRONT-PAGE VARIETY

The front pages shown here point out the degree of variety which characterizes today's page one. All have some attractive features to draw the reader, but in each case there may be elements that work for one individual newspaper and not for others.

The *Winnipeg Tribune,* another of Peter Palazzo's designs, represents the modern front page in transition. Better yet, the front page is a combination of some of the most contemporary graphics and the tested ideas of yesterday. The striking contrast of extremely bold and light typefaces gives the reader one definite lead story around which the rest of the page will be designed. Notice the unusual, and somewhat confusing, use of various column widths. The lead story follows a six-column pattern, but other items on the page may have two and three wider column combinations. The index highlights the bottom of the page effectively, and the nameplate resembles an automobile license superimposed on the page. Although the page definitely lacks a sense of directional order, it is unusual enough to create interest through the use of column rules, large photos, and unorthodox placement of copy and headlines. This is certainly not the type of design that beginners should experiment with! (The Tribune discontinued publication in 1980.)

A clean, easy-to-read newspaper, the *Midland (Tex.) Reporter-Telegram* relies on sans serif headlines, large photos, and an almost totally horizontal format for its front page. The nameplate continues to use Old English typeface but has been surrounded with white space and underlined with a distinctive rule. Few stories are played up on page one, but they are packaged to provide comfortable reading. The headlines show little size variation, although italics are used to create contrast. This type of front page is easy to design and easy to look at. The absence of gimmicks should make it popular with its readers.

The *Providence Journal* was redesigned by Peter Palazzo, who prefers center positioning of photographs. This page clusters photo content in the center, surrounding the photos with copy. Obviously, the *Journal*'s front page is a showcase for photos as primary graphic elements. Headlines and copy become secondary in the editor's priority. Notice the use of news summary directly below the nameplate. Packaging strategies allow for easy reading, and two-thirds of the page is packaged as a unit.

Some front pages will follow the all-inclusive format, which allows many stories to be displayed equally on page one. The *Austin (Tex.) American-Statesman* shows that approach here, except that it lacks bold headlines and enough photos to keep the page from looking gray. The use of two horizontal packages at the top and bottom of the page tends to squeeze the middle.

Color dominates the Sunday *Toronto Star.* The page is broken up into two structures, one of which is devoted entirely to an impressive color photograph. Headlines and copy blocks attempt to grab the reader's attention at the bottom two-thirds of the page. This front page shows that a good designer can manage quality, quantity, and overall graphic impact in one front page.

This front page relies on vertical placement for an attractive packaging of news and photos. Notice the photo dominance at the top, contrasting with the horizontal display of a feature item at the bottom. The nameplate uses a distinctive border arrangement. On a more traditional note, the *Times* centers its headlines and accompanies most of them with a flush-left kicker. The index feature is not as prominently displayed as in some of the other front pages profiled here. The overall impact of this front page is brought about by the use of white space and simple design. (The *Times* was redesigned totally in 1979.)

These front pages from the *Miami* (Fla.) *Herald* and the (Albany, N.Y.) *Knickerbocker News* show effective use of index items as potential graphic tools to highlight an otherwise routine page. In the *Herald's* example, color is used as part of an illustration. The *News,* however, relies on the index color exclusively to carry the page.

These pages from the *Des Moines Tribune* and the *Free Press* display alternative methods of carrying a page-one content to a prominently displayed inside page. Both pages are ad-free and follow a format similar to that of page one.

## EYE MOVEMENT AND PAGE ONE

Newspaper designers must recognize the importance of eye movement when they design a page. On page one, particularly, initial attraction precedes any other action by the reader. The designer's objective is twofold:

1. To grab the reader's attention the moment he sees the page.
2. To create sufficient visual interest to keep the reader's eyes moving on the page.

Traditionally, newspaper editors in making up a front page assumed that a reader's journey through the newspaper inevitably began at the upper right corner and continued in a circular motion around the page. It is no wonder that so many editors often saved their lead story for that priority area, assuming that if they caught the attention of a reader there, the reader would move to the left, where a photo would await her, and from there she would proceed accordingly. Many editors still use this plan to make up their front pages, but the concept has become less popular with more experimental editors.

The new front page, then, emphasizes a more creative and artistic visual approach to the placement of elements. Greater freedom has led to the abandonment of traditional rules for the positioning of copy, headlines, and photos. It has given the designer new dimensions and created a free form for newspaper design.

*Free form* refers to a nonstationary design concept in which graphic packaging of news and photos is adapted to the day's available content as opposed to a set or stationary format ruled by the same positioning from day to day. Free form encourages the designer to play up copy when the content deserves such graphic dominance or to emphasize a photo or illustration if either is the best graphic possibility for the day. Content dictates the use of graphics in free-form design.

Newspaper designers must be aware of the changing nature of the news. Events which alter page design may occur at any time, and the designer must be flexible enough to change accordingly, giving a news item the importance it deserves regardless of how it may affect the design.

Samuel V. Kennedy, who teaches news editing at Syracuse University, often reminds his students that unlike the mason who piles up his bricks on one side and picks up one at a time to build a structure, the newspaper editor seldom knows what his "pile of bricks" will look like each day. Each brick is likely to be different from the next. The only day-to-day constants in a newspaper are the nameplate, the standing signatures, and white space. The rest of the elements revolve and take turns in commanding the attention of the reader.

In a sense, free form reassures the designer that he is doing something right as long as the day's news is displayed in a manner that will be pleasant to look at and easy to digest. There is no set of predetermined rules to obey, no stationary eye movement techniques to hinder the creative process. Offset printing, cold type, and other innovative technological advances are making it possible to carry this new creative freedom in newspaper design beyond what could have been imagined twenty years ago.

But no matter how creative the new technology allows him or her to become, the beginning designer must realize that planning and consistency of graphic style are still the framework of any successful newspaper format. A designed newspaper does not happen overnight. It requires months of preparation leading to an acceptable-to-all format for which a graphic stylebook must be prepared (see Chapter 6). This stylebook will deal with such day-to-day specifics as the consistent style for cutlines, bylines, jump lines, and other constants. It will explain how to handle the front page on days with many news items or days with heavy emphasis on photography, what typefaces to use, and how to use them harmoniously. Most important, once a particular design has been adopted for the newspaper, the stylebook will show designers how to implement the basic format page by page. Such planning does not mean that a certain degree of improvisation will not remain as part of the day-to-day production of a newspaper. Nothing can be more changeable or seemingly "improvised" than the day's news. And besides, how many newspaper editors are willing to give up those fascinating guessing games that often take place in the back shop while they try to fit last-minute copy and photos into place? Ideally, however, a page should not be completely improvised minutes before deadline. Planning is precisely what establishes the difference between design and makeup.

## DESIGN VERSUS MAKEUP

When the traditionalist makes up a newspaper page he simply finds a space for every story, headline, and photograph, working from the top to the bottom of the page. Usually he has no preconceived idea of how the final product will look. He simply hopes for the best results.

The changing nature of news and the many last-minute items that sometimes must be accommodated on page one explain the practicality of making up the page. Many attractive newspaper pages are the result of last-minute efforts by a makeup editor whose most exciting graphic creation took place right in the composing room on deadline.

Designing a page, on the other hand, implies organized planning—*how* each element will appear, *where* it will be located, and *what effect* it will have on the overall appearance of the page. Designing a page also means harmonizing the various graphic elements. It calls for a blending of typography, photography, and white space to create total graphic impact and effortless reading.

## A CASE FOR THE CENTER OF VISUAL IMPACT

Creative and harmonious page design begins with the placement of what I call a strong *Center of Visual Impact* on the page. At the expense of adding three more initials to a field that is already saturated, let's refer to this concept as the CVI.

What is the CVI?

A better question might be, "*Where* is the CVI?" The answer is anywhere the designer wishes to place it. Obviously, the designer controls the way he wants the reader to proceed visually on the page. One of the basic rules of page design is to create instant attraction for the reader. The CVI should generate enough interest or magnetism to command the reader's visual attention at a glance. An article published in *Art Education* (Spring 1941) by the noted psychologist B. F. Skinner—a name seldom linked to publication design—offers insight into the behavior of looking that is applicable to newspaper design, particularly the initial attraction of a reader to a page. Skinner points out that a uniform surface (which translated to our study of newspaper typography might be described as a gray page) does not cause the observer to behave in any very definite way. However, he writes, if we place upon it a single dot of contrasting color or value, we may be said to have established a rudimentary design, because almost invariably the eye will move in the direction of the dot and stop there, at least temporarily.

Let's assume that instead of a dot we place a single photograph on the page, no matter how small. It would be safe to assert that the reader's eye will move in the direction of that photograph, whether it is at the top, middle, or bottom portion of the page. The photo has created attraction, has generated movement, and therefore, has become a CVI.

Skinner explains that if a second dot is introduced into the design, immediately the effect is enhanced. The eye now tends to move from one dot to another, establishing the two design constants of *direction* and *distance*. As we position a second photograph on the page we immediately give the first one competition. We also must place the second photograph in a strategic position that will make direction and distance functional tools for moving the reader through the page.

Skinner's final observation on the behavior of looking is that if the designer increases the number of dots, the repetition weakens the effect of the overall design. In other words, pages with an overabundance of photographs, where sameness has led to a lack of direction and distance, ruin the design and do the photographs an injustice.

Skinner's observations should help us understand that eye movement on a printed page—and even on a television or movie screen—does not begin with a set or organized pattern. In simpler terms, the reader does not have an itinerary before he begins his journey through the page. Consequently, he may be attracted to one area of the front page first, from which he may proceed. He may move from top to bottom and left to right (the preferred order) but will also move from bottom to top and right to left.

The reader finds a target spot on the page and aims at it first. The target spot becomes the CVI, a movable structure that aims at attracting the reader, regardless of where it is placed. The designer positions the CVI where he feels it will be most functional to attract the reader and to promote further reading on the page. Options here may be as variable as the content of the page, but in all cases, the CVI must not be isolated from the rest of the page. It should be designed as a distinctively unique graphic structure that will attract the most attention. If a second area of the page offers competition to the CVI, the reader becomes confused by the graphic demands placed upon him. In other words, there should be only one strong CVI to a page, and no other element should weaken its total effect. In terms of content, the CVI can be any of the following:

## Photographs

The most common and dramatic way of creating instant graphic appeal is with a photograph. Large horizontals and dramatically cropped verticals can become effective CVIs:

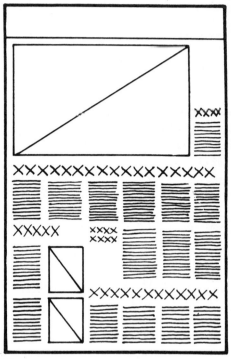

**Horizontal CVI**

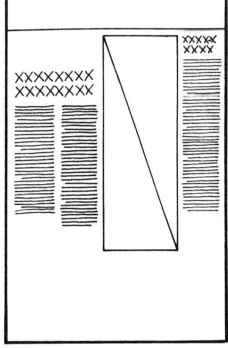

**Vertical CVI**

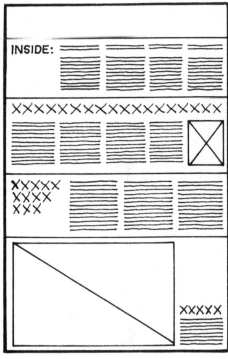

**Lower-half CVI**

## Typography

Large, bold, and properly placed display type can become an effective CVI. Especially when photos are not available, type can create graphic interest for the page. Its most practical application, however, is on inside pages dominated by a single, lengthy article with little possibilities for photo or art. Another example where typography may serve as a CVI is in the case of an attractive nameplate that will create reader interest for a page one, even when the day's contents do not lend themselves to creative graphics.

## Packaging

Packaging refers to the concept of combining photo(s) and copy for special effect and easy identification of subject matter. Such combinations, well packaged into closed or open boxes, can also create graphic dominance. The packages may be horizontal, vertical, even rectangular, or uneven. Many times a package consists only of a photograph and cutline. (More detailed information concerning packaging strategies appears in Chapter 7.)

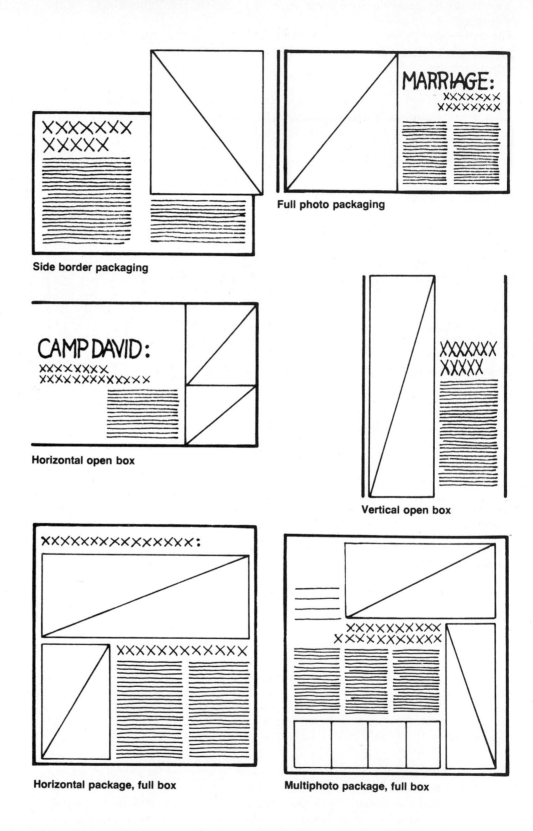

Side border packaging

Full photo packaging

Horizontal open box

Vertical open box

Horizontal package, full box

Multiphoto package, full box

# ANALYSIS OF FRONT PAGES DESIGNED WITH CVI

The front pages shown here include strong CVIs that create initial attraction while generating interest and promoting further movement on the page.

### Vertical CVI

Overall vertical placement dominates the design of this page. The photo used for the CVI also follows vertical movement. Notice how the CVI encourages further movement on the page and allows for proper distance and direction leading to the photograph at the bottom.

### Horizontal CVI

The *Milwaukee Sentinel* uses an eight-column format with a prominent lead story carrying a banner head at the top. A strong horizontal photograph of a cold mid-February day dominates the design as the CVI, receiving in this case generous competition from the banner above it. Notice how other photographs on the page have been kept at minimal size to keep them from competing with the CVI.

### Top-of-page CVI

The CVI at the top of the page is what many editors may call the preferred position, creating interest above the fold and providing for natural left-to-right reading flow. Notice that this page does not include other photographs but is successful in bringing the reader to the bottom half of the page through the use of sigs for "weather outlook" and "tonight's times." Box arrangement for berry festival also helps pull the eye down.

### Mid-page CVI

Not only is this an example of a mid-page CVI, it is also a packaged CVI with almost perfect symmetrical balance reminiscent of the 1950s.

# the structural approach and page one

Although many newspapers have made the technological switch from hot metal to cold type, some editors still have not adjusted their ''hot type'' thinking to accommodate the unlimited design potential of cold type. These editors hesitate to become designers who deal with the general available space, and continue to be makeup men who deal with inches and columns as isolated units on the page.

Cold type makes designing each page easier, since it allows for more graphic strategies than does hot type. Some of these strategies we have already discussed in Chapter 3 as ways to make the front page more readable and graphically appealing. We have also outlined the importance of a single target spot or Center of Visual Impact on the page to generate initial reader interest in the page's contents. Now we should turn our attention to designing the rest of the page. Just as a reporter works until he comes up with the best possible lead for a news story, the page designer does the same in terms of his CVI.

Both the lead and the CVI serve the same purpose—that of attracting a reader—but in the same way that a story cannot depend on a lead alone to communicate all the facts effectively, a front page is not likely to survive graphically on the basis of a striking CVI. Other graphic elements around the CVI must be organized harmoniously to create good overall design.

The structural approach to newspaper design is probably the easiest way to organize unrelated content in an orderly and harmonious manner. It is also the most natural way to place elements on the page. In its most natural form, a newspaper page is nothing more than a vast open white area, receptive to almost anything the designer wishes to locate on it. To treat a page structurally means to incorporate horizontal and vertical structures in the available spaces while creating visual order.

Order is paramount to contemporary newspaper design, at least for Americans, who tend to devote a limited amount of time to reading newspapers (see Chapter 2).

Nothing can be more disruptive to the reader who has only a few minutes to read the newspaper than a totally disorganized page in which extremely bold headlines clash, and heavy borders and odd-shaped photographs appear in ambiguous positions. The day's news itself provides enough chaos for the reader. Let the designer present this chaos in as orderly a fashion as possible.

## CREATING GRAPHIC ORDER

Structurally designed pages emphasize order as their most basic principle. Design order is accomplished through a logical progression of elements on the page, from large to small and from small to large. That is, the page is broken up into equal or unequal structures, which should vary in size to create visual appeal.

All photographs, copy blocks, and headlines maintain a sense of order by restricted placement in certain areas of space: they are squared off. No copy blocks turn or twist around other elements. Uniformity in shape creates order.

The success of structural design is based on the principle of creating order and visual harmony with one-level stories, while emphasizing balance and contrast with progression from large to small and small to large graphic elements, and from vertical to horizontal and horizontal to vertical copy blocks.

Several patterns of design progression can be incorporated into the page as follows.

### Patterns of Design Progression for Graphic Elements

*Small to large.* When this pattern is used, the bottom of the page will probably be the target for the CVI and consequently for page dominance. The top of the page relies on a small photograph or package. Positioning of graphic elements can be centered, traditional, or marginal. The illustrations on this page show how all three work in the small to large pattern:

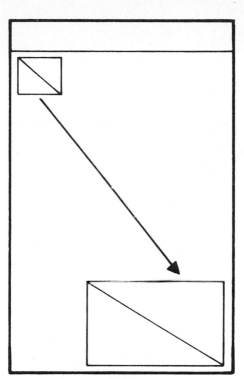

**Small to large—traditional**
This pattern calls for the small element to be placed near the upper left-hand corner of the page, while the large element, placed below the fold, serves to pull the reader's eye down to the bottom of the page.

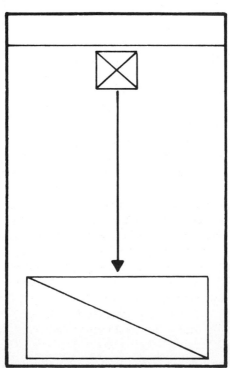

**Small to large—centered**
Effective centered positioning relies on the center of the page for impact. The main graphic display is framed by headlines and copy blocks.

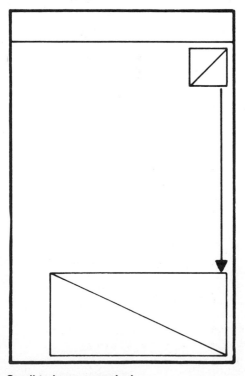

**Small to large—marginal**
Marginal positioning depends on a flush right or flush left approach, allowing an open center area for copy and headlines or perhaps a small photo.

***Large to small.*** Because a large element is placed above the fold, this may be a designer's best way to draw the reader into the page. Logically, the small to large combination carries more powerful motion, but when a photograph deserves space, this option may be worth considering. Let us examine how the large to small progression of elements works for the three positions: centered, traditional, and marginal.

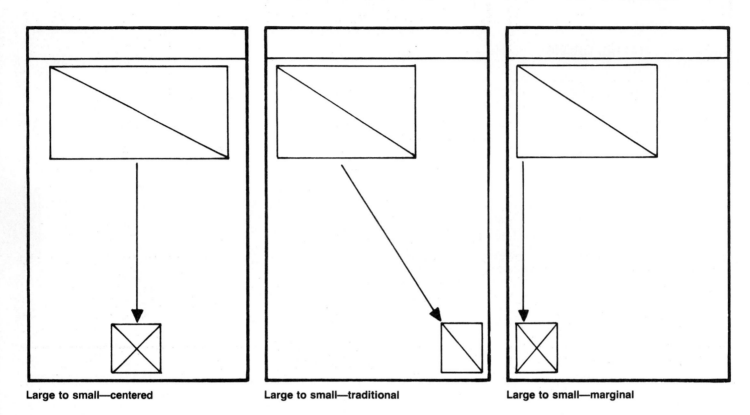

**Large to small—centered**       **Large to small—traditional**       **Large to small—marginal**

***Horizontal to vertical patterns for entire front page.*** As mentioned earlier, a structurally designed page can be divided into equal or unequal areas. When the progression of elements follows a horizontal to vertical pattern, the page opens visually at the top and narrows down to a vertical emphasis below the fold. The combinations shown at the top of the next page are possibilities, but many variations of the same concept can be adapted to individual situations.

***Vertical to horizontal combinations.*** An actual reversal of the procedure just outlined takes place in the pattern shown opposite, with the upper section of the page emphasizing vertical splits while the bottom carries the reader forcefully from left to right.

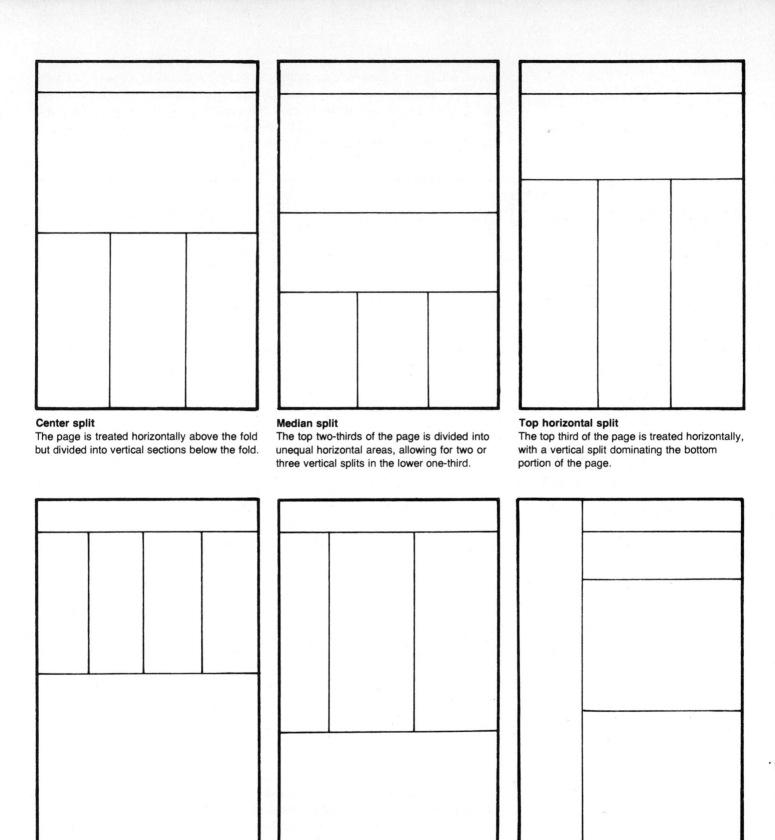

**Center split**
The page is treated horizontally above the fold but divided into vertical sections below the fold.

**Median split**
The top two-thirds of the page is divided into unequal horizontal areas, allowing for two or three vertical splits in the lower one-third.

**Top horizontal split**
The top third of the page is treated horizontally, with a vertical split dominating the bottom portion of the page.

**Center split**
When there isn't a single story or photo worth highlighting as a lead item on the page, this vertical center split can become most effective.

**Median split**
The top two-thirds of the page is divided into unequal vertical areas, allowing for two or three horizontal splits at the bottom of the page. This is a useful design, ideal for occasions when more than one story deserves top-of-the-page prominence.

**Side vertical split**
Perhaps the most common arrangement, as exemplified by the front pages of many well-designed newspapers, is the strong vertical column that cuts down one side of the page and from which a series of horizontal structures originate.

*Other patterns.* Although perhaps we should not label the designs below patterns of progression, nonetheless they are options available for designing a page structurally.

The progression patterns presented in this chapter should not become absolute rules to be followed at all times. Graphic design is an art, and its practitioners should allow themselves room for creativity and innovation. Many times, alteration and adaptation of the patterns presented here may lead to a variety of successful and graphically appealing page designs.

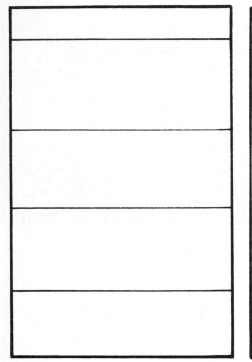

**Complete horizontal**
The page is *sliced* or cut through to form equal or unequal horizontal areas. No vertical emphasis appears anywhere, and the result can be graphically boring, although it is an ideal situation for placing long copy. This pattern definitely works better in tabloids than in full-sized newspapers. If it is used in the latter, two-way splits, where the page's natural fold becomes a visible partition, should be avoided.

**Complete vertical**
This is what readers of the *Wall Street Journal* find on page one of that newspaper daily. It is definitely up-and-down reading all the way. It should be used with caution and provided with a generous dose of white space.

## FRONT PAGE WORKSHOP

One of the newspaper editors consulted during the research for this chapter confessed that he could turn his discussion of front-page design into another version of *War and Peace*. Anybody who has ever tried to present the many aspects of designing a front page will agree that it has to be a mammoth production. For this reason a series of essentials not discussed in the last two chapters appear here as a page-one workshop.

### On the Use of Wider Columns

With few exceptions, *most* American newspapers have abandoned the use of narrow columns and *adopted a wider-column format* for their pages. Six columns seems to be the most readable and widespread format today, although several newspapers have successfully switched to four columns, at least for their front and other open pages. The six-column format was used by the *New York Times* from its debut on September 18, 1851, until December 3, 1865.

*Many* newspapers, however, *have not* been able to make the switch to a wider-column format on their inside pages because of advertising space committed ahead of time or because of mechanical limitations. What many newspapers in this situation have found practical has been to change the front page first, and then to adapt inside-page format when possible. Still, some contemporarily designed newspapers, such as the *Toronto Star*, continued to use a nine-column front page until the late 1970s.

A few newspapers, such as the *Winnipeg Tribune* (illustration on page 36 in Chapter 3), use column width combinations throughout the page, a practice that may create graphic interest but will surely guarantee some degree of confusion for typesetting and other production areas. In fact, a plausible trend among newspapers using the six-column format is to set all stories, and even cutlines, on the page the same width. This facilitates page design and maneuvering of copy when pasting up the page.

The following front pages illustrate various column formats:

**The six-column format**
*Times Union*, Rochester, New York.

**The four-column format**
el *Miami Herald*, Miami, Florida.

**The eight-column format**
*Daily Times*, Mamaroneck, New York.

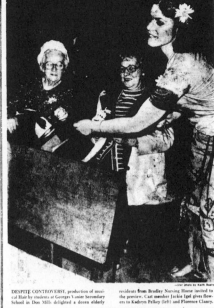

**The nine-column format**
*Toronto Star*, Toronto, Canada.
(This is the old *Toronto Star*; the paper switched
to a six-column format October 11, 1978.)

## On Column Width Alignment

If a sense of graphic order is to prevail, the column width of any given story should remain the same throughout the length of that story. Two-column leads that merge into a single column do nothing to create graphic order. They are time-consuming in that copyfitting must allow for a certain number of lines to be set at a different width; and, of course, structurally designed pages would not allow column width variation within the same story.

## On Maintaining a Smooth Copy Flow

Once the story has captured the attention of the reader, all he wants to do is to read until he gets the information he is looking for. The graphic designer should not create any graphic noise by placing quotes, lines, photographs, or any other elements in the midst of the reader's copy flow. If any such elements, such as a news analysis or opinion sig, are included, they should be positioned where they will not interfere with copy continuity.

## On Photo Relativity

How many times have you looked at a photograph that interested you only to find yourself struggling to identify the story that accompanies it? One of the most common offenders in the art of page design is failing to create "relativity" for a photograph. The result is usually a photograph framed by stories all of which could accompany the photo.

The reader who is in a hurry will not stop to decipher what the designer should have done for him, but the previously mentioned concept of packaging can solve the problem. (Refer to illustrations on page 42 for further explanation.)

## On the "Sprinkling" of Small Items

Brighteners and short two-paragraph items have always been as much a part of the American newspaper's front page as the nameplate and the banner headline. But when six or seven such items land on page one (often without much editorial justification), the result can be instant graphic disaster. While not advocating the elimination of these usually popular brief items on page one, we recommend that they be graphically organized into one column where the reader may find them neatly packaged for fast and convenient reading. The *Miami News'* front page carries all its small page-one items in a column entitled "Etcetera."

## On the Distribution of Weight Around the Page

Display type, standing sigs, and photographs are some of the elements used to give the page its weight, visually speaking. How one distributes these elements will determine how well each story and photograph will be displayed on the page. For example, a page in which every element is placed in perfect symmetrical proportion will probably result in a boring experience for the reader and a time-consuming chore for the pasteup crew.

Even the *New York Times*, whose trademark for many years was its continuous use of perfect symmetrical page makeup, has now radically departed from such typographic perfection. If there is any use for perfect symmetrical balance today it is

Even the traditionally conservative *Times'* front page displays a readable and surprisingly asymmetrical design, as opposed to the perfect balance that was part of its daily fare in the 1950s.

This jump page is attractive, easy to index, and includes a photograph for a story started on page one. Notice the ad space.

probably for special sections, particularly those dealing with political elections and other topics where equal coverage by the inch for all candidates and issues is of utmost importance. Some modernly designed newspapers may find symmetrical perfection handy sometimes. If nothing else, it is guaranteed to provide a bit of nostalgia for those readers old enough to remember the newspaper design of the 1950s.

The weight of the page should not be placed all on one side or all above or below the fold. Unequal, but balanced, distribution should be the designer's basic criterion when distributing graphic elements.

## On Multilevel Column Depth

Throughout the first three chapters we have emphasized the concept of making it easier for the reader to get his or her information. Few readers enjoy a story that begins at the top of the page, then runs nine inches down the page, forcing him to go back up for the start of the second column, which then plunges eleven inches before it makes the reader return to the original point. Multilevel column depth can only result from improvisation in page makeup. The alternative? Create one level for the story and maintain it regardless of how many columns that story extends across the page. Preferably, the reader will not have to descend more than six inches before he will go up again, and so on; at any rate, he should not be expected to move outside of that six-inch depth range.

## On Story Jumps

Page-one stories that jump to an inside page are a necessary evil. Studies indicate that if a story deserves it, 25 percent of the readers will faithfully move with the jump to continue reading. The designer should create order for any jumped stories by trying to place all the jumps together on an inside page. The jump page should be clean, well organized, and attractive. Photos and illustrations that cannot be incorporated on page one where the stories originate may very well be prominently placed on the jump page. The *Providence Journal* even labels such a page "From Page One."

## On Justified Versus Unjustified Columns

Justified columns work best for the front page. There is a certain informality about unjustified columns that should not be present for every item carried on a typical front page. Unjustified, or ragged right type, works effectively for special features or even on a regular basis for such standard items as index or summary boxes. One story or feature set in ragged right may create variety and help the page visually; an entire page so set may tend to look disorganized.

## On Graphic Consistency

The front page not only sets the mood for the entire newspaper in terms of how it looks, but also becomes a primer of style consistency for every other page. Whether a headline is centered, flush left or flush right, or even staggered may seem insignificant to the average reader, but he will be the first to notice if the paper fails to maintain a consistent style throughout the publication. The same principle of continuity applies to cutlines, photo credits, standing sigs, bylines, column format, and other constants. If a newspaper staff cannot be consistent in its day-to-day presentation of graphic elements, why should the reader have reason to believe that the editors will be consistent in maintaining content and editorial policy?

The front page today may not be the hard-sell ''marquee'' that it was twenty years ago, but it continues to be the newspaper's showcase, the privileged spot for which reporters and photographers still aim when covering an assignment.

A newspaper editor describes the front page as ''strident chaos, a five-car collision with all horns stuck and honking, a frenetic whorehouse on a subway platform during rush hour, an eight-way intersection where all impacts impact and none has real impact.''

Structural design says it doesn't have to be.

## 5 the typography of newspaper design

### DEFINING TYPOGRAPHY

Although the term *typography* is often used within a limited definition, referring to type only, many editors and designers are apt to use the term in an all-inclusive manner, referring to all the elements that go into designing a page, such as white space, photos, charts, and illustrations. When one hears an editor discussing a newspaper that uses poor typography, the editor is probably using the general definition of the term.

Purists and laymen who are not directly involved with the production of newspapers and magazines may continue to adhere to the term as narrowly defined. In this book, however, we shall use the more general definition: typography as the application of various elements on the page.

### HOT, COLD, ET AL.

Both hot and cold type continue to be used in many printshops, sometimes even as part of the same job. Many small dailies have converted their editing and typesetting operations to the modern use of Video Display Terminals and photocomposition but have retained their letterpress printing equipment for economic reasons. The result is a teamed effort between the old and the new, a combination likely to remain for a few more years.

*Hot type* refers to machine-set type, a method which involves casting type from molten metal. It is a direct outgrowth of an invention by Johann Gutenberg, who in

1448 set a line of type (metal) by hand. Many printers continue to set type by hand. The printer holds the composing stick with one hand and picks type from a type case with the other. Whenever he wants to insert space he simply inserts metal strips—called *leads* (pronounced ledds)— between the lines. The exercise is time-consuming but fun; in fact, many instructors include units of study in setting type by hand, insisting that there is no better substitute to give students "a feel" for the handling of type: spacing between lines, spacing between letters, positioning of each line, and so forth.

The handset method of setting type is obviously not a practical one for most newspapers. A faster method developed from the invention of the Linotype machine by Ottmar Mergenthaler in 1886. The term *Linotype* is an appropriate description for the machine that casts lines of type. An operator sits at a keyboard, and the machine is adjusted to set type to a desired pica width and to a prescribed leading (spacing between lines). When the operator strikes the keys, the matrices (or letter molds) fall into place, forming a line of type. When the operator is ready to cast a line, he pulls a lever which, among other things, forces molten metal into the matrices, and the line of type is ejected onto a pan.

Other machines used to set hot type include the Monotype, invented in 1887 by Tolbert Lanston, and the Ludlow, designed primarily for casting type from twelve to seventy-two points. As its name implies, the Monotype casts characters one by one rather than as a complete line. It combines a perforating keyboard with a typecaster. The Ludlow, a combination of handsetting and casting, is used most often for headlines.

In 1978, when the *New York Times* made the complete transition from hot to cold type, an editorial heralded the historic event which ended 127 years of hot type and gave way to the new technology. The editorial's description of hot versus cold typesetting methods is as pictorial as any illustrations we could use:

For the past 127 years, The New York Times' type has been hot, set like this paragraph, with each letter summoned to align itself beside the next until a whole line of words could be cast in molten lead. At the direction of a linotypist, the letters danced into place with the precision of the Rockettes, but to the discerning eye they were always individuals. Look closely and you can see one tilting left or right, or a wounded one with a nicked shoulder, or a drunken one refusing to toe the mark. This morning we say farewell on this page and the page opposite to these hot characters that so often seem to have the printer's devil in them. Within a month they'll be gone from the rest of the paper as well.

We switch to cool electronic characters that look like this. They dance lightly into line, choreographed and disciplined, head to toe, by computer. . . . But in the head, alas, we remain hotly fallible, like the old characters, condemned to a life without buttons that automatically delete error, misjudgment and other outrages. . . ."

Hot gave way to cold with the advent of offset lithography as a printing process, which is why we associate hot type with letterpress printing and cold type with offset. In its simplest definition *letterpress* is synonymous with relief printing, because the area to be printed is raised. When the surface is inked, the area to be printed receives ink, but the surrounding area, because it is lower, receives no ink and thus does not print.

Unlike letterpress, *offset* requires the transfer of an image from a plate to a blanket cylinder and then onto paper. The use of offset has brought about many new methods of typesetting, because anything that can be photographed can be used in offset printing.

The term *phototypesetting* (or photocomposition) is often used to describe the new typesetting methods. In phototypesetting, letters can be imprinted directly on photosensitized film or paper. Typically, most phototypesetting systems are made up of a keyboard for input, a computer for processing the tape and executing such action as justifying copy and allowing for leading space, and an output unit for paper or film reproduction. Many different systems are available to newspapers today, but the basic steps of production outlined here are likely to be the same.

In simple, comparative terms, cold type is cheaper than hot type, and cleaner. Also, because everything that can be photographed can be reproduced, it offers greater design possibilities and creates greater availability of typefaces—both the readable and the not-so-readable. Untrained eyes may be overwhelmed by the variety of typefaces available in the market today.

In the days of hot type the design and manufacture of typefaces was an extremely expensive enterprise. Today, with the use of cold type, it is cheaper and quicker for manufacturers to produce film faces. The result is what John Peter, of John Peter Associates Inc., describes as the greatest flood of new typefaces ever. In an article for *Folio* magazine, Peter described this avalanche as both a blessing and a curse:

> Most of today's newly designed typefaces are considered fashion faces, with the life span of a butterfly. Some of these are considered unreadable. And most of them are display faces which can serve a useful purpose in advertising and promotion where attention-getting and novelty play an important role.

But there are advantages to the greater availability of typefaces and to photocomposition generally. It is easier to reduce space between letters, the lower cases are designed with large x-heights (height of the lowercase letter exclusive of ascenders and descenders), and therefore bigger type sizes can be used more economically on the page.

In Syracuse, New York, the *Post-Standard* uses a combination of cold type and letterpress printing, which means that page pasteups are photographed and the negatives produced are used to expose the printing image on a thin, flat sheet of plastic. The plastic sheet is shallow etched, creating a relief image. This plate is then wrapped around a "saddle" and run on the printing cylinder of a rotary press.

Pasteup artist for the *Post Standard* pastes all type, art, and photos in page form, creating a mechanical.

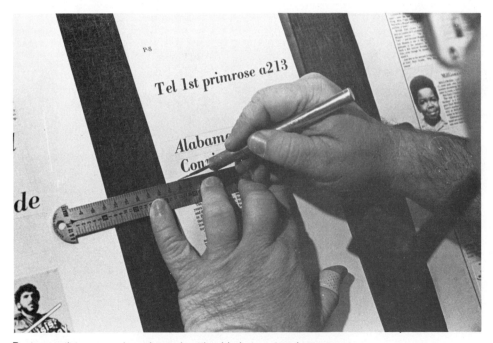

Pasteup artist uses a pica ruler and cutting blade to cut and arrange copy.

Almost completed is the pasteup of page one.

The completed pasteup of page one is now ready to be photographed to make negatives.

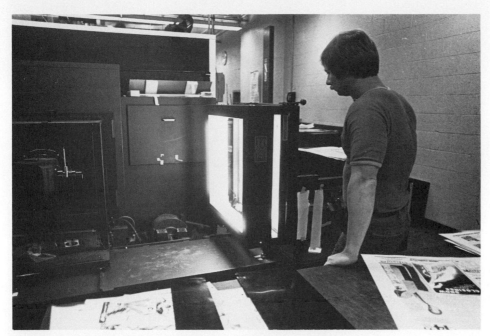

Pasteups are placed in front of a camera and photographed for negatives.

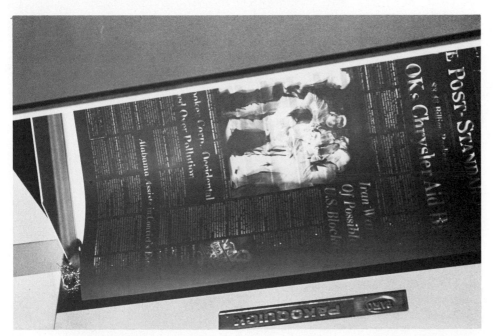

This is a close-up of a negative of page one.

Page negatives are stripped into a mask to form a flat.

The plate (a plastic sheet) has been shallow etched to create a relief image suitable for letterpress printing and put on press cylinder.

Notice the printed page emerging from the bottom of the printing cylinder.

Proofreader checks one of the first copies off the press. (Photos by Bill Thompson.)

## SEEING TYPE AS "LETTERS"

When the makers of the alphabet conceived each of the twenty-six symbols that provide us with the tools to express our thoughts, little did they know that their creation would result in the art and science of typography. The Egyptians, who started it all with picture writing, and the Phoenicians, who adapted their writing system from the Egyptians, desired only to express their most concrete thoughts about everyday living. The Greeks and the Romans, who perfected the work of the Egyptians and Phoenicians while adding vowels and modifying some letters, established the alphabet as a vehicle for literary expression.

But by the time the alphabet became printable, approximately twenty centuries later, the size, form, and shape of each letter became as important as the meaning of the letter itself. Today when a newspaper designer makes a type selection, he scrutinizes each typeface for what it offers in visual appearance and readability.

The designer should first look at *individual* letters, then at the combination of several letters forming a *word,* and finally at a *line.* Readers will seldom see isolated letters, but letters that look crowded when standing alone in printers' guidebooks are likely to look more so when combined in a word in a front-page headline.

Let's analyze the anatomy of a letter, an exercise that will help the designer contemplate design possibilities based on the structure of a certain letter.

*Ascenders,* the part of the lowercase letter above the body, provide the designer with a straight line from which to design borders or as a point of support for the other type material.

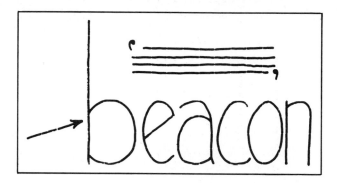

*Descenders,* the part of the lower case letter below the body, also provide unlimited possibilities for design.

*Counter* refers to the hollow part of certain letters, such as *b* and *p.* Often a designer will fill up the counters with photos.

*Serifs* are probably the most often mentioned parts of a letter. A serif is the stroke projecting from the top or bottom of the main stroke of a letter. Serifs have evolved into a subject of controversy among designers, especially with regard to readability. Originally, however, serifs were a physical necessity more than an esthetic choice. Imagine the Roman masons who carved letters in a slab of stone; as they finished each stroke they looked for a way to correct the often uneven appearance left by their tools. Serifs developed as a finishing touch to each letter. The Romans' solution for their primitive typesetting method evolved into modern typography as an esthetic matter of choice.

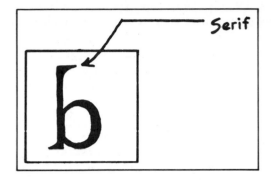

## MAKING TYPE WORK FOR DESIGN

Type is the single most important element in newspaper design. Be it through *body type* (type twelve points in size or smaller and normally used for text) or *display type* (type fourteen points in size or larger and ordinarily reserved for headlines), letters become the visual framework that gives readers their first overall impression of a printed page.

A designer who learns to use type well is prepared to cope with any other design problems. In fact, little designing can occur unless the *selection* and *use* of type are properly handled. The study of newspaper typography is a fascinating field, one which veteran typographers and editors admit has become more challenging with the advent of technological advances in typesetting and printing.

Although readers are likely to recognize effective content and syntax, they are not usually trained to determine the good, mediocre, or bad use of typography in their newspapers. But they can definitely be turned off when the typographical presentation of their newspaper is not *organized, harmonious,* and *easy to read,* three important qualities in the selection and use of type. Anyone involved in the design of newspapers today has a responsibility to guarantee the presence of these elements.

## Using Type to Produce Organization

Type organization is a paramount requirement in the design of each page. The designer should select one typeface and use it consistently through the newspaper, establishing visual continuity and order (see Chapter 6). He selects other typefaces for special effects (quotes, feature headlines, editorial page), and he uses them consistently. Organization creates typographic continuity, providing the reader with a typographic "thread" throughout the newspaper. In a sense, *organization* is closely linked to *corporate identity* for the newspaper. Large corporations have always emphasized the concept of corporate image (the manner in which their product establishes itself with prospective buyers and/or users). Newspapers today also need to create their own sense of corporate identity, and *type* can easily become the most important and recognizable symbol for such identity (see Chapter 6).

### Using Type to Produce Harmony

Typographic harmony is secondary to organization, which serves to create a visual framework for the entire newspaper. Harmony blends various tones and sizes within a typeface (bold, medium, light, extra bold) or even among different typefaces. Perhaps one of the most revolutionary aspects of newspaper typography in recent years has been the abandonment of such traditional rules for establishing contrast and harmony as the use of italics (slanted type) on a regular basis or the use of light and bold headlines throughout the page. In other words, today's designer doesn't have to create contrast by alternating between roman and italic or light and bold headlines.

Many newspapers have adopted a particular typeface, let's say Helvetica Medium, and simply use that face (in different sizes) throughout the newspaper, reserving Helvetica Light or Bold for special effects and perhaps not using Helvetica italics *at all*. Other newspapers have gone in the opposite direction, purposely emphasizing contrast of bold and light or roman and italic, as does the *Yakima Herald-Republic* (see illustrations, Chapter 7).

Harmony becomes a desired quality, one which will be easier to apply when the designer knows how to identify and recognize typefaces.

## RECOGNIZING TYPE

Today's newspaper designer is constantly exposed to an overabundance of typefaces, with new ones being designed all the time. Making selections from this seemingly endless avalanche of typefaces is a difficult task. (For a sampling of frequently used typefaces, see appendix, page 235.) Intelligent choices can be made if the designer understands the various ''families''—or commonly used classifications—of type. Because newspaper designers make more limited use of various typefaces than other print media, we have chosen to classify type on the basis of those typefaces most often used by American newspapers.

### Roman: Old Style, Transitional, and Modern

The roman typefaces are distinctive because of their thin and thick strokes, plus the use of serifs at the ends of letters. They should also be of interest to us because of the mileage they've received from American newspapers. Within the roman classification we may separate type according to its style, or how each letter is shaped.

*Old style* continues to be used today, but a printer may refer to it as *Garamond,* simply because a Frenchman, Claude Garamond, is credited with its design, although recent findings tell us that the face was designed by Jean Jannon in 1615. Garamond type is open, round, and readable. There isn't much contrast between thick and thin strokes. Another readable old style typeface that newspaper designers are likely to use is *Caslon,* not so much for primary use (as the standard headline type throughout the newspaper) but for a special one-liner and perhaps even for the nameplate and standing sigs. Caslon reads well and looks contemporary, in spite of its old style classification.

*Transitional* typefaces represent the in-between period, evolving from old style to modern. An Englishman, John Baskerville, designed a representative transitional typeface, showing greater contrast between thicks and thins than old style, and more vertical stress. Baskerville approximates Bodoni, but somehow manages to look more elegant.

ITC Garamond
Light

ITC Garamond
Bold

ITC *Garamond*
*Bold Italic*

ABCDEFGHIJK
LMNOPQRSTU
VWXYZ abcdefg
hijklmnopqrstuvw
xyz1234567890&?
!ß$£()«»°

BASKERVILLE OLD FACE

*Modern* typefaces display the strongest contrast between thick and thin strokes. The serifs are sharp fine lines, with no bracketing. In the world of newspaper typography, modern is synonymous with Bodoni, but there is little "modern" about it. The last few years have seen the demise of Bodoni type as the ultimate headline type in many American newspapers. Bodoni type was designed by Giambattista Bodoni in the late 1700s, but it has had a long and healthy run through the headlines of American newspapers, to the point where some designers never see an end to its use.

Designer Frank Ariss, who redesigned the *Minneapolis Tribune,* often carries his anti-Bodoni movement (via slides) to newspaper editors and publishers who remain loyal to the eighteenth-century typeface. Ariss reminds editors how ironic it is to tell the world about such historical events as the Lindbergh flight (1927), Roosevelt's election (1932), and man's landing on the moon (1969) with the same old typeface. Ariss argues that while newspapers are constantly reporting change, their typography remains resistant to changes and innovations in graphics.

Obviously not all newspaper editors are guilty of typographic anachronism, and many of Ariss' listeners argue that there is no need to change "a good thing." Concerning Bodoni, however, we agree with Ariss. It is definitely not an easy-to-read typeface, especially when used in large doses across the top of a page or in its bolder versions, but it can work well in one-line headlines or when surrounded by generous amounts of white space.

# Bodoni No. 2
# *Bodoni Italic No. 2*

## Sans Serif: Gothic/Contemporary

Sans serif typefaces, as the name indicates, are designed without serifs. Usually the strokes are the same thickness throughout. Generally speaking, sans serif type—referred to as Gothic—is easier to read, especially in headlines, than serif type. Sans serif type originated in the early 1800s, but it didn't enjoy much popularity until almost a hundred years later when a group of artists at the Bauhaus in Germany began to experiment with it. The very plain sans serif letters must have looked almost invisible when the first serifless letter was created. Perhaps as a reaction to the more elaborate Baskerville and Bodoni, sans serif type is free of visual distractions.

Newspapers started by adopting sans serif typefaces for inside pages, supplements, and special occasions. Soon, however, upon realizing the greater readability afforded by the simpler style of type, many editors made the switch to sans serif for their primary typeface.

Of the sans serif typefaces used by American newspapers, two in particular are probably the most popular: *Futura* and *Helvetica.*

*Futura* is a readable typeface, but it often requires large sizes and heavier than medium weight for impact on the page. Futura Light, for example, is not strong enough to hold a long headline. Futura Medium and Bold do a better job of creating instant attraction for the reader. Basically, Futura works well only in the 36- to 72-point size range.

*Helvetica* is a Swiss sans serif typeface that has all the visual requirements most newspaper typographers look for. It is clean, contemporary, easy on the eyes, and strong on the page. Helvetica has impact and readability even when used in small sizes.

Two other sans serif typefaces that also look and read well are *Helios* (very similar to Helvetica) and *Univers* (elegant and uniform).

ABCDEFGHIJKLM
NOPQRSTUVWX
YZabcdefghijklmn
opqrstuvwxyz123
4567890&?!ß£$
FUTURA LIGHT

ABCDEFGHIJKL
MNOPQRSTUV
WXYZabcdefghi
jklmnopqrstuvwx
yz1234567890&
?!ß£$(;)≋«»⋮
FUTURA MEDIUM

ABCDEFGHIJK
LMNOPQRST
UVWXYZabc
defghijklmno
pqrstuvwxyz
1234567890&
?!ß£$(;)≋«»⋯
FUTURA BOLD

ABCDEFGHIJK
LMNOPQRSTU
VWXYZabcdef
ghijklmnopqrstu
vwxyz1234567
890&?!ß£$(;)⟨⟨⟩⟩

HELVETICA EXTRA LIGHT 60

ABCDEFGHIJK
LMNOPQRSTU
VWXYZabcdef
uvwxyz123456
ghijklmnopqrst
7890 &?!ß£$(;)

HELVETICA BOLD

ABCDEFGH
IJKLMNOP
QRSTUVW
XYZ &?!ß£$

abcdefghijkl
mnopqrstuv
wxyz 1234
567890(;)

HELVETICA LIGHT

ABCDEFGHI
JKLMNOPQ
RSTUVWXY
Z&?!ß£$

abcdefghijkl
mnopqrstuv
wxyz12345
67890;

HELVETICA MEDIUM

# Helios Bold *Helios Bold Italic*

ABCDEFGHIJ
KLMNOPQR
STUVWXYZ
abcdefghijklm
nopqrstuvwx
yz123456789
0&&?!ß£$(·:)⟩⟨⟩⟨

UNIVERS 53

ABCDEFGHIJKL
MNOPQRSTUV
WXYZabcdefg
hijklmnopqrstuv
wxyz12345678
90&&?!ß£$(·:)⟩⟨⟩⟨`

UNIVERS 55

ABCDEFGHIJKL
MNOPQRSTUV
WXYZabcdefg
hijklmnopqrstuv
wxyz12345678
90&?!£$ß(·:)⟨⟩⟨⟩~

UNIVERS 45

**Miscellaneous: The "Be Careful" Category**

This is the catchall bag of typefaces that do not qualify for inclusion in any of the other categories listed here. It is this group that may provide the designer with the perfect typeface for that two-page spread on summer travel or the half-page feature on Old World wines. It is also the category that will give the designer his greatest share of frustration and temptation, since he'll be forced to make choices from an endless selection of type.

One of the advantages of photocomposition is that the designer who wants to go the extra mile can even create his own typeface and have it set to his own specifications.

69

## Enter Mellis Bold

In an earlier chapter we mentioned Robert Mellis, former graphics director at the *Miami Herald*. When Mellis served in the same capacity at the *St. Petersburg Times,* he came across a typeface that he liked very much.

The typeface was called Neil Bold, and it was the closest thing to what Mellis had in mind for the *Times*—but not close enough. Mellis decided to alter Neil Bold to fit his own specifications. In its original form Neil Bold's slots tended to be too narrow, so Mellis redesigned each letter in more open forms (almost squares), adding 150 percent more space inside each slot. Mellis had the original letters blown up photographically at 600 percent; then he used a razor blade to cut each letter. The result is *Mellis Bold,* a full but readable letter that is not practical for primary use in headlines but works well as a contrasting typeface for standing sigs.

Here is a sample sheet of Mellis Bold in transfer letter form. Notice the fullness of the letters, especially the lowercase.

## sports

### Sunday
**Great Teams/Great Years** — The undefeated 1972 Miami Dolphins are the subject of this week's retrospective. 11 a.m., Ch. 7.
**Tennis** — World Invitational Tennis — Mixed Doubles Finals from Hilton Head, S.C. 3 p.m., Chs. 10, 12, 26.
**Tennis** — World Championship Tennis — $200,000 Tournament of Champions. 3 p.m., Ch. 7.
**Golf** — IVB Philadelphia Golf Classic — Live from Whitemarsh Valley Country Club, Lafayette Hill, Pa. 4 p.m., Chs. 4, 11, 34.
**Golf** — U.S. Women's Open — Live coverage of the final round from the Indianapolis Country Club., Chs. 10, 12, 26.

**Sportsworld** — Diana Nyad attempts to swim from Cuba to Florida. 4 p.m., Chs. 7, 5, 20.
**Tennis** — Washington Star Gran Prix Tennis. 5 p.m., Chs. 6, 33.
**German Soccer** — REPEAT. Fortuna Dusseldorf vs. Shalke 04. 7 p.m., Ch. 2.

### Monday
**Major League Baseball** — Monday Night Baseball. 8:30 p.m., Chs. 10, 12, 26.

### Saturday
**NBC Baseball '78** — Teams to be announced. 2 p.m., Chs. 7, 5, 20.
**Florida Wrestling** — 3 p.m., Ch. 51.
**Golf** — US Women's Golf Classic — Live from the Indianapolis Country

Club. 4 p.m., Chs. 10, 12, 26.
**Golf** — Sammy Davis Jr. Geater Hartford Open. Third-round play from Wethersfield Country Club in Wethersfield, Conn. 4 p.m., Chs. 4, 11, 34.
**CBS Sports Spectacular** — Gold Cup Hydro-Plane race from Owensboro, Ky.; Women's Junior Gymnastic Championships from Tokyo, Japan. 5 p.m., Chs. 4, 11, 34.
**ABC Wide World of Sports** — Live coverage of the AFC-NFC Hall of Fame game between the Miami Dolphins and the Philadelphia Eagles, from the site of the Professional Football Hall of Fame in Canton, Ohio. 3:30 p.m., Chs. 10, 12, 26.

## seriously

### Sunday

**Face the Nation** — 11:30 a.m., Chs. 4, 34; 12:30 p.m., Ch. 11.
**Issues and Answers** — Noon, Chs. 10, 12, 26.
**Meet the Press** — 12:30 p.m., Chs. 7, 5, 20.

tee a chairwoman, chairman or chairperson? 7 p.m., Chs. 4, 11, 34.
**Destination America** — "City of Big Shoulders" The Poles make up nearly a third of the population of Chicago. This show examines the people that helped make the to the metropolis that

## for children

### Sunday
**Wonderful World of Disney** — Conclusion — "Whiz Kid and the Carnival Caper" Three youngsters uncover a plot by members of a traveling carnival troupe to rob the local bank. 7 p.m., Chs. 7, 5, 20.

### Monday

Now observe how Mellis Bold integrates well with other type in this television section. Mellis Bold is used for the standing sig, while Helvetica is used for the headlines. As for the rest of the *Miami Herald,* it is Bodoni all the way. As Mellis put it: "The Herald and Bodoni are intertwined—it would shock the readers if we switched to a different typeface for primary headline use."

70

## USING TYPE TO PRODUCE READABILITY

Readability—the quality that makes type easy to read—is the single most important factor in selecting and using a typeface. The most readable type is that which moves the reader quickly and easily from word to word and from line to line. Any typeface that does not have instant readability is not worth considering, let alone using.

One of the greatest frustrations newspaper typographers face today is the ever-increasing avalanche of available typefaces, some of which *look attractive* but lack readability. The designer, faced with countless type books, might be wise to put "stop signs" next to any such typefaces, to avoid temptation.

Many factors affect readability, the most important of which are (1) the use of all caps versus lowercase, (2) the use of serifs versus sans serif, (3) justified versus unjustified lines, (4) letterspacing and leading (spacing between lines), and (5) type size and weight (variations in letterform such as light, bold, extra bold, and so on).

### All Caps versus Lowercase

Generally, headlines set in all caps are difficult to read. But it is not fair to condemn all headlines set in all caps as unreadable. The exception is the use of one word set in all caps to bring attention to the subject, while the rest of the headline is set in lowercase. Especially if a word is short (such as *war, end, love*) there is nothing graphically wrong with calling attention to it through the use of all caps. Size becomes important, however. If a key word is set in capitals, it should be large enough to draw attention and create better readability. For example, the capitalized word should be set at least two times larger than the size of the headline. Various design possibilities are available:

Vertical treatment of the same story calls for the word LOVE to be set in all caps with accompanying headline directly underneath, but indented at least six picas from the left.

Here is a sketch using one word in all caps with surrounding headline and copy.

Especially when no photographs are available to illustrate a feature article, typographic design can enhance the overall look of the page. Notice how a three-dimensional package emerges from the letter E in Love.

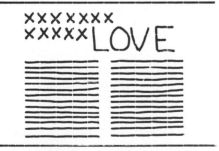

In this example the smaller headline leads reader into the large all-cap LOVE. This is an effective arrangement to use when white space is desired.

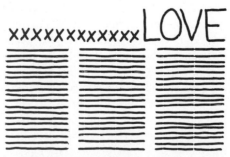

An arrangement more difficult to design includes the use of a capitalized word at the end of the headline, at least doubling the size of the original headline for the last word.

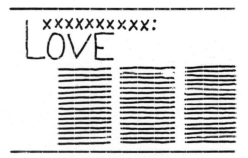

In this sample (suitable for at least a four-column area), the word LOVE is set large enough so that the ascender on the letter L will serve as a support line for the accompanying headline and also for the other letters in the word.

Obviously the examples presented here are more suitable for features than they are for news, but this does not preclude the possible use of one of these patterns on the front page to highlight a special item. Let us clarify the fact that all the patterns shown here depend on type selection for visual impact. If, for example, the word LOVE is set in Futura Demibold and the accompanying headline is set in Futura Bold, there is little contrast to guide the reader's eye through the design. However, a combination of Futura Demibold and Futura Medium would provide the needed contrast. (Physically the human eye jumps, or skips, as it scans printed material—thus the benefit of incorporating some degree of contrast among typefaces.)

In fact, the reason masses of headlines in all caps become unreadable is because of the lack of contrast in the shape of the capitalized letters. Lowercase letters are more distinctive in shape than all caps and therefore tend to make reading faster.

# MAYOR TO SIGN PACT TODAY

# Mayor to sign pact today

## Serifs versus Sans Serifs

Many American newspapers have switched to sans serif typefaces for their headlines. Sans serifs, as the name implies, are faces with no serifs terminating the lines. Esthetically, sans serif typefaces are unimpressively simple and, some say, monotonous. For the hurried American newspaper reader, however, simplicity of style may be the quickest way to get through the day's headlines. *Helvetica, Futura,* and *Univers* are the sans serif headline typefaces most widely used by American newspapers. Few newspapers use sans serif type for body copy, on the assumption that large masses of type are going to be more easily read with the aid of the serifs. Some newspapers, including the *Minneapolis Tribune,* are experimenting with the use of sans serif body copy for special content, such as the "Lifestyle" page. In some instances, the *Tribune* will run a story set in sans serif type at the bottom of the front page, providing a pleasing contrast.

Most students of typography agree that the serif versus sans serif argument is somewhat relative. If one runs a legibility test in a country where people are accustomed to reading sans serif body type since an early age, chances are that it will test better than in another place where people are less exposed to that style of type. Informal testing conducted in Minneapolis by the *Tribune* yields little significant difference between the legibility of sans serif versus serif typefaces. However, American newspaper readers are accustomed to those serifs in their body copy, and any changes should be considered carefully.

Designers are constantly trying to come up with new typefaces that will humanize sans serif as much as possible. The most successful attempts to date include such compromise typefaces as New Text and Serif Gothic. These faces combine the traditional serif with the modern simplicity of sans serif. For editors who prefer italics, Eras Bold offers a slight slant to the right.

# Newtext Regular

## ITC Serif Gothic Bold

## ITC Eras Bold

The choice of serif or sans serif in a typeface cannot be made arbitrarily. We have already mentioned that serifs add variety to each individual letter; they are decorative, too. Sans serif typefaces tend to be simple and more visually monotonous. Therefore, a newspaper designer who uses a serif typeface throughout *must* tone down the number of elements included in a page, since the serif typeface will ordinarily give the page a busier look. When serif headlines are used, it is important to allow more space between the lines than is necessary between lines of sans serif type.

Sans serif headlines, because of their simplicity, allow the designer to include more elements on the page without necessarily giving the type major competition. In simpler terms, serif headlines occupy more of the visual space on the page than do sans serif headlines; thus, the designer should exercise caution when selecting and using a typeface because it affects the overall design of the page.

### Light, Medium, Bold

The weight of the typeface has considerable impact upon its readability. It also affects the way a page is designed. Weight refers to the roundness or thinness of each letter, and type specimen books use such terms as *light, medium,* and *bold,* or in superlative terms, *extra light, ultra bold,* or *heavy bold.* Designers learn not to apply these terms generally, and few will order type without first *seeing* a sample of what it looks like. A medium weight for one type manufacturer may be the next manufacturer's bold. When it comes to the selection of typefaces, *optical perception* is a more adequate method of evaluation. One must see type before one selects it, paying attention to the shape of round letters (*o* and *c*) and tall letters (*l* and *j*) and to the length of ascenders and descenders.

# Friz Quadrata

# Friz Quadrata Bold

Notice the weight gradation from medium to bold in this sample of Friz Quadrata, a typeface worth considering for special use in an inside page article or as part of a supplement.

Avant Garde Gothic X-Light

ITC Lubalin Graph X-Light

Compare the sample at left (Avant Garde Gothic Extra Light) with Lubalin Graph Extra Light. Notice how the serifs help to make the lighter type more readable.

ITC

# Bookman Bold

# Excellence in typography is the result of nothing more than an attitude. Its appeal comes from the understanding u

As a two-liner, Bookman Bold is pleasing, creates impact, and attracts readers to the page; as a four-liner, however, the same typeface creates a crowded mass of type.

# ITC Souvenir Bold

ITC Souvenir Bold

Notice how the spacing between the lines affects readability here. The sample at left is Souvenir Bold set solid, somewhat difficult to read at a glance. Notice the difference when a small amount of spacing is allowed between lines.

Since most typefaces available today can be used in light, medium, or bold, it is up to the designer to make the right choice. The following considerations are in order:

1. Select a weight that will convey the mood. The boldest typefaces are not necessarily the easiest to read nor the most elegant. The lighter typefaces tend to be frail but elegant, and not readable at a glance. For the selection of a primary typeface for use throughout the newspaper, neither one of these extremes in type weight is recommended. Medium weight works best on the eye and on the page.

2. If type is to accompany a page heavy with photographs and illustrations, the designer can afford to select a lighter typeface. However, if type alone will carry the page, graphically speaking, then it should be medium or bold.

3. Sans serif light becomes less visible on the page than serif light.

4. Heavy or ultra bold type should be used sparingly; for example, no more than a two-line headline. Three or more lines would create a mass of type that inhibits readability.

5. The heavier the weight of each letter the more space should be allowed between lines.

6. The bolder the type the greater need for white space around the headline.

## Typeface Style

When a designer discusses the *style* of a typeface, he is usually referring to the way each letter stands, that is, in *italic, condensed, expanded,* or its superlatives, *ultra condensed.* And, yes, a typeface may be *italic* and *condensed italic*.

The style of a typeface has everything to do with the way it will communicate to the reader. In addition, some styles are more readable than others. As in the previous discussion of type, let us repeat that some italic typefaces are more readable than others, some condensed easier to read at a glance, and so on. Again, it is optical perception that counts.

*Italics.* Elsewhere in this chapter we referred briefly to these slanted typefaces created by the sixteenth-century designer Aldus Manutius of Venice. Italic typefaces can be very beautiful indeed. They can add a touch of elegance to a special feature or even to a standing sig or nameplate. As a general rule, however, italic headlines are not the most readable.

*Condensed.* Condensed letters are a narrower version of the regular typeface. These are extremely upright letters that emphasize a vertical look, and they should not be used in large quantities or in all capitals.

*Light Condensed Italic*

# to use
# Garamond
# Bold
# Condensed

**Extended.** Also known as *expanded*, these letters are a wider version of the regular typeface and obviously take up more space than regular or condensed type. For special effects—such as a story on *stretching the dollar* or *dieting (to eliminate fat)*—extended type may be used, in limited quantities, to make a point through type. In such examples the word *dollar* may be set in extended type, or the word *fat*, or even *diet*, can be extended.

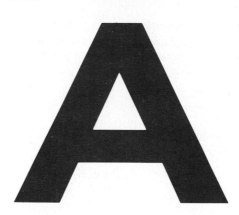 

## Body Type

Although many newspapers have made drastic changes in their display type, they are slower to make changes in body type, probably because editors feel such a transformation may have a negative effect on their habitual readers. However, the designer needs to pay attention to body type, and especially he should:

1. Select the most readable typeface, preferably one with serifs, since all indications point to the higher readability and reader appeal of serifs for body type. Lately, however, many newspapers are experimenting with sans serif body type for special articles, features, or cutlines.
2. Analyze the x-height of the typeface. The x-height is the vertical distance between the top and bottom of letters without ascenders and descenders—letters such as *a, c, e, m*. A typeface with a large x-height will look larger than one in an identical point size but with smaller x-height.
3. Emphasize either medium or light faces, as opposed to extremes of bold, which produce eye fatigue.
4. Avoid large masses of italic body type that slow down the reader.

5. Think twice before using body type smaller than eight point and remember that nine-point body type is more comfortable on the eyes.

6. Avoid reversing type. White letters on a black or dark background are not easy to read.

7. Be careful with screens, that is, gray or colored shades on the background. Screens are distracting and seldom functional. There is nothing more legible than black letters on a white background. Offset printing, however, makes screens more visually tolerable, as long as the screen does not exceed 20 percent.

8. Determine standard widths for body type. For example, the *Minneapolis Tribune* standardized body type to two column sizes throughout the newspaper: one column, 9.9 pica print area; second column, 20.9 pica print area, except for special use in what the editors term ''custom'' layout of inside sections and/or supplements.

One of the advantages of standardizing line widths is that it facilitates computer operations, as well as providing a visual framework for the newspaper as a whole.

While on the subject of line width, let's reemphasize the fact that readers do not feel comfortable skipping through very narrow columns—as found in nine-column format—but it is just as impractical to make the eye extend over widths of more than 22 picas. Ideally, columns should be set to widths between 10 and 18 picas whenever possible.

The designer should realize that column width can be used as a graphic strategy on a page. Let's say that a newspaper continuously uses 9-pica columns throughout; the use of eighteen-pica columns for a story on the page will immediately make that story stand out. However, that story must be worthy of such prominent display. Designers do not assign column widths arbitrarily or for the sake of design alone. If the content deserves it, then the wider column strategy is justified.

The designer should avoid placing a wider column in the middle of the page, where it will stand out even more. Wide columns work best at the top or bottom of the page.

White space plays a significant role in determining the line width of a column. The designer must allow white space on each side of the printed line. At the *Minneapolis Tribune* the column margin is without exception 1.3 picas, but it goes up to 2 picas in some newspapers.

9. Paragraphs should be separated by one line of space to avoid wide gaps. If the copy is set at 9.5 points, there should be 9.5 points of space between paragraphs.

10. Indented paragraphs are easier to read than those set in block style. The indentation space helps the reader and provides much-desired white space throughout the page.

**Serious crime declines 10 pct. from year ago**

United Press International

*Serious* crime in Minnesota in the first quarter of this year was down 10.3 percent from a year earlier, the State Bureau of Criminal Apprehension reported in St. Paul.

Paul Tschida, superintendent of the bureau, said this continues a trend that began in the first quarter of 1976, when the percentage of increase in serious crime began to fall. The over-all decrease in actual offenses since the first quarter of 1976 is 9 percent.

"The downward trend in serious crimes appears to be the result of a declining juvenile population, specifically in the 15-17 year old age

**New lease on life for Delta Queen**

WASHINGTON, D.C. (AP) — The House voted 367 to 9 Monday to give another lease on life to a half-century-old Mississippi River steamboat, the Delta Queen.

The paddle-driven steamer, one of the last remnants of the age of passenger river craft, has been designated a historic monument.

Present law in general denies licensing to a craft of its kind with wooden superstructure. However, Congress gave special reprieves to the owners of the Delta Queen while they undertook to build a replacement that conforms to safety legislation.

The bill passed by the House and sent to the Senate would extend until Nov. 1, 1983, permissible operation of the Queen.

## Rules, Borders, and Lines

In the days of hot type the use of a line or border required more maneuvering of metal than many editors were willing to allow precious time for. In fact, a printer had to go through eight operations to miter four rules. With today's cold type and photocomposition, a line or rule is as close as the border tape dispenser. Some newspapers with the latest computer technology have done away with border tape, allowing computers to provide borders and rules! Much of the thinking related to the use of rules, borders, and lines on a page can be summarized as follows:

1. Column rules—vertical lines running up and down on the page—can probably create more visual confusion than order on the page. They occupy what could become white space, and as we have mentioned earlier, white space can act as a visual cushion on the page. Used properly, however, they can bring order out of typographic chaos.

2. Borders and lines are the designer's best tool to show relationship, to create packages (see Chapter 7). As with other typographic elements, they should be used functionally, primarily to show relationship or to link related copy, headlines, and photos. Richard Curtis, assistant managing editor for graphics for the *Baltimore News American,* advises his staff to use boxes and lines ''for good reason, to separate, to join, to compartmentalize, to emphasize—but never to confuse.''

3. Borders and lines can also help in extremely gray areas by providing a visual magnet for a mass of type that could otherwise go unnoticed.

4. Heavy or decorative rules that detract from the overall look of the page should be avoided.

5. The size and content of the story should determine the thickness and style of border to be used.

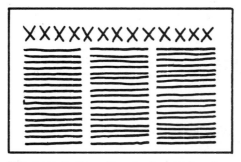

This example shows the standard *enclosed box.*

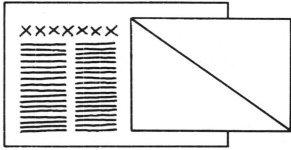

The *open box* needs heavier lines to show the reader the extent of the story in depth and width.

Here is a sample page from a catalog of available border tapes. The average newspaper can do well by simply ordering a few of the thinnest (hairline to 4 point) and avoiding the highly ornamental.

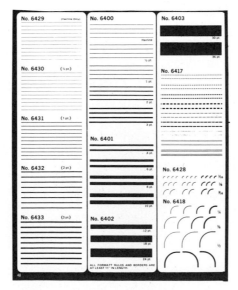

The *interrupted box* calls attention to a word or picture.

So far this chapter has offered some insight into various theories concerning readability and has provided ideas for typographical design. The examples that follow will apply some of this information to the design of the newspaper's nameplate.

The nameplate is the most constant typographic element in the newspaper. As an identifying link between newspaper and reader, it should convey at a glance the personality of the newspaper and offer a glimpse into community characteristics. The nameplate is the one item that the newspaper will wear every day. It has to be typographically *durable* and *appropriate*. It must be able to develop enough longevity so that readers will become familiar with it, and it should convey to the readers—local people or out-of-towners—the degree to which a newspaper is conservative, liberal, youth-oriented, contemporary, or traditional.

Redesigning a nameplate must include serious consideration of how it will blend with the rest of the newspaper. The following examples—based on the imaginary *Town News*—accommodate a variety of choices and possibilities.

## The Town News

Whero sei fro                              ua   AIA     fdidikkfk                              12345

This is the simplest nameplate available. The name of the newspaper is centered, set in Garamond Bold, with the folio lines centered directly under it and underscored by a 2-point rule.

## The Town News

didisi udnkkdj  a
Wed he
345  2345

Scourna yracuse Universi
tyraphic of Jarch
197

hool
lism
16

This nameplate features Eras, a sans serif typeface with a slight forward slant. The typeface proclaims contemporary thinking. Notice how the word *The* is set in smaller size and accompanies the illustration of an *orange* (the town's primary crop). The line is set in lightface to emphasize the boldness of the type and illustration. Folio lines are placed in the right-hand side of the nameplate.

## The Town NEWS

Now 12345
How1 bout to it
fidig|f⌐ wwwwwkdl

School of Journalism raphic Arts
eidra Delano niversity
26, 19

Marc Syra D
cuse Uh G
70

Lubalin Graph Bold has a large x-height, especially appropriate for this nameplate. The editors wish to emphasize the word *News*—which is what most readers call the newspaper. This typeface implies strength and permanence. Notice how the nameplate is flush left but the line extends to accommodate the teaser photo on the right.

the
Town
News

Indy For the
xmxnmc|helk lsls

12345  345
Anytown fjfjdk

The designer here wanted to bring white space to the nameplate, which means that he could afford a bold version of Serif Gothic. The type is simple but elegant. White space on both sides provides a clean look for the entire page.

*The Town News*

Wed e sksyf For  sist
119df|e/lkuwpqpelr  skdkfy

For a newspaper that does not use italics elsewhere, the italic type here provides a pleasing change from the routine. Notice how the designer has provided relief by injecting white space on both sides.

TOWN
The News

to iK  Wed  Wed
Century  Goyywotja
12345  12345

The designer has combined two typefaces, an outline type for the word *Town* and ITC Tiffany Medium for *The News*.

**MONDAY**

the Town News

2345  2345
Anytown, Any Day In the
ti  fro ti  ro ti

This nameplate capitalizes on double lines for emphasis, with the day of the week interrupting the top line at right. The typeface used is ITC Serif Gothic Black.

## CREATIVE APPROACHES TO NEWSPAPER TYPOGRAPHY

Although most students of newspaper typography can learn the basic guidelines for readability and apply them properly, the ultimate touch of creativity in typography will rest with each individual designer. Three editors faced with the same story content will come up with three different treatments, and only one may add the creative touch that will make it extraordinarily different. The examples on the next page show all that is possible through the use of what we have presented in this chapter, plus an added creative touch that is impossible to teach through a textbook.

Experimenting with type and with the various typographic elements of white space, borders, and rules, the designer has unlimited possibilities. The new technological advances make those possibilities more accessible and easier to accomplish today than at any other time in the history of newspaper typography.

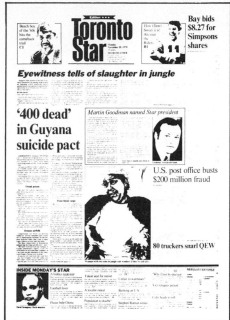

The teaser for an upcoming story uses typographic color for the word *Guyana*. Notice how the letters cut into the line at the bottom of the package.

This inside page from the *New York Times* draws attention to each story through the use of bold initials set in square serif typeface.

In its new format, the *Toronto Star* uses a condensed typeface for its nameplate and accompanies it with two photo teasers for inside stories.

A type-only inside page from *Scene*—the *Louisville Times'* entertainment supplement—alternates between bold and light typefaces, lines, and an attractive standing sig to carry what could otherwise be a very dull and gray page.

This paper capitalizes on large, all-down-style type for its column, "tip-off."

Notice how the election story package uses an idea from the voting machine to create attractive lines.

## order and continuity

Organizing the newspaper's content is the first step toward improving its graphic presentation.

All newspapers—small or large, those with dazzling graphics or those with simple typographical styles—should follow an orderly design plan beginning on page one and continuing through the last page of classified ads. The first step in creating organized content is to think rationally about the way most people approach a newspaper. As we pointed out in Chapter 2, it is getting increasingly difficult for newspapers to get their share of the reader's extremely busy day. With few exceptions, the average American newspaper reader who holds a full-time job does not spend more than twenty-five to thirty minutes on his daily newspaper.

Even without much training in newspaper typography, the reader can usually tell when news, features, photos, and headlines are thrown together. She dislikes typographical chaos in her newspaper, which is what happens when a police news item appears next to a church announcement, or when a photo on page 6 refers to a related story on page 32, or when a story starts on page 16 and jumps to page 7.

When the reader sits down to his daily half hour of newspaper reading, he must be presented with an orderly package that requires little deciphering on his part to find what he wants. It is the responsibility of the page designer to offer the reader orderly content and graphic continuity.

### PROVIDING ORDER

*Order* begins with an honest appraisal of the newspaper's typical content. Let's say that a newspaper carries heavy emphasis on local news, including many small items related to people and events. Instead of sprinkling these items anywhere they can be accommodated through the newspaper, it appears more logical to find a page or series of pages for them and to label the page accordingly, thus *packaging* all this related content as a structure.

Many large dailies have eliminated a good number of short world and national news stories from page one and have positioned them on a special page, usually page two, under such headlines as ''News Briefings,'' ''The News Today,'' ''Monday's Sampler,'' or ''News at a Glance.'' The immediate graphic result is a less congested page one with room for larger photos and fewer, but more important, news and feature articles. Several newspapers, including the *Detroit Free Press,* have created a second ''front page'' as a graphic buffer to page one. By relieving page one of several inches of copy and photos, the editors have accomplished two important goals:

- to showcase the best available news on page one.
- to create news interest beyond page one by using the second front page.

Another successful attempt to organize content has been the *Providence Journal's* ''Second Front Page,'' officially labeled as such and designed in an organized and attractive manner to carry jumps from the front page. We have always thought that the actual jumping of a story is not what bothers readers so much as the time it takes to locate the jumped portion of the story. Organizing all the jumps does not guarantee that readers will follow them, but it allows for easier reading—which is what newspaper designers should regard as their primary goal.

The illustrations shown here indicate how organization of content leads to an orderly appearance on the page. Visual order can also be accomplished through design unity, the type of structural order discussed in more detail in Chapter 4. Structural design provides visual order by keeping stories rectangularly shaped, without twists and turns to confuse the reader. The same visual order provided for news must be created for ads through the design of rectangular advertising structures. Consistent rectangular format promotes order on the page even though editorial matter is unequally sized and advertising content is unequally shaped. The confusion of multilevel stories disappears, giving the reader self-contained visual units that speed up his journey through the page and give a more attractive overall appearance to each page.

Robert S. Mellis, former graphic arts director for the *Miami Herald,* who also participated in the redesign of the *St. Petersburg Times,* is a strong advocate of graphic order for newspaper pages:

> There can never be adequate justification for disorder. Any size of newspaper and any production system can be used to produce rational organization of editorial matter and advertising.

Pages designed by Mellis show effective use of rectangular structures for both copy and advertising. The ads on the page are positioned so that they form a rectangle at one side of the page, avoiding what Mellis describes as ''the stairways to typographic hell.'' More information on the positioning and design of advertising appears in Chapter 8.

## PROVIDING CONTINUITY

Nothing is less continuous or more inconsistent than the content of a daily newspaper. Yet readers unconsciously demand a framework of continuity in the way their newspaper appears every day.

Continuity should begin with the newspaper's nameplate and should remain evident on every page. Typographic continuity is achieved through the visual design

The *Free Press'* second front page relieves page one of many short items and organizes these in an easy-to-find, easy-to-read manner.

The *Journal's* ''Second Front Page'' is an example of orderly content, the result of clean, attractive graphics.

A sports page from the *Miami Herald,* also designed by Mellis, shows all ads stacked up vertically on the right side of the page, allowing a similar structure for news copy on the left side.

and unvarying presentation of the following standard elements:

1. The nameplate.
2. The use of type.
3. Cutline and byline styles.
4. Standing sigs for columns and special features.
5. Graphic strategies that become a part of the newspaper's format.
6. Departmentalizing.

## The Nameplate

The nameplate sets the mood graphically for anything else the reader may find in a newspaper. A well-designed newspaper relies on the nameplate as a graphic ally, one that can enhance anything else placed on the page or that will help to carry the page when photos, art, or other elements do not stand out graphically. Editors should not place the nameplate on the page as a necessary evil. Instead, it should be integrated into the overall design of the page.

Graphically appealing nameplates are simple, readable, and uncongested. Modern newspapers have clipped the ears from their nameplates. Gone also are exaggerated drawings of buildings, flags, city insignias, and seals. Nameplates today are clean and elegant. The use of the traditional Old English type for nameplates is also becoming rarer, giving way to more legible and contemporary typefaces.

Nameplates also make more appropriate use of white space. If used properly, white space around the nameplate will draw the reader into the page. In addition, assuming that there is no opportunity to use white space elsewhere on the front page, white space around the nameplate will often provide enough air to give the page breathing room.

Nameplates serve their purpose best when used at the very top of the page and at full width (six columns across for a six-column newspaper, four columns across for a four-column tabloid, and so on). However, many newspapers display their nameplates attractively by setting them two, three, or four columns under the full width of the page.

Floating nameplates are often used to highlight a late-breaking story or feature above the nameplate or in situations where the editors feel two stories on page one deserve top billing. A floating nameplate should not be lowered more than five inches from the top of the page. Nameplates should not be placed near the page's fold since their primary purpose is to identify the publication at the reader's first glance. If the nameplate gets lost on the page, it has failed to accomplish its primary mission.

The nameplate sets the graphic continuity of the newspaper because the typeface used for its name will also be used for other standing sigs throughout the publication. If the nameplate design calls for a circular box, the same pattern should be repeated for second headings, such as "Viewpoints," "Sports," "Local News," and so on. There are some exceptions, however; the *New York Times'* nameplate has not changed throughout the years, but its inside sections—such as "Home," "Weekend," and "Living"—depart from the Old English typeface to display square-serif bold.

Old English remains a standard type for the nameplate of many American newspapers. Notice how the *Times* maintains Old English as part of the nameplate but uses a more modern square serif bold for other section openers.

Nameplates should be placed at the top of the page, preferably running the full width of the page.

Dropping the nameplate one inch will often allow for a teaser headline to run over it.

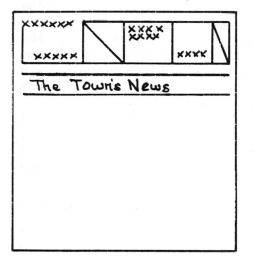

An index to inside pages (with pictures) may be carried above the nameplate.

Dropping the nameplate a few inches from the top of the page and setting it two columns narrower than the full page width is a common practice among tabloid editors. The result, however, is often a "trapped" or "floating" nameplate that makes the rest of the page much more difficult to design.

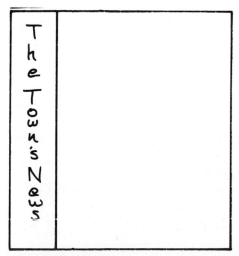

Although most newspapers refrain from running a vertically placed nameplate, this practice has become popular with newsmagazines. Not only is this positioning difficult to read, but it also creates design problems for the rest of the page. When the newspaper is folded and placed on a newsstand, only half of the nameplate becomes visible.

Nameplates should never be dropped so low on the page as to interfere with the natural fold.

Although the *Chicago Tribune* also uses Old English, its nameplate displays a more contemporary use of white space and type boldness that makes it readable at a glance. In many cases the editors of a newspaper whose nameplate continues to use Old English type are aware of how difficult it is to read letters set in Old English. They also know that in some communities a change in the nameplate, especially to a contemporary and more sophisticated typeface, could mean the loss of some subscribers. A word of consolation is in order: The variety of type available today allows designers modern typefaces that preserve the formality and style of Old English.

New newspapers, and some old ones that apparently did not fear losing a few subscribers on the journey to contemporary typography, display attractive and unconventionally designed nameplates.

For its Spanish daily section, the *Miami Herald* designed a modern nameplate where variety is the key graphic element. The word *el* (for *el Miami Herald*) is lowered, *Herald* has a capital *H,* and *Miami* is set in all caps, sans serif in color. The nameplate is packaged with two rectangular structures to highlight inside stories and is underlined with a column rule. Ironically, the parent publication (the *Miami Herald*) continues to use Old English type, ''ears'' for the weather, and other vestiges of the past.

Unconventional design describes the nameplate for the *Toronto Star,* which uses condensed caps and lower case, plenty of white space, and a solid column rule to underline its nameplate. At least two teasers for inside stories run with the nameplate.

Simplicity, sharpness, and effective use of white space characterize *Newsday*'s nameplate. It creates a sense of graphic identity for this pioneering newspaper. Circular packaging is also used for framing the entire front page.

Readers relate to a newspaper's nameplate in the same manner they relate to the trademarks of other products they use daily. Sudden typographical and design changes in the nameplate can provoke reader reaction, as was the case when the editors of the *Miami News* decided it was inaccurate to continue carrying a palm tree as part of the newspaper's nameplate, since most palm trees in South Florida had died after an insect epidemic. One day the palm tree was also gone from the *News'* nameplate, a disappearance which created stronger reader reaction than the editors had ever anticipated. Not that the palm tree "grew" back into the nameplate of the *News,* but the issue generated enough reader interest, shown in letters to the editor, to warrant page-one coverage for a few days.

Such reader identification or sense of familiarity with nameplates may be the reason that such well-established newspapers as the *Atlanta Constitution,* the *Boston Globe,* and the *Providence Journal* have adopted modern, attractive designs for standing sigs through their inside sections but continue to carry their original nameplates on page one.

Notice, however, that even when the typeface for the nameplate is different from other standing sigs, a sense of typographic harmony and continuity prevails.

This sectional front page from the *Milwaukee Sentinel* shows typographic continuity, beginning with the standing sig, "Friday's Woman." Notice the similar typeface used for "The Working Woman," "Children," and "Going Places." Articles open with a highlighted initial letter. Cutlines use sans serif lightface.

## The Use of Type

Type is the single most important graphic element in newspaper design. It is a constant, whether it be used for copy, cutlines, bylines, or headlines. Type is the blood of the newspaper, the framework of the total visual experience created for the reader (see Chapter 5). Continuity through typography can be achieved through the following means:

1. Select one typeface to use for body type and do not depart from it. The size can be changed, let's say from 9 point to 10, as well as the leading (space between lines), but not the typeface itself.

2. Select one typeface for headlines and use it predominantly. If an additional typeface is used on the same page to highlight a special article or feature, it should be harmonious with the rest.

3. The type used for such standing sigs as "Inside Stories," "Weather," or "Letters to the Editor" should be the same throughout the newspaper.

4. All special copy elements, such as quotes pulled from stories, indexes, or charts, should be set in the same typeface.

## Cutline and Byline Styles

Attention to detail is a prerequisite in creating graphic continuity and order. Cutlines and bylines represent constants throughout every page, which is why a style should be provided to maintain graphic consistency. Every photograph must carry a cutline, although the amount of information included may vary. If the photo accompanies a

*Today* (Cocoa Beach, Florida) combines italic and roman headlines on the same page, establishing contrast and continuity through standing sigs, such as "Brevard Today," which carries the consistent nameplate design.

Abe Fortas

The News American
**KAMALVAND: Strong beliefs.**

**PRESIDENT CARTER**
**Asks sweeping changes**

For head shots, usually the name of the person photographed is all the information that is needed. It may be set *flush left, centered,* or in *two lines.* Notice the prevalence of caps and lower case as more readable for cutlines: flush left (*Chicago Tribune*, above left); centered (*Baltimore News American*, above center); two lines (*Times Union*, Rochester, N.Y., above right).

story, a skeleton cutline (one or two lines) should suffice. If the photo runs independently of a story, a full cutline is needed.

Editors should set guidelines for determining when a full cutline becomes a story. If the copy explaining a photograph requires fifteen or more lines of type, then a story will be more adequate than a cutline. If the copy block under a photo is as deep as the length of the photo itself, a story will do the job more effectively and more attractively.

Skeleton cutlines are the easiest to handle, as they require two lines at the most. For the sake of continuity, editors should select a style and a typeface and adhere to those throughout.

For photos three columns or more, it is usually better to break the cutline into two or more columns, to avoid the unreadable mass of type that results when lines of type run 24 picas or wider. The minimum space between columns should be two picas, to avoid the confusion that results when narrow margins cause the reader to read across the cutline.

Vince Garrity as a Cub bat boy in 1938.

Some cutlines run the full width of the photograph, as seen in the *Chicago Tribune.*

FORD 'FUTURA' — the first of a new breed.

Other skeleton cutlines combine all caps and lower case within the same line, as seen in the *Providence Journal.*

Charlie's on Hand for Edgar's 75th Birthday
It was birthday number 75 for famed ventriloquist Edgar Bergen Thursday and even his old sidekick Charlie McCarthy showed up for the party. Charlie joined the rest of the family, son Chris, wife Frances and daughter Candice, to wish Edgar the best.
—UPI

**Overline centered, *Milwaukee Sentinel*.**

## Cole takes note

Alberta skip Betty Cole had reason to smile Tuesday afternoon after beating Manitoba's Chris Pidzarko in the afternoon draw of the Canadian ladies' curling championships in Sault Ste. Marie, Ont. In the evening draw, though, Penny Larocque of Nova Scotia handed Cole her first loss in six outings. Manitoba, meanwhile, won once in three starts yesterday and is at 4-3. For more, see Page 50.

**Overline flush left, *Winnipeg Tribune*.**

WONDER BEHIND THE SCENES — Blind entertainer Stevie Wonder (second from right, foreground) posed with members of the cast of "Timbuktu," a new Broadway musical, during a visit backstage in New York City. On hand were (from left) Melba Moore, Gilbert Price, director Geoffrey Holder and Eartha Kitt.
—AP Wirephoto

**Introduction all caps, *Milwaukee Journal*.**

**Full cutline on the side, ragged right, *Atlanta Constitution*.**

One of the most popular styles for full cutlines is that which utilizes a phrase as a key into the copy. This phrase may be placed as an *overline* or, immediately preceding the cutline, as an *introduction*.

Many newspapers find it practical and less time-consuming to establish a set pica width in which to set all cutlines, thereby permitting flexibility when pasting up the page. Let's say that all cutlines in a six-column page are set 14 picas; the measurement allows for the cutline to be used as follows:

    1. For a one-column photo:

    2. For a two-column photo, with use of overline:

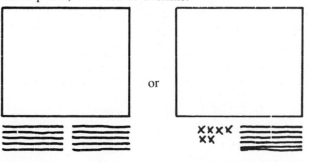

3. Three-column photo:

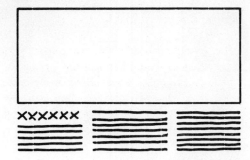

4. Four columns:

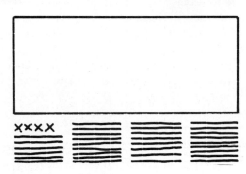

5. Side placement:

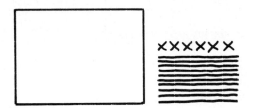

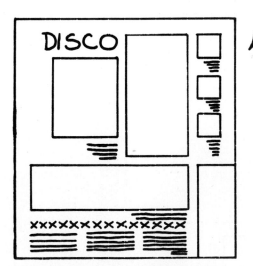

The photo essay includes individual cutlines under each photograph or next to it.

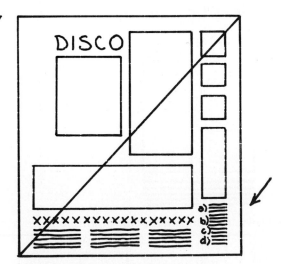

A poorly designed arrangement of photos stacks cutlines at the bottom of the page.

*Cutlines and photo combinations.* The most functional consideration in the placement of a cutline is that it must provide instant access to information related to a photograph. Logical proximity requires that the cutline be placed directly under (or to the right or left of) the photo it describes.

When more than one photo is used as part of the same content, it is advisable to write separate cutlines for each photo. For example, a photo essay involving eight photographs should have individual cutlines under each of the photos to avoid the "stacking" of cutlines, which is what happens when they are all placed as part of a block. The reader should have immediate access to information about a photo without having to move to a different area of the page to find it.

*Bylines.* Although some readers may think that bylines are significant only to the writers who claim them, page designers think differently. Those small and seemingly escapable elements become graphic constants on the page. In terms of design, the byline allows for a pleasant typographical break between the headline and the lead paragraph of a story.

Good designers will use the byline to provide typographical contrast and to inject white space in and around a story. If the style for bylines is maintained consistently, the inclusion of several bylines on a page guarantees typographical contrast and much-needed white space. Some recommended byline styles include the following:

**By Richard Conrad** Toronto Star

Spontaneous cheers punctured the silence in the bus as a sleek Boeing-707 glided to a halt on the icy tarmac. The huge stylized trillium on its tail was clearly visible through the darkness shrouding the remote corner of the airfield at Toronto International.

**One line/bold-light**

**By Michael Crabb**

Very few classical ballet companies can lay claim to five ballerinas able to dance the acutely demanding role of Giselle. The National Ballet became one of them Saturday when Vanessa Harwood made her long-overdue debut as the dance-loving peasant girl who looses her heart (and eventually her mind and life) to a double-dealing young prince from the neighborhood castle.

**Flush-left/name only**

By Michael Edgerton

**"NOBODY HERE works 100 per cent of the time," says Joe Troc, a repairman in Illinois Bell Telephone**

**Indented byline/light**

**by Jim McManus**

With the Hendrick Hudson
Sailors and the John Jay Indians
pulling major upsets over their
Conference B-North opponents
(Peekskill and J.F.K. respectively),
it would have been appropriate
for the Somers Tuskers to follow

## Double-line/bold

By JANE BRIGGS-BUNTING
Free Press Staff Writer

Eleven days ago, Bloomfield Hills court bailiffs moved all of
Thure Rosene's worldly possessions to the backyard of the
crumbling, 150-year-old brick home he had been living in on
Woodward Avenue north of Lone Pine Road.

## Flush-left/light/all capital letters

By Stephen Wermiel
Globe Washington Bureau

WASHINGTON — If you are waiting for a significant shift when Sen.
Edward M. Kennedy takes over the Ju-
diciary Committee next year from Sen.
James O. Eastland (D-Miss.), you may
have a long wait.

## Flush-left/same as body copy/capital letters and lower case

**By Bonnie Miller Rubin**
Staff Writer

There's something about dining
outside that makes even junk food
taste healthy.

## Flush-left/bold-light/sans serif

**By Robert C. Cowen**
Natural science editor of
The Christian Science Monitor

British cosmologist Sir Fred Hoyle has made
a career of audacious speculation that
encourages new lines of research. But his
boldest suggestion yet has so far had few
takers. Together with his Sri Lankan colleague
N. Chandra Wickramasinghe at University
College in Cardiff, Wales, he has developed the
theory of the cosmic cradle — the proposition
that living organisms have arisen in outer
space.

## Centered/bold-light

**By BOB ROSS**
St. Petersburg Times Staff Writer

A raft of rafts — as many as 2,500
assorted floating vehicles — are expected to jam 3.8 miles of the Hills-
borough River from 11 a.m. to 3 p.m.
Saturday.

**Single line/bold**

**By MIKE BARRETT**
Staff Writer

**(First of two-part series)**
In ancient Greece, the council
of elders examined infants and
ordered the weak or deformed
thrown from the mountain top.

**One size up/9 pt. copy - 10 pt. byline**

**By KEN PARKER**
Journal-Bulletin Automotive Writer

The day of the real auto inspection is at
last with us in Rhode Island, and in spite
of individual inconvenience, it's a good
thing.

**Centered/all bold**

## Standing Sigs

Standing sigs—also called standing heads—are daily reminders of regular content in a
newspaper. They provide the greatest opportunity for graphic order and continuity. In a
sense, standing sigs can become visual links that hold a newspaper together, giving it a
look and personality.

It should be natural for editors to design a standing sig format or style and stick to
it throughout (i.e. for columns, regular features, classified page subheads, sports, and
business sections). Instead, many newspapers use a mixed bag approach, allowing
each regular feature to display a uniquely different sig; and if three pages from the same
newspaper were to be separated, it would be difficult to see a relationship. These are
the newspapers in which the book editor's column appears under a sig showing a stack
of books; letters to the editor run under a sig displaying a gigantic mailbox with a
chirping bird perched atop it; the women's or lifestyle editor uses a head shot with
her name under it; and the outdoors editor fancies his favorite snapshot of a familiar
fishing pier. The result is a graphic smorgasbord that translates into visual congestion
and lack of continuity.

Standing sigs should be simply designed and used consistently. Many newspapers design their standing sigs as a visual outgrowth of the nameplate. If, for example,
the nameplate uses a single rule as an underline, each sig should follow the same style.

Sigs should use the same typeface as the nameplate, although obviously reduced in size to fit the various areas where they are positioned. Consistency also applies to the positioning of elements within each sig. A newspaper in which most of the elements, such as headlines, bylines, cutlines, and even paragraphs, are flush left should position type within a sig accordingly.

White space must be part of the design for each standing sig. It guarantees breathing room on the page and allows for easier reading.

In summary, designing sigs requires careful attention to detail and should include such considerations as the following:

1. *Space requirements*—Large sigs are not attractive and result in wasted space.
2. *Harmony with other elements on the page*—Sigs should complement the page's content without producing a visual clash.
3. *Graphic meaning*—How does each sig reflect the format or personality of the newspaper? What visual elements make the sig distinctive, recognizable, and unique?
4. *Flexibility*—How can the sig adapt to often necessary changes when it must be enlarged, reduced, or used with color?

Sigs are as much a trademark for the newspaper as the nameplate. To the habitual reader, standing sigs provide stepping stones for easy and quick travel from item to item on the page.

## Graphic Strategies

Ask a typical daily newspaper reader what his newspaper looks like and he is apt to quickly respond by describing such variables as color, boldness, large photos, or large headlines.

These are all graphic strategies that through constant application have become identifying features of a particular newspaper. For many years the *Chicago Tribune* carried a color cartoon on page one, an element that became as familiar to the *Tribune*'s readers as the American flag it still carries on its nameplate. In Florida, the *St. Petersburg Times* includes some form of color on page one daily. Its readers expect it, whether it is a large four-color process photograph or flat (spot) color on a map or chart. The *New York Daily News'* photo cover could be recognized by thousands of New York City commuters even if the nameplate were to be deleted. Likewise, habitual readers of the *Wall Street Journal* can identify their newspaper's strong vertical emphasis at a glance.

Graphic continuity, as described here, is not to be confused with sameness of design, however. The newspapers mentioned have developed graphic continuity through a chosen format, through the creation of a visual image or personality; but they continue to change the day-to-day design within their format.

The *Yakima Herald-Republic* established itself graphically as a "large photo" newspaper, developing the design of each page around a large and dramatically cropped photograph around which every other element centers.

Thursday, November 17, 1977

# Yakima Herald-Republic
a daily part of your life

Saturday, March 11, 1978

# Yakima Herald-Republic
a daily part of your life

● Price 20 Cents

## Farm size limit
### 'Un-American,' say 160-acre rule opponents

By BOB TUCKER

Cragg Gilbert of Yakima listens to testimony at hearing on proposed regulations governing farm lands

## Fire
### Blaze destroys Yakima warehouse

By CHARLES LAMB

Firemen battle blaze at the Pacific Fruit and Produce Co.

City's snorkel rig put to use

### Good Morning

The weather

INDEX

### Lucky for him, pilots poor shots

By BARRY SCHATZ

## Oil prices
### Shah to push for 12-month freeze

### Good Morning

The weather

Swimming for life

## Wilderness
Lumber firm opposes Forest Service proposal for Bumping Lake region

By FRED COOMBS

Coin flip may decide

## Coal strike
Union, industry bargainers resume talks after 2 weeks

## Migrant housing
Gov. Ray backs proposal for Yakima Valley to jar loose funds from federal government

By BILL LEE

---

These two pages from the *Yakima Herald-Republic* show the use of a format developed around major photographs. Notice how type, white space, and photography combine to present an easy-to-read package almost like a magazine in approach.

The *Miami News* emphasizes order throughout the newspaper, as shown by these illustrations. Notice the effective distribution of such items as "people," "world," "nation," "Florida," and "Washington" together with "Weather." Notice the "Tomorrow" teaser at the bottom of the page. At right, the *News'* "columns, etc." groups popular columns and some standard comic strips.

The *Detroit Free Press'* "Feature Page" packages syndicated and local columnists in easy-to-read and attractively designed structures.

## Departmentalizing

The grouping together of stories with related content—departmentalizing—provides unlimited possibilities for designing visually attractive pages. The illustrations above reveal the importance of combining related content, thus making the task of reading the newspaper simpler and quicker for today's hurried reader.

## GRAPHIC STYLE SHEET

Continuity and order are not new words to newspaper editors, most of whom have applied these concepts to writing and editing the day's news. Many American newspapers follow the Associated Press and United Press International stylebooks closely in an effort to maintain consistent style for capitalization, abbreviation, and spelling.

It is only recently, however, that the same criteria have been applied to graphics. This chapter has already presented sufficient justification for establishing visual continuity and page-by-page sequence. Developing a graphic style sheet suggests that this sense of continuity and sequence will become as permanent for the visual presentation of news as the editing stylebook is for word usage.

Following is a sample graphic style sheet from the *Midland Reporter-Telegram* (Midland, Texas) (see also Chapter 3, page 36). Each newspaper that adopts a distinct graphic format should prepare its own style sheet, adapting and changing it so that it always reflects a detailed listing of the newspaper's visual strategies.

*Page Size:* Front page and section lead pages are six columns wide by 21½ inches deep. (13 pica col with a 1 pica alley.) Inside pages are eight columns wide by 21½ inches deep. (9½ pica col with a 1 pica alley.)

*Compugraphic Typography:* All headlines and picture captions are in Futura type; all editorial and regular news are in News type. Headings for regular features are in all caps Futura Bold Condensed plus a standard 1 agate rule format.

*Front Page:* The nameplate, "The Midland Reporter-Telegram" remains the same. However, it has been enlarged to the full width of the live matter for stronger identification and a new look.

We have regrouped the folio lines, including the ad slogan (a good one) centered line-on-line in all caps, between the new format stripe (rule) and the name. This is aired out for stronger eye appeal and a cleaner more contemporary look.

The right-hand ear is one agate line above the bold rule and includes the day, date and abbreviated weather report. This information is important to all readers and should help to promote the new visual personality of the newspaper.

On this front page layout, as is true of all layouts in this presentation, the news and ad copy are made up of scrap to demonstrate a look. (Not for reprint.)

This front page includes several important elements: downstyle headlines (in which only the first word in a sentence and proper nouns are capped); five or six summarized stories with references to inside pages; "The Permian Basin Oil News" feature, plus a picture to add punch; the "Weather;" an "Index" box; and for the good news, a universally-enjoyed comic strip. With these common denominators, this page could be laid out a hundred different ways, even in color when desired, and still have plenty of excitement and layout follow through.

*Section Pages:* In order to maintain a professional format we have designed a standard for section headings. They should include as many different subjects as the editor feels necessary to make the paper easier to read and help the reader to locate material.

*Editorial Page:* This page is almost identical to the one furnished from your make-up department. However, the masthead was changed slightly to a full two column width; the stripe was added at the top for continuity; the headings for the regular features were standardized with the name just below in all caps and placed 1 agate line below the stripe on the left. Two of the features were boxed, only to give a more organized look. The main editorial was indicated in a larger type face, 27 picas wide, which we feel would add visual conviction to the message.

*Business Section Page:* This page includes further demonstrations of the section heading, flush-left and downstyle headlines. A variation of the six column format to include art and square cut photography. Even a continuation from page one of your energy feature.

*Classified Section Page:* Maintains the regular six column format and should include well laid out display ads selling advertising for the daily and Sunday editions.

The style sheet shown above is a simple and brief one. Many newspapers create more extensive graphic manuals, complete with illustrations and step-by-step instructions to maintain consistent style.

Consistency of style should be at the top of the designer's list of priorities. It is not enough just to use the same typeface throughout the newspaper. Such other elements as cutlines, bylines, spacing between elements, use of photography and white space must show evidence of the continuity and sequence that result when the design of the newspaper is planned and organized.

## 7
## graphic strategies

Today's newspaper editor must also be a graphic strategist.

As soon as the content for each page becomes available, the editor will use his knowledge of graphic strategies to present that content in the most appealing manner. A strategy is often defined as a plan or technique for achieving some end. In the case of the newspaper editor, his graphic strategies are part of a plan for overall visual impact.

This definition of strategy includes the word *plan*. And planning is what this chapter is about; not using graphics for the sake of graphics, but taking into consideration that each of the strategies presented here can—and should—be used to serve a specific purpose.

Many of the strategies described in this chapter may be new to newspapers, but they have been used successfully by magazines for years. Earlier in this book we mentioned the influence of magazine graphics on today's newspaper, emphasizing the need for editors to become more open-minded in accepting the need for graphically appealing newspapers.

Geoff Vincent, former Sunday editor of the *Courier-Journal and Louisville Times,* reinforces both statements:

> I once declared that people with newspaper mentalities had no business producing magazines. I will now amend that to say that in these dangerous times of dying daily newspapers, people with traditional daily newspaper mentalities have no business producing newspapers, either.

### STRATEGIES FOR POSITIONING BODY AND DISPLAY TYPE

You may not be certain what news stories you'll read tomorrow. But you can be certain of two things about them when they appear in your newspaper. They will be set in body type and they will carry a headline. They may be accompanied by some art.

Body type and display type are recurrent elements on a newspaper page. As such, the designer can count on their presence for unlimited possibilities in effective and harmonious placement of page elements.

Most newspapers have set styles (format) for the pica width of body type, depending on the number of columns per page and sometimes on the individual page where the material is to appear. For example, newspapers often set their editorials wider than other elements on the editorial page, using larger type and more leading between the lines. The strategies presented here are not meant to alter format or continuity but to offer insight into other possibilities and to provide variety, especially for handling feature and other specialized material.

## Long Copy and Horizontal Movement

The first strategy to learn here is that the longer the copy to be positioned, the greater the need to move horizontally rather than vertically. Let's say that a news story runs 12 or more inches. Placing such copy vertically will make it look longer than it is, but horizontal placement will give the reader the optical illusion that the copy is shorter.

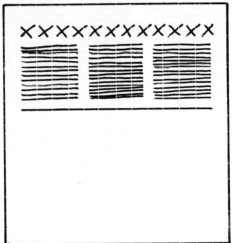

## Long Copy and Wider Column Measure

Another strategy to make long copy appear shorter is to set articles 12 inches or longer in wide measure. Long and narrow columns will take up more space and give the impression of an extremely long and unpalatable piece of copy that few readers will want to tackle. Copy set wider, to run in fewer columns, contributes positively to the overall appearance of the page:

## Long Copy and the Use of Breakers

Page designers have a responsibility to maintain proper distribution of weight around each page, which means that there will be no congestion of display type anywhere on the page, but at the same time there will be no *gray areas* of body type. A gray area can be defined as a block or section of the page in which the designer has placed body copy exclusive of bolder elements. Several alternatives are available to avoid gray areas whenever possible.

*Quotations.* Most well-written stories will include direct quotes. The page designer can capitalize on these quotes as a design strategy by pulling them out of the story and setting them as *breakers* or *grabbers*, depending upon placement in and/or around the copy block, as illustrated in the examples that follow.

Stories set with an odd number of columns give the designer space for placing a direct quote in the middle columns, directly under the headline.

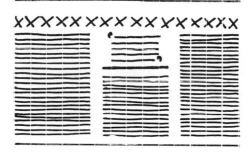

A direct quote can also be placed over the headline, either flush right or flush left. Designers may even prefer centering the quote over the headline, especially if abundant white space is desired.

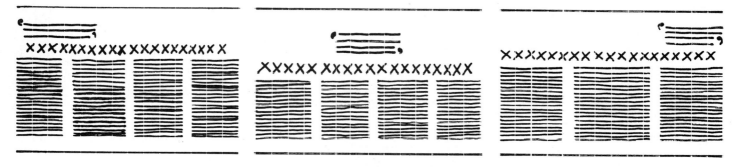

A quote on the side can make an attractive package but not a very practical one on front or other news pages.

The quote as breaker is recommended only for extremely long articles, the type that would occupy an entire page. The quote should be placed in strategic places where the writer's train of thought is not suddenly interrupted.

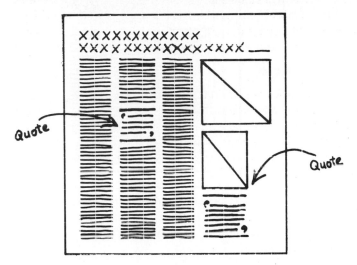

The horizontal quote usually runs at the bottom of the article, ideally with at least a six-pica indentation on each side.

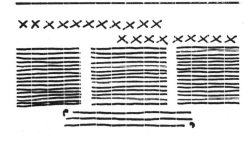

*Quotations and head shots.* Quotations alone can break gray areas and create graphically appealing packages for stories when photos or art are not available. However, another strategy worth considering is the use of a direct quote accompanied by a head shot of the person being quoted.

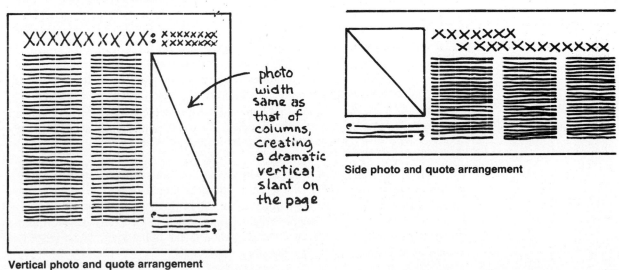

**Vertical photo and quote arrangement**

**Side photo and quote arrangement**

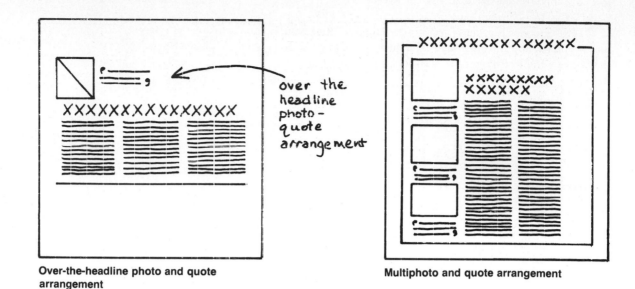

**Over-the-headline photo and quote arrangement**

**Multiphoto and quote arrangement**

### The Use of Art and Illustrations

Many news and feature stories for which photographs are not available may be graphically illustrated through the use of art. Newspapers are using staff artists more than ever before. The staff artist is no longer limited to creating large and impressive illustrations to go with a full-page Sunday feature. Instead, the artist may, and should, be called upon to create simple and small illustrations that will help the reader relate to a variety of stories, from the news story dealing with the economy to the three-paragraph human-interest "brite."

The newsroom artist is becoming an integral part of daily newspaper production, especially if he or she is a news-oriented person who can understand the news and pass on this understanding to readers.

A pioneer in the use of graphics on a daily basis is the *St. Petersburg Times,* whose front page is one of the most graphic in the country. The *Times'* artist, Frank Peters, says that the use of newspaper graphics must not be restricted to process color or charts. In addition, the *St. Petersburg Times* has experimented with the following:

1. Three-dimensional art forms utilizing paper sculptures, arrangement of props, clay sculpture, baking dough, acrylic paint, colored felt, or other material. The finished artwork is photographed in color.
2. Paintings that are copied through a direct reflection process in the photo lab, producing color separations.
3. Fluorographic drawing and artwork, with colored ink applied to Mylar (plastic) overlays. Color separations are done on the artist's drawing board, with overlays for each basic color on top of the black artwork.
4. Mechanical separations, probably the most widely used process in producing color graphics. Amberlith overlays are used, with the artist cutting away areas of the Mylar film base to achieve color effects.

Sometimes a simple dollar sign, which won't occupy more than 8 picas across a column by 6 picas in depth, will serve to attract potential readers to a story about inflation or the state of the dollar abroad. If the story is in a predominantly gray area at the bottom of the page, this simple graphic strategy will immediately isolate it in the eyes of the reader. If a touch of color is applied to the dollar sign, its presence has become more visible, and so has the story.

These three graphics were used by the *St. Petersburg Times* to help the reader identify with complex stories on the front page. Color, type, a clear strategy to convey the message at a glance, and simplicity combine to make an otherwise routine story more graphically appealing. All three samples were designed by Frank Peters.

Maps, charts, and instantly recognizable symbols should figure prominently in the graphic designer's strategies. A word of caution is in order as we discuss available strategies for page design: they work successfully only when not abused. In fact, the use of any of these strategies in conjunction with another may create an overcrowded page that will confuse, rather than attract, the reader. For example, if a photograph has been used to accompany a news story, perhaps the additional map or chart available to go with it can be eliminated or placed elsewhere—where the story might be continued, for example, or where a sidebar (related story) is carried.

## Placement of Headlines

Many alternatives exist today for the placement of headlines. Obviously not every headline must cover the story—umbrella style—from left to right. Although such may be the preferred and perhaps most practical positioning, other strategies can help the designer in a bind, and provide the page with some attractive display.

*Headline on the side.* Headlines on the side, as shown below, serve an important purpose, that of keeping a completely horizontal page from looking overcrowded. Let's compare the sample dummy labeled Dummy A (next page, top) with the one labeled Dummy B next to it. In one example we see a series of horizontal structures slicing the page, whereas in the other, the designer has alternated between headlines over the story and headlines on the side, creating interest and making each story more distinctive and attractive.

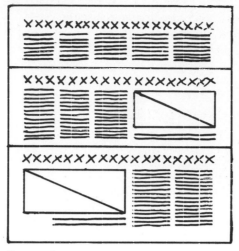
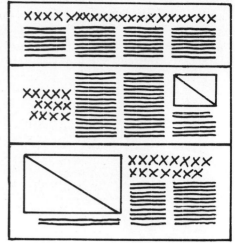

**Dummy A**          **Dummy B**

Within the *headline on the side*, the designer may choose to use a *full depth headline* or a *reduced depth headline*, the difference being one of allowing white space in the latter.

**Full depth headline**          **Reduced depth headline**

*Dutch wrap.* Nobody knows for certain whether the Dutch came up with this interesting and not-so-widely-accepted arrangement, but *Dutch wrap* is what most designers term it when the headline runs the width of the first column of a two- or three-column story. The Dutch wrap requires a line running above the entire width of the story; otherwise the columns not covered by the headline may run confusingly into stories above and below it. Avoid using such headlines in the middle of the page.

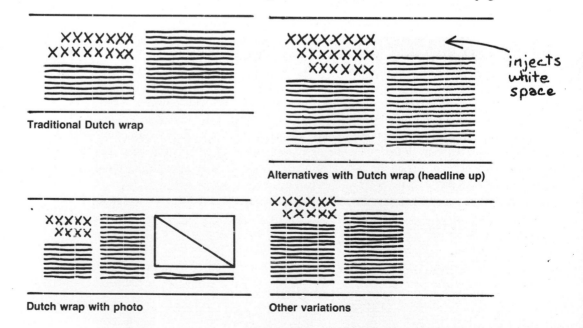

**Traditional Dutch wrap**

*injects white space*

**Alternatives with Dutch wrap (headline up)**

**Dutch wrap with photo**          **Other variations**

***U-shape wrap.*** The idea here is to create a U-shape with body copy around the headline, which is placed in a centered position between two or more columns. As in the case of the Dutch wrap, this arrangement requires that the copy block be kept in rectangular shape, with lines above and below to keep those columns not covered by the headline from running into other copy.

**U-shape wrap**

***Reverse kicker.*** Although the traditional kicker—a small line that simply adds a bit of information to the headline—has become less popular in recent years, the *reverse kicker* continues to be a strategy worth considering. One or two short words usually provide maximum impact.

The reverse kicker (also referred to as *hammer head* in some newsrooms) consists of a large and usually bold kicker, positioned flush left, which accompanies a smaller and lighter headline, positioned flush right.

The reverse kicker is an effective strategy because it injects white space where otherwise none might exist. It may also call attention to one area of the page where the lack of photos, art, or illustrations may have created grayness.

As with other headline-positioning strategies mentioned in this chapter, it is best to maintain the reverse kicker at the very *top* or *bottom* of the page, areas where the built-in white space will lead the eye into the page.

This sample front page from the *Yakima* (Wash.) *Herald-Republic* shows effective use of a centered reverse kicker.

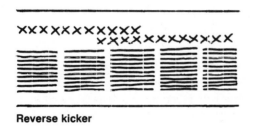

**Reverse kicker**

Flush left or flush right is the most common arrangement, especially useful to inject white space into crowded areas. An unusually long piece of copy for which no art or photos are available presents the ideal situation for the reverse kicker strategy as suggested here.

***Tripod headline.*** A variation of the reverse kicker, but emphasizing the same contrast of large and small type, is the *tripod headline,* in which one key word or phrase is set in bolder and larger type than its accompanying line or lines, which do not exceed the depth of the bolder line.

Refer to the front page from the *Yakima Herald-Republic* and see the "Migrant housing" headline at the bottom of the page. Notice how the boldness of type and placement of head create visual interest in an area that could otherwise have been neglected.

One of the greatest challenges presented by graphic design is the freedom to experiment. We have presented various alternatives, but certainly not all that are available to the designer. As long as the design is functional and allows for easy reading, it is worth trying. When it comes to newspapers, the period of graphic experimentation is in its infancy.

## STRATEGIES FOR EFFECTIVE USE OF WHITE SPACE

Designing with white space has never been unusual in the world of magazines, but only in recent years have newspaper editors become aware of its usefulness as a graphic strategy to improve readability. White space should act as a cushion on the page, especially in overcrowded or totally gray areas, and as such, provide visual relief for the reader. For practical reasons, newspapers may not use white space as openly or freely as magazines do, except perhaps on inside sections. However, there is room for effective use of white space throughout the newspaper in a variety of ways.

Newspaper designers may categorize the use of white space in two specific areas:

1. Day-to-day use.
2. Special use.

In the first category, the designer provides a series of strategic places where white space can become a constant for the page. In a sense, white space as described here would be part of the newspaper's graphic style, another consistent element to follow throughout the publication. Then the following areas become especially important:

*In and around the nameplate.* Because the nameplate is a constant on page one, it also becomes the ideal place to inject appropriate amounts of white space to allow breathing room for the page, even on days when it appears crowded otherwise.

*Between the nameplate and the rest of the page.* The nameplate and the rest of the page should be separated by an almost invisible strip of white space, ranging between ¼ and ½ inch, space that will help the reader make a visual transition from the nameplate to the content of the page.

*Between the lines of headlines.* Determining the appropriate amount of white space between the lines of headlines is difficult simply because not all headlines are alike; some include more letters with ascenders (such as the letter *b*) and descenders (such as the letter *p*) than others. If a staff is to assign a set amount of white space between the lines of a headline, a headline without ascenders and descenders will look more open than one with such elements. All that can be said here is that too much space between the lines of a headline can be as visually undesirable as too little. The designer should trust his eye on this one.

# July election set for county bonds

Closed headline (no space)

# July election set for county bonds

Same headline (more open)

***Between the byline and first paragraph of the story.*** Bylines can help the designer by providing an opportunity to inject a small dose of white space between them and the lead paragraphs.

***Between paragraphs in a story.*** Readers need adequate spacing between paragraphs. It may seem insignificant to provide at least ⅛ of an inch of space between two paragraphs, but the situation changes tremendously when one multiplies that figure times the number of paragraphs that appear on the average page of a daily newspaper.

So far we have discussed the day-to-day areas where white space can be injected into the page in a consistent manner. Perhaps it will help to mention here that it is not only designers who are concerned with the use of white space. Recent research conducted by John M. Smith of the University of California at Los Angeles and Maxwell E. McCombs of Syracuse University shows that of two versions of the same page—one with low white space and one with high white space—readers preferred the high white space version, which showed significant improvements in readability.

Designer Robert Mellis agrees that white space is a must for a well-designed newspaper page:

> I look at a page as a creative rectangle in three colors—black, gray and white. The black comes from the headline elements and the art, the gray comes from the body type and *the white is the space that is pumped into a page to act as punctuation or breathing room.* . . .

**Symmetrical framing**

Mellis admits that American newspaper editors have traditionally been shy about the use of white space. He questions the use of kickers above the main headline, explaining that the kicker has been a traditional means of forcing precious white space into the layout.

> I urge that the kicker be eliminated but that the white space be maintained in the area occupied by the kicker.

## SPECIAL USES OF WHITE SPACE

This second category deals with the special use of white space, probably more suitable for features than for news pages. In all cases, let's understand that application of white space is part of a strategy, meant to ease readability while creating a more attractive page.

### Framing with White Space

White space is the one graphic element that is present on a dummy sheet long before any designing takes place. It is, as we shall see here, one of the most important graphic elements, one that can be used strategically to move the reader's eye in whatever direction the available content dictates.

When the designer frames with white space he creates an all-around margin to highlight copy and art or photographs. Framing can be perfectly *symmetrical*—when the margin is the same width on all four sides of the arrangement—or *asymmetrical*, creating visual contrast by using two different sizes for the margins around the main copy and art block.

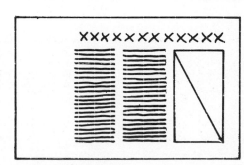

**Asymmetrical framing**

## Blocking with White Space

Blocking with white space involves the use of white or neutral space to push copy and photographs to one side of the page, or up or down. Blocking is ideal for extremely long pieces that are likely to run from the top to the bottom of the page. Let's say that the designer is working with a tabloid page of five columns, placing a single article and photos on that page. Why not plan to work with four (instead of five) columns, thus providing a block of white space to move the reader more easily into a long reading piece?

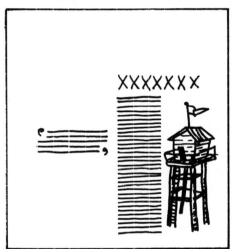

Editors for whom too much white space continues to be taboo may begin by designing the page with the full white space blocking. Then they can try to incorporate elements, such as a small photograph or a direct quotation, that will take up some of the space but allow enough white space elsewhere.

## Indenting with White Space

To indent with white space the designer creates the shape of a letter L or an inverted letter L on the page. The idea is to incorporate white space and to make better use of the available space than when blocking is applied.

Notice how these special strategies for the use of white space make it easier to develop creative positioning for other elements, such as art and copy.

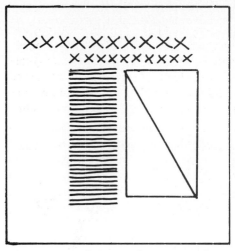

**Indenting (top of the page)**

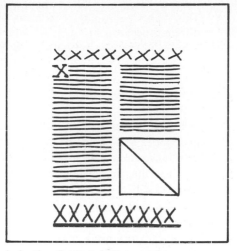

**Indenting (bottom of the page)**

## Some Rules about White Space

The lack of white space can be visually detrimental to a page. But the poor use—or abuse—of white space can be even worse. White space should be gained on the outside, not the inside, of the page. That is, the designer should "cluster" his copy, headline, and photos, allowing any white space to fall on the outside of the package.

Never trap large amounts of white space between photos or between headline and copy.

## STRATEGIES FOR PACKAGING

Packaging is probably the most urgently needed graphic strategy for today's newspaper. It is through packaging that related content is linked so that the reader will find it easier to absorb the material.

Strategies for packaging can be divided into two categories: the packaging of entire sections, for example, "Lifestyle," "Business," or "Real Estate"; and the packaging of a single story and photo or two related stories within a given page. In addition, we may create a third category for the full-page package.

## Packaging of Entire Sections

In this category, the designer will organize content within a specific area, devoting an entire section to one subject. Ordinarily, newspapers arrange their content in such a way that there will be daily packaged sections, such as sports and lifestyle. Recently, newspapers have started to publish special sections ranging from sports (seasonal) to consumer topics, using packaging as the best strategy to create continuity and organization of content.

Louis Silverstein, assistant managing editor of the *New York Times* and art director for the corporate Times Company, supervises the design and packaging of the *Times'* weekly sections (sports, business, home, leisure, and weekend entertainment). He thinks that packaging is a sounder alternative than simply pouring news into available holes:

> The editors and advertising staff must settle on certain configurations—a prearranged flow of ads and news—and develop a structure or architecture

for each section in order to permit attractive graphic treatment of stories. This makes packaging a cooperative, creative endeavor that cuts across different departments such as production, circulation, promotion, news, advertising and the business office.

### Packaging of Individual Stories and/or Photos

Today's hurried reader expects visual organization from his newspaper. The packaging of related stories and photos provides such organization. A package on a newspaper page may range in size from a small (two columns by four inches) to a full-page package, depending on content and space availability. Earlier (Chapter 4), we mentioned the possibility of creating a Center of Visual Impact through a package, in which case there would be no other CVI on the page. That suggestion is worth remembering during our discussion of packaging.

Not every story needs to be packaged. The moment we mention the word *package* we are assuming that column rules or borders will be used to show content relationship. The positioning of such rules and/or borders, however, may vary, as shown by the following examples:

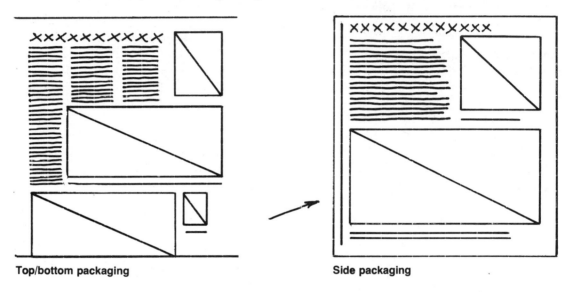

**Top/bottom packaging**                    **Side packaging**

Open packages depend on top and bottom lines to show content relationship. Ideally, these packages will make long copy look shorter while providing access into the page.

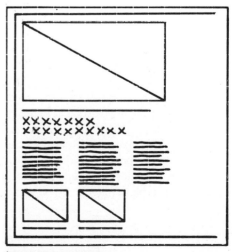

**Three-dimensional**

A *closed package* boxes all of the story and/or photos. Closed packages are recommended when the copy does not exceed thirty inches. Enclosing long copy tends to make it look longer. An open box, however, gives readers the optical illusion of shorter copy.

Closed packages may allow a graphic element to protrude, creating more attractive graphics and letting the reader's eye gain access to the inside of the package.

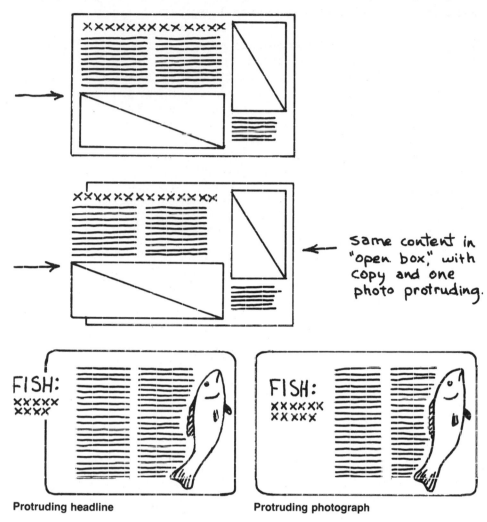

same content in "open box," with copy and one photo protruding.

**Protruding headline**          **Protruding photograph**

If more than two stories are positioned inside a package, the designer will treat their placement with the same considerations he would apply to an open page. For example, two stories within a package should be placed using contrasting elements (horizontal and vertical). A package is visually perceived as *one unit,* except that such a unit will also be perceived as part of a total page—in which case it may help to remember that if the package is large and prominent, other elements on the same page should be underplayed. Most importantly, the designer should avoid packaging too many other elements on the page. If other packages do appear on the same page, only one package should carry the most visual impact.

Once the concept of packaging is mastered, the designer may begin to package related content and photos without actually using any borders to keep the material together. Notice how the page from the *Knickerbocker News* (Albany, New York) packages a story at the top with related art but does not use borders. In this case, however, the package at the bottom of the page is attractive enough to create some competition.

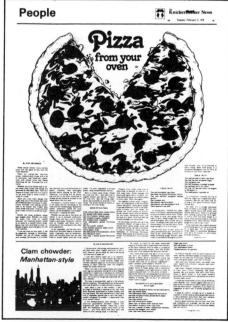

Notice how this page, the second one for section A of this newspaper, packages national, international, state, people, and weather structures by forming the shape of a letter U around a cluster of wire photos.

This page includes comic strips (reduced to 34-pica widths), television listings, horoscope, bridge column, crossword puzzle, and brief television news, all under the heading of "Leisure/TV."

This business page uses a photo arrangement of cars as a CVI, packaging one main story while making the rest of the page well organized and easy to read.

The entire page is devoted to a calendar of events in the local area. Notice the use of a standing sig at top, with photos of two or three main events for the week. The rest of the page forms the U-shape design around a cluster of photos.

Full-page packaging results in easy-to-read and economical pages, as shown through these sample pages from the *St. Cloud Daily Times* (St. Cloud, Minnesota).

This chapter has presented various strategies for designers to make newspaper content easier to grasp while they create more visually appealing pages. These strategies are not universal, however, because they may not work for all newspapers. Design evolves from content, and design strategies must be flexible enough to adapt to the day's news.

The most effective graphic strategies will be those that enhance communication and create maximum legibility. Just as important is that such strategies be economical and easy to execute.

We opened this chapter by describing today's newspaper editor as a *graphic strategist*. However, participants at an American Press Institute Seminar on Newspaper Design not only concluded that editors should become graphic strategists, but also acknowledged the need for what they term the newsroom's emerging specialist, a *graphic journalist*. A graphic journalist, the API participants say, is a hybrid, a person who combines the skills of an artist or designer with those of an editor. For most American newspapers of the future it is safe to assert that there will be a demand for such a combination of skills.

# 8
# inside pages

Inside pages have gained a new status in American newspapers. Editors give them more attention than ever before, especially through the use of large photographs, better packaging of news and photos, and more effective placement of advertising.

Saul Pett of the Associated Press describes the new status of inside pages eloquently:

> Television gives them the front page. If that's all we give them, they have no reason to come to us.

> It is the inside that will save the newspaper, the inside that will sell subscriptions and make the product a profound habit. Not the fast headline for the fast buck on a newsstand that will fast disappear because nobody lives at the newsstands; they go by. It is the inside that will attend and nourish the human soul, and there was never a time when the soul needed more attention and nourishment. Or, was more willing to pay for it.

Page one captures the reader. Inside pages keep his attention. Today's editors are more willing to emphasize good design for inside pages and to allocate open pages free of ads whenever possible. For example, page two or three in the first section of many newspapers is used as a second front page. For the *Miami News, Yakima Herald-Republic,* and *Boston Globe,* among others, page two offers the reader an attractive package with many of the national and international news items that didn't make page one. The style of writing is easy to read, and the graphics abets fast consumption of the many items on the page. Appropriately, the *Yakima Herald-Republic* labels its page ''Just A Minute,'' the *Miami News* uses the day of the week plus ''Briefing,'' and the *Boston Globe* calls its page ''In Brief.''

One inside page that has almost gained the graphic status of a front page is page three of the *Providence Journal*. It is labeled "The Second Front Page" and includes the typographical variety and editorial content that allow it to compete with a front page anywhere.

This is unquestionably the *Journal*'s second front page and it is so labeled. Notice how photo packaging becomes a CVI for this page. The copy frames the photo arrangement, forming the shape of a number 7.

Page two of the *Herald-Republic* displays four structures in addition to two ads at the bottom of the page. Note the "Just a Minute" section, where regional, national, and international briefs are combined.The opening sentence for each item is in boldface.

Page two of the *Miami News* is divided into two vertical structures that cut the page from top to bottom. The structure on the left is divided into five substructures for brief items about people, the world, the nation, Florida, and Washington. The right-side structure is divided into unequally sized horizontal structures to highlight other important news items. Note the effective placement of weather at the bottom of the page and also the "Tomorrow" teaser which brings a sense of horizontal movement to an otherwise totally vertical page.

The *Globe* also uses page two as an open page of news, features, and brief items. Notice the use of the two narrow vertical structures on both ends of the page, balanced by a center structure and an interesting use of photographs.

The *Chicago Tribune*'s open news page appears as the last page of the newspaper's first section. Notice the effective use of four vertical structures dominating the top portion of the page. White space, boldface lead-ins, and properly positioned photographs create an easy-to-read and graphically exciting page. More important, the page packs a tremendous amount of information.

## FORMAT FOR INSIDE PAGES

An inside page of the *Tribune* shows effective use of a six-column format.

This eight-column inside page from the *Journal* is built around one major photograph that serves as a CVI. The use of clean type and white space gives the reader an attractive page.

Design experimentation among newspapers in the last few years has brought about format changes, especially in the number of columns. As newspapers made the changeover from hot metal type to photocomposition, their staffs found it an appropriate time to introduce major improvements in page and column widths, and in design generally.

The early 1970s and the inflationary cost of newsprint forced newspaper executives to consider ways of saving money. Reducing page size became the most obvious way to do so. For example, the *Los Angeles Times* reduced its page width by about three-quarters of an inch for an estimated saving of 18,000 tons of newsprint a year. A smaller page made the eight-column format a difficult one on the reader's eyes, however, as the narrow columns appear even narrower within the more limited page size.

In Minneapolis, the *Star* and the *Tribune* switched to a six-column format and also cut the page by half an inch for a substantial saving in newsprint and a breezy, easier-to-read page. Obviously, what started as a management strategy to save money and paper led to the redesigning of many newspapers. Newspapers thus have benefited both economically and graphically from the resulting changes.

Although column format changes have little effect upon the design of page one and other open pages, they create problems for inside pages. A new column format may mean restructuring advertising space, or provide an excuse for it. The advertising agencies that distribute ads to newspapers are pleading for standardization of column widths, citing the difficulty of coping with more than forty different page sizes and/or formats when putting together print ads. Many newspapers have been forced to use a six-column format exclusively on their front and open inside pages and to maintain eight or nine columns on the other pages.

The two most prevalent formats for inside pages today continue to be six and eight columns. Other formats include four and nine columns, although these are rarer and more difficult to design.

### Six-Column Format

Wider columns of type are easier to read. They are less tiring on the eye and produce a clearer and more attractive design for the page. Ideally, when a newspaper makes a column format change on page one it should be able to carry out the change throughout the newspaper, as did the *Los Angeles Times* and the *Minneapolis Star* and *Tribune*.

The six-column format allows for less crowding of headlines, especially at the top of the page. Ads designed to cover wider columns also enhance the overall look of the page, since there is no room for congested or small ads. The total graphic atmosphere of a page using the six-column format is more inviting to the reader, an argument worth mentioning to advertisers who might be skeptical of the format.

### Eight-Column Format

The eight-column format is still around, even on the inside pages of newspapers that have abandoned it for their front pages. As one defender of this format puts it, "It allows the reader to sweep through the page, not dance on it (as is the case with six columns)." And sweeping may very well be the proper description. Usually there is plenty of visual sweeping to do when the reader finds fourteen or twenty small three-line headline items on the page, surrounded by an equal number of small ads.

The worst offense of the eight-column inside page is the congestion of eight headlines, tombstoned side by side at the top of the page. However, a page designed around a major story or photograph will create reader interest and eye movement for other items on the page. An advantage of the eight-column format is that it facilitates the use of 1½- and 2-column combinations to create visual variety throughout the page.

## Four-Column Format

The four-column format is clean and readable but impractical for the design of inside pages. There is no way to avoid gray blocks of copy on a four-column page. This format is ideal for an open page where one single story and illustrations are to appear, but it won't serve the editor who has four or five stories of unequal length to place on the page. And there is virtually no attractive way of getting a two-inch story on the page, since it will end up as four lines of type when stretched out to fit the column width.

These two inside pages from the Quakertown, Pa. *Free Press* show the effectiveness of a four-column format for a single story page (left) but its less practical application for multi-story and ad displays.

## Nine-Column Format

Few newspapers today use the nine-column format. Narrow columns, the use of many stories on the page, and an overall congested look characterize this format. The *Toronto Star* used the nine-column format effectively until 1978, when it switched to six columns. The very narrow columns present a problem in hyphenating words for newspapers using cold type, another probable reason this format has become unpopular in the last few years.

This inside page from the *Journal* shows
effective use of a photograph as a CVI. The
subject in this photograph is looking into the
page, which also helps to bring the reader into
the page. Advertising content, in this case, is
graphically secondary.

In this example from the *Times,* advertising
content dominates the page graphically, leaving
the designer little space for major display of
editorial content.

## DESIGNING INSIDE PAGES

The designer should approach each inside page in terms of two important considerations:

1. Editorial content.
2. Structural positioning of advertising content.

Inside pages cover a variety of content that ultimately affects their appearance.
Obviously a designer is not going to treat a jump page the same way he would handle
an inside section opener. As with other pages, editorial content determines what design
pattern to follow.

The designer should attempt to create a CVI on the page. The attractive inside
page will revolve graphically around one major item, be it a photograph, a story, or a
combination package of the two.

An inside page may be designed structurally by following the same graphic
considerations already discussed for page one. The designer should determine the
number of items to be included on the page, identify one item as a CVI, and then place
the rest according to their editorial significance. One difference, however, is the
consideration that must be given to advertising space to make it harmonious with other
elements on the page.

An inside page is usually dominated either by editorial or advertising content.
When 90 percent of the page is occupied by advertising, the designer's task becomes
that of placing editorial content as ''secondary'' material.

The most difficult inside pages to design effectively are those where advertising
content takes half of the available space, leaving the other half for editorial display. In
such situations the page will be divided into either vertical or horizontal structures. Of
the two, it is easier to work with a horizontal than a vertical structure. The upper half of
the page can be emphasized without interfering wtih advertising content. When the
page is cut vertically in half, however, the designer hasn't much chance to avoid
mixing photographs with the photos or art in an ad. This is one reason designers should
have an idea of what the ads look like—to create page harmony.

We have seen how the relevant position of advertising affects the outcome of a
page design. In fact, when advertisements are placed raggedly on a page, it becomes
difficult, if not impossible, to design a page structurally, because structural design calls
for squared-off columns. The traditional double-pyramid pattern (below left) for
placement of ads or the exaggerated ragged half pyramid (below right) make readable
and attractive design impossible. The so-called allocation for editorial copy ends up as
a triangle at the top of the page, with one news story forced into the ''well'' created
where the two half pyramids of advertising material meet.

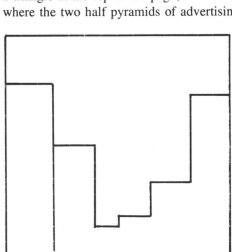

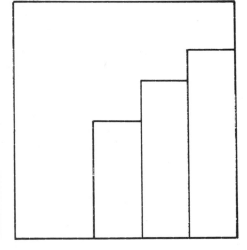

An inside page from the *Boston Herald American* shows a double-pyramid pattern for placement of ads. Notice the "President" story that falls into the "well" created where the two pyramids meet on the page.

An inside page from the *Winnipeg Tribune* displays a half pyramid that lends structural support to news items on the page. Notice how ads are placed in solid blocks to avoid a ragged look and make the placement of editorial content easier and more attractive.

An inside page from the *Times* illustrates how the block placement of ads allows a major story display at the top of the page, in spite of heavy advertising content.

## PLACEMENT ALTERNATIVES FOR INSIDE PAGES

Editors want their content to be read and advertisers want their ads to be attractive and eye-catching.

Harmonizing both contents graphically is not an impossibility as long as the ads can be arranged in "blocks" or "structures." The designer must be willing to abandon the rigid and disorganized appearance caused by double pyramids and to shape half pyramids so that they will provide solid blocks of support for the rest of the editorial content. These two steps mark the beginning of graphic harmony and consequently more attractive inside pages.

No news story should be trapped inside a well created by two ad pyramids. Advertisers who still insist that their ads be touched by news copy should spend more time creating attractive design for their ads, to make them visible no matter how removed they may be from news content. The editor of a small daily says he has stopped worrying about placing news copy next to ads. "The readers are going for the ads first now, to get the coupons, so I am not going to struggle with a set of arbitrary rules that no longer apply to today's newspaper."

Other patterns that allow for effective and structural placement of news content are the following:

1. *The inverted* L *pattern*—Although ad space dominates the page graphically it usually allows enough room for horizontal display of one or two stories, as illustrated here.

Inverted "L" pattern

Vertical blocking—Notice how space has been used effectively to display several photographs and cutlines.

2. *Vertical and horizontal blocking*—Depending on how much space is allowed by ad placement, the editor may display one or many stories following vertical or horizontal patterns.

## ADVERTISING DESIGN

The actual design of each advertisement affects the way advertising and news content create a sense of graphic harmony on the page.

Ads designed with heavy and elaborate borders are the worst offenders. In addition to creating an eyesore on the page, these heavily ornamented ads block entrance of the reader's eye into the ad's contents, which is probably the last thing the advertiser wants.

It is true that in many cases the advertiser who does not know much about typography or design may request an ultra-heavy border for his ad. In such cases, it is up to the advertising salesperson to educate his client, emphasizing the higher visibility, greater clarity, and more effective communication of a message that is simply and cleanly designed.

The use of an extremely heavy border creates typographic congestion here.

The same ad designed with a lighter border becomes a more readable and harmonious element on the page.

Many newspaper advertising design departments would do well to limit the variety of border tapes they have in stock, concentrating on those that are thin, simple, and visually appealing, not on those that are highly decorative and obtrusive. The thickness and boldness of the tape used to border an ad should work in direct relation to the size of the ad. A large ad, three columns wide by 8 inches deep, will obviously hold a heavier border better than a one-column by two-inch ad.

The subject of advertising design is too broad to discuss fully in this book. However, one more hint is in order. It's difficult to read ''reversed'' ads, those black squares with white type on them that do little to attract the eye and communicate a message. Reverses, heavy borders, and congested ads alienate the reader. They also create typographic congestion on the page and defeat the important concept of graphic harmony between advertising and news content.

In the long run, the design of an inside page is only as good as the ads on that page allow it to be.

## INSIDE PAGE VARIETY

Not every inside page is a second front page or an ad-dominated structure. Other categories of inside pages include the section opener, the open feature page, and the picture page.

### The Section Opener

Section openers usually include a label to classify their content, such as ''Entertainment,'' ''Sports,'' ''Finance,'' or ''Lifestyle.'' The overall look follows closely that of the newspaper's front page. Consistent use of type for standing sigs makes the section opener identifiable with a particular newspaper even if the section becomes separated from the rest of the newspaper. Section openers often have fewer stories than page one, giving designers a greater opportunity for exploration of graphics. The opener usually includes an index to the inside of the section, along with large photographs, a variety of display types to accommodate specific content, and color in many cases. Some section openers include at least one ad; most are open pages.

### The Open Feature Page

A designer's delight is the open feature page, which allows unlimited creativity. Probably the only way to make a long article readable is by surrounding it with a generous amount of white space and producing an effective package of photographs and copy. The designer tries to create an optical illusion that will make the copy look shorter than its actual length. Most designers use the open feature page to bring magazine design into the newspaper (see Chapter 7).

### The Picture Page

Readers want more pictures in their newspapers, and as a result, editors are using more picture pages. The *Des Moines Tribune,* for example, devotes its back page to pictures. Graphic interest is created through the use of unequally sized photographs. Horizontal and vertical shapes combine to provide movement and balance for the page, and copy is kept at a minimum. White space is included to bring attention to each photograph, but it is maintained outside, not trapped between photos. (See also Chapter 9.)

This "Entertainment–Travel" section opener displays one major story and an index to inside content. Notice the dominant use of photography.

For its local news section, the *Herald-Republic* uses an open page section opener. Notice the dominance of type and the use of horizontal structures throughout the page.

This feature page is based on one single story but includes a sidebar (bottom of page) which allows the designer to increase graphic interest by placing a column rule above the headline. Note the photo treatment: three connected photographs, one of which dominates the page. The headline is ragged right, flush left, and the entire page content is boxed.

Only the top two-thirds of this page is used for a main feature story. Photos help break the gray created by long articles. The main headline is reversed at the top of the page, but enough white space is injected directly below it to create a pleasant atmosphere around the main story. It is an economical design, allowing for placement of two unrelated stories at the bottom of the page.

Design options are as many and varied for inside pages as they are for page one. Now that front pages have become more attractive through better design, the reader expects the same treatment throughout the newspaper. The reader also expects the designer to make reading easy for him—one element dominating the page and other elements maintaining harmony throughout.

Inside pages offer designers the challenge of arranging copy, photographs or illustrations, and advertising content in a harmonious graphic pattern. The successful designer is one who pleases his editor, his readers, and the newspaper's advertisers.

This photo page is labeled "The Back Page/ Pictures" and offers the reader a mixture of local and national photos that stand alone, relying on a full cutline to tell the story. The photos are well organized, with emphasis on the clustering of elements in the center and white space on the outside.

# 9 photographic impact

More than a hundred years have passed since a practical method was invented for halftone photoengraving, making it possible for newspapers and magazines to include photographs as part of their coverage. During those years photographs have served newspapers as visual communicators of the news. The standard newspaper fare in this country includes the refreshing human interest photograph of a child and his pet or the dramatic image of a plane crash, earthquake, or other disaster.

Photographs create a mood for the day's news and become mirrors that reflect the facial expressions of politicians, sports heroes, celebrities, and ordinary people. Photos make us smile or weep. They entice us into a story we might otherwise ignore or tempt us to buy a newspaper through visual impulse.

While magazines have always capitalized on photography to create visual appeal, newspapers have relied more heavily on the printed word. In some newspapers, however, photographs become a tool to break gray matter on the page, stepping stones placed on a page to help the reader's eyes jump from story to story.

Today, with newspapers adopting magazine-style design, and with more advanced technology making it easier to print photographs, many editors treat photographs as design elements, an integral part of the overall presentation of each page. Some newspapers have hired directors of photography to coordinate assignments and work closely with page designers.

Earlier we mentioned that photographs—and not headlines—are doing most of the shouting in American newspapers today. But not all photographs are meant to shout, and this chapter points out some strategies for assigning, selecting, and editing photographs.

## THE EDITOR AND PHOTOGRAPHER AS A TEAM

The key to the effective use of photography in newspapers is a good working relationship between the editor (or page designer) and the photographer. "The team most likely to achieve the happy blend of words and pictures consists of an editor who thinks visually and a photographer who thinks editorially," write Gerald D. Hurley and Angus McDougall.*

Most photographers appreciate an editor who thinks visually and can describe mental images to be captured through film. This does not mean that the photographer won't be able to use his creativity in recording the subject as he perceives it, but at least he will receive a head start from the editor, who will be the ultimate judge of the photograph and how it will be used.

The moment when the editor assigns a photograph is a crucial one, especially in the hurried world of newspaper photojournalism, where there is seldom time for the photographer to go back and reshoot what he missed. If the assignment can be made orally, with the editor describing what he wants and how he plans to use the photograph, the chances are greater for a usable photograph. *Usable photographs* is the phrase most newspaper editors use to describe their expected return.

Frank Hoy, a former news photographer for the *Washington Post* who teaches photography at Arizona State University, describes the news photographer on the scene as "the eyes of the editor"—a visual reporter who thinks editorially. The editor, for his part, organizes the photos into a strong communication for the reader. Hoy explains,

> This teamwork calls for a delicate balance between specific requests of the editor and the initiative of the photographer on the scene. Although the editor has the final decision on picture use, teamwork is best when the photographer goes beyond specific requests to provide other choices. Usually in searching for the right photograph, the newspaper photographer chooses between long shot, to show the entire scene, or close up, to show some storytelling detail. Often he takes both as part of the search for the essence of the story. When he does he gives the editor a choice of visual alternatives during layout.

For today's photographer-editor team, the widest choice is necessary. The photographer must have shots of the *entire scene*—in case the editor wants to use a large and dominant overview of a subject; *close-ups*—when there is a need for detail, for the specific rather than the general; *horizontals*—when the design strategy calls for the reader to move from left to right; *verticals*—to pull the reader's eye down to the bottom of the page or for contrast with extreme horizontals; and the *imaginative*—for what Hoy describes as "something different," the icing on the cake, a shot that the editor never planned for but that is too good to pass up.

Many photographers complain about this last category, arguing that some newspaper editors follow the photographic clichés, selecting the mundane as opposed to the out-of-the-ordinary.

Let us analyze the photographs opposite. At top is one used by the *Washington Post* for a back-to-school picture page. Hoy took this picture of a sad little boy who refused, with tears in his eyes, to be left alone in school. His mother and teacher are trying to offer some comfort, but to no avail. Below is a photograph that was not used by the *Post* that day. In it, a young girl is left alone outside the school building while her mother walks away. The photo expresses the loneliness of a child who is feeling

*Hurley, Gerald D. and Angus McDougall, *Visual Impact in Print: How to Make Pictures Communicate: A Guide for the Photographer, the Editor and the Designer,* American Publishers Press, Chicago, 1971.

(Photo by Frank Hoy, the *Washington Post*.)

(Photo by Frank Hoy.)

isolated. Here's how Hoy explains how he was moved to shoot it:

> After the coverage of the usual first day activities on that first day of school, I heard a child crying, looked back, and saw this scene. The child was crying after her mother shouted for her to get back to school. She did, turning and sprinting over the crest of the small hill to the school beyond. . . . For publication that day, the photograph lacked connection to school, or more photo-journalistic meaning. But every time I look at this photo, I think of my reaction to this momentarily lost child.

Although the photo of the little boy, his mother, and his teacher was more appropriate to communicate the visual feeling of opening day at school, the photographer gave his editor other possibilities, which if not usable with the specific story of the day, could be considered for future use. Often the photographer's imaginative photographs will be used, even when enough samples of the requested assignment are available.

The best news photograph is that which combines the *familiar elements* and the added dimension of the *creative,* a quality that only the photographer can contribute to his work.

The system that Frank Hoy has used successfully as a news photographer, and which he now teaches to would-be photojournalists, takes into consideration both the photographer and the editor and, as he puts it, "leads to a balance between extremes." The system is based on the photographer as a creative representative of the editor. It can be summed up in the acronym EDFAT: Entire, Details, Frame, Angles, and Time.

In practice this means that the photographer

1. Observes the *entire* scene, or subject, and shoots general views.
2. Dissects the scene into specific *details,* shooting as he moves in.
3. *Frames* those details into a strong, even radically strong, composition.
4. Shoots, as he moves in, from a variety of *angles:* high, low, and so on.
5. Makes maximum use of the *time* available and applies the system within realistic newspaper deadlines. On news stories, the photographer shoots for the widest choice of shots possible despite the lack of time. On stories involving more time, she shoots in much wider variety. She also uses different lenses to change the focal point of art.

The relationship between photographer and editor begins with the original assignment and continues through the selection process, but it does not end when the selected print is turned in. Photographers should receive feedback about their work. They should also be exposed whenever possible to the actual *editing* of the photograph and should observe the designing process. A photographer who knows how his work will be used is more likely to produce usable photographs.

Part of what makes the editor-photographer relationship meaningful is their willingness to learn each other's craft. The photographer for today's newspaper, and magazine, must possess some basic knowledge of design. He should know that the manner in which photographs are placed on a page determines to a certain extent how those photographs will relate to each other and to the reader. Photographers need to know about type selection, white space, page dimensions, and other design strategies.

Similarly, editors must learn as much as possible about the art and science of photography. Both the editor and his photographer must also learn to compromise. The editor should realize that her best design plans were meant to be altered if the photographs available lend themselves to a different treatment. Likewise, a photographer must understand why his "best" photograph did not get on page one, or even in the newspaper at all.

The relationship between these two practitioners is vital to good newspaper design. Teamwork, good communication, an open mind, and mutual respect foster such a relationship, which today's visual newspaper cannot afford to be without.

## SELECTING PHOTOGRAPHS

Many important considerations enter into the selection of a photograph, but the following four elements should help designers make better choices:

1. *Appropriateness*. The foremost criterion in selecting a photograph is whether it says what it is supposed to. Does the photo enhance the story visually instead of repeating what the words say?

2. *Impact*. Does the photograph possess a quality that would cause the reader to stop and look? Even when the subject may be considered routine, such as a car accident, a meeting, or other standard news fare, the best photograph will be that which is out of the ordinary, the one that turns the very familiar into the creative dimension of the not-so-familiar.

3. *Design possibilities*. Photographs ultimately become part of the total newspaper page, which is the reason they must be evaluated for their design possibilities. What can this photograph do to enhance the overall visual presentation of the page? Sometimes the editor looks for a photo that she can use horizontally or vertically on the page. Often she wants a photograph that can be cropped closely or a small picture that will carry impact. A photograph that lends itself to several design strategies is certainly more worthy of consideration than one that must be used in one specific shape. Although it is possible that a photograph will help determine the way a feature page design will evolve, designers more often build their new pages around story content.

4. *Quality*. Photos that are too dark, too light, grainy, out of focus, or otherwise difficult to look at create the kind of graphic noise the designer can do without. With the many possibilities available for designing with type that were described in the chapter on typography, it is better not to have a photograph on the page at all than to use one of inferior quality.

## EDITING THE PHOTOGRAPH

Few photographs are ever used in their original size: 5 × 7 or 8 × 10 inches. Instead, photo sizes are made to conform to a preconceived page layout. Some basic mathematical rules are all the designer needs to size a photograph, and the quickest and most commonly used method is the *proportional scale*.

Using a proportional scale (or cropping wheel), a low-cost instrument which is easy to use, the designer can adapt the size of a photograph from the original to the desired width and length. Here is how the process works:

1. The proportional scale consists of an outer and an inner wheel: The outer wheel represents the *desired* size, the inner wheel the *original size*.

2. If the designer knows the new width he wants for a photograph (to accommodate his layout space) and wishes to determine the new height, he aligns the original width with the desired width—inner wheel against outer wheel—and then reads the figure opposite the actual height, which will be the new height. The same principle applies when the designer knows the new height and would like to know the new width.

3. Without moving the wheel, the designer will also be able to know the percentage of the enlargement or reduction, which shows through a window on the proportional scale.

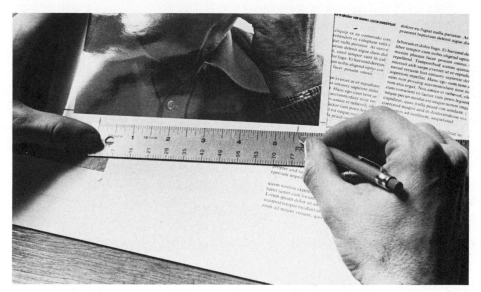

The designer is ready to crop the photograph when he knows what space the photo will take on the layout. In this case the layout calls for a width of 2¼ inches, but the designer wishes to preserve 5⅝ inches of the original (as cropped). By matching 5⅝ on the inner wheel against the desired width of 2¼ inches on the outer wheel and checking likewise for depth, the designer can make sure that the photo will fit into the space allowed.
(Photos by John Scott.)

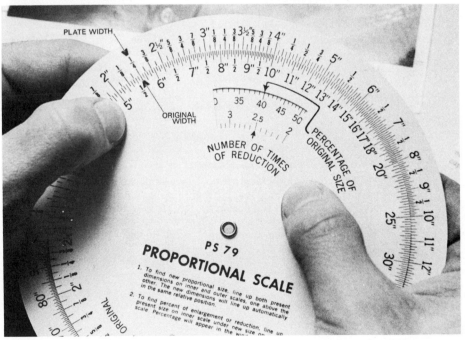

The mechanical task of sizing a photograph is simpler than the more esthetic task of editing it. A few basic suggestions should make the job easier:

1. Determine what elements in the photograph are needed to tell the story.
2. Eliminate any elements that detract from the center of interest.
3. Consider design strategies that can enhance the use of the photograph—emphasizing a close-up, cropping closely around a face, creating a strong vertical or horizontal.
4. Edit the photograph so that the end result will be the most dramatic treatment possible.

For example, let us look at what some newspaper editors have done with *head shots*. Traditionally, newspaper editors converted head shots to thumbnail status, making them almost invisible. Today the head shot has become one of the strongest photographic elements on the page.

Nothing can be more impressive than a well-cropped head shot. Readers who like to have *names* sprinkled in their daily newspaper copy like *faces* just as much. Photographers have always capitalized on faces, but now editors are beginning to recognize their worth as design strategies. Let us examine the following examples:

The editor here decided to eliminate the subject's forehead in order to bring attention to the lips. Cropping should be used to bring out the highlight of a photograph, an exercise which often requires the elimination of distracting elements—in this case the forehead. The idea here is to create a "mask" through cropping. (Photo by John Scott.)

Ears are an expressionless part of the body, which is the reason we don't feel there is anything missing in this special treatment. (Photo by John Scott.)

The examples shown here and opposite illustrate convincingly that head shots can not only save the editor's day but can also create visually interesting pages, especially when staff photographers realize the many possibilities presented by an informal or candid head shot, the type in which the subject is not posed.

If the subject is shown in a pensive mood, what may be called a "portrait" shot, a horizontal slant will enhance the photograph and the page, as shown in the *Miami News*.

No two faces are alike, even if they may seem that way to a frustrated photographer shooting a boring news conference. Notice the special treatment given to this head shot of a weary participant during a press conference. Close cropping of the head brought out the hand-to-eye motion the editor wanted to emphasize.
(Courtesy of the *Toronto Star*.)

Faces can carry a page, as shown through these all-head shot pages from the *Toronto Star*. At left is the front page, showing various approaches to the use of faces. At right is an inside page with nine head shots in various sizes for contrast and impact. Far right is the use of a portrait head shot as a CVI.

This page from the *Minneapolis Tribune* uses a large head shot with the background dropped to make it look larger on the page. The subject almost talks directly to the reader.

## RETOUCHING AND FLOPPING

A photograph that needs too much retouching or doctoring before it is printable probably should not be published at all, and one that requires flopping probably could be replaced by one that doesn't. Retouching and flopping involve altering the original photograph—in a sense, an alteration of the facts.

Newspaper editors do not always have time to carry out these tasks, but often it is not a matter of choice.

*Retouching.* Sometimes the photo editor will retouch a photograph to improve the quality of a good print. For example, there may be a bright spot somewhere on the photo which attracts the reader's eye to an area away from the center of interest. In such cases, a simple airbrush can take the bright spot out without affecting the rest of the photograph.

*Flopping.* Flopping means turning over an image in the photograph so that it faces the opposite way. It is usually done to conform to layout standards, since faces should look into the page and not off it. The problem here is that not every photograph can be flopped. For example, any photograph showing symbols, letters, or numbers should not be flopped, unless the editor wants player number 70 to come out as 0Γ. Similarly, photographs showing subjects signing contracts or swinging bats cannot be flopped.

Backgrounds, microphones, cables, outlines formed by a door or window can all become distracting elements that the editor may remove by a simple airbrush. Notice how the photo on the left includes trees and people in the background, detracting from the action up front. The photo at right has been retouched to eliminate this distraction.
(Photos by John Scott.)

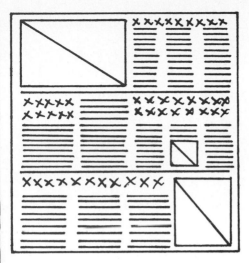

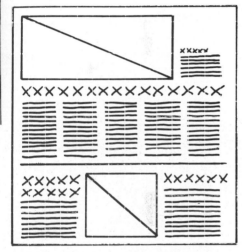

Notice what happens to the letters on the crate when the photo is improperly flopped (right).

Usually many recourses are available to the designer to eliminate unnecessary flopping. One is to use a different photograph.

## PHOTOGRAPHIC DESIGN STRATEGIES

If properly integrated, photographs help pull a design together. The designer's primary task is to create *order* through the placement of photographs on the page. The following suggestions will help to establish order while providing various approaches to design:

1. Emphasize a combination of large and small photos on the page, avoiding the same size for unrelated photographs (above, right).

2. Distribute photographs so that both the top and bottom of the page receive photographic impact (center).

3. When only one photograph is used, make it a *page stopper*—a Center of Visual Impact (right).

4. Let photographs move the reader in whatever direction the designer wishes. The example at left shows the double truck horizontal, creating a dramatic CVI for the two-page spread. The example on the right shows a strong vertical, pulling the reader to a horizontal story at the bottom of the page.

5. Place related photos in a cluster, but size them differently for much-desired visual contrast. One of the strongest advocates of the cluster approach is Peter Palazzo, whose redesign of the *Providence Journal* is based on a cluster of unrelated photo-

The pages here and opposite from the *Yakima Herald-Republic* show the maximum impact of photographs as dominant elements.

Notice that these photo pages use type as a secondary element; the page on the left reverses type on photograph. One large photo becomes the Center of Visual Impact, the rest are smaller. The page on the right displays a dominant photo at the top with a thin typeface used to provide contrast.

graphs for page one. Palazzo defends his approach: "Pictures are collected throughout when possible for maximum impact and to show them to their greatest advantage. The design renders obsolete the practice of having to use filler pictures to separate stories or help brighten up the page."

6. Let white space lead the reader's eyes into photography. Do not always use all available space. For example, use a five-column photograph in the space of six columns. The placement of the cutline at the left of the photo allows valuable white space at top. When using a cluster of photographs, position them to allow white space on outer areas.

7. Coordinate photography and type. Both are important elements competing for the reader's attention. Sometimes type wins. The designer's job is to avoid competition, to make the elements complement each other. If type is the primary element on the page—bold and large—make the photographs smaller. However, if a photo is the highlight of the page, deemphasize display type, making the headlines smaller and less bold. Designers must realize that only one element becomes primary to the reader; anything different will probably create a congested page.

Most readers follow a certain order when they read the newspaper. For example, they look at a photograph and then search for its corresponding cutline and copy. Do

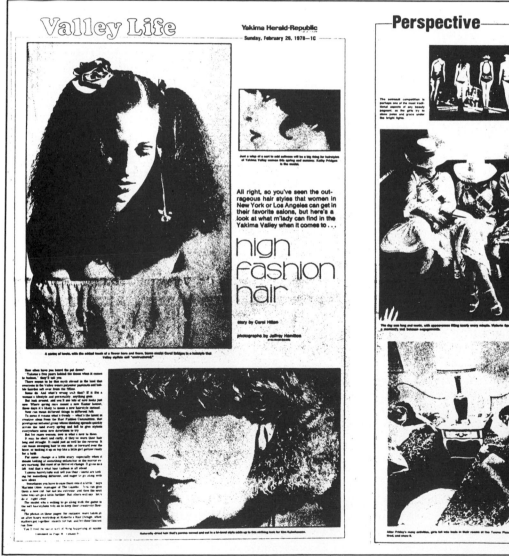

not place headlines over photographs. Normally the reader sees the most dominant element first (the photo); then his eye travels down to the cutline, not up to the caption.

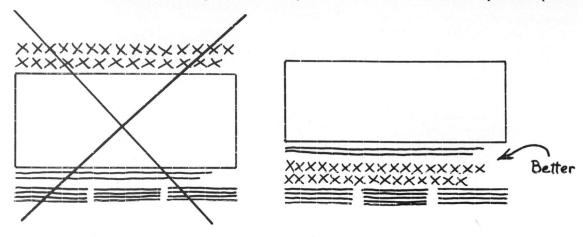

Every photograph must have a cutline, even head shots. Place the cutline directly under the photo or as near to it as possible, as shown in the following sketches.

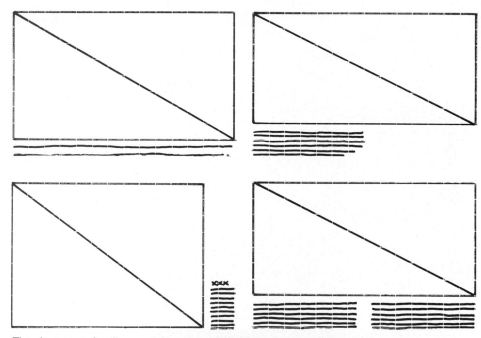

The placement of cutlines may be approached differently, depending on size, position, and use of photographs. As a rule, the cutline should be placed directly under the photograph.

8. Borrow ideas from magazines for the placement of photos on the page. Today's newspaper designer should have a ''swipe file'' handy. This is where she keeps tear sheets from magazines, and from other newspapers, to refer to when looking for design ideas. Magazine advertisements especially are a major source of ideas.

Not all ideas must be used in their original form. What the designer should do is to take the original idea and turn it upside down or sideways. Suddenly he will begin to gain a new perspective on what was in the original.

## SPECIAL EFFECTS

Graphically attractive inside sections and the popularity of special supplements are making today's newspaper editor more aware of the need for special photographic effects—things that can be done to turn a mundane photograph into one that is arresting. In many cases, photographic tricks can actually enhance the presentation of a photograph. Here are some of the most widely used tricks of the photographic trade:

*Line conversions.* Line conversions use special line screens to convert continuous-tone copy to line copy. Special screens (horizontal wavyline, circle-line, horizontal round dots, woodgrain, linen, vertical straightline) are used for special effects. Often, when an editor wishes to disguise the identity of a subject—as in the case of a story about teenage mothers in which a model was used for the illustration—these line conversions can add a dramatic touch to the photograph while also obscuring the subject's face and identity.

*The Photogram.* The photogram is a camera-less picture made completely in the darkroom. It consists of placing any object on the unexposed paper and exposing the paper in the enlarger. A leaf, a pencil, or a razor blade can suddenly become abstract elements through this special treatment.

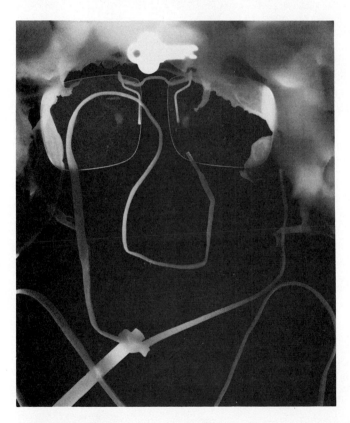

*Double-printing.* Two or three different negatives are printed on a single sheet of photographic paper. The result can be dramatic and creative and is especially suitable for feature photographs, in which two images are combined into one photograph.

*Negative image.* In this case a single weight print is contact-printed onto another sheet of photographic paper, developed, and fixed. A positive print is then placed face to face with an unexposed sheet and developed.

***Excessive grain.*** The illustration from the *Minneapolis Tribune* (below, left) was made through the excessive grain technique, achieved by "abusing" the film with drastic temperature changes during developing. The photo has the look of a sketch. Notice the photograph of a child made with the same technique (below, right).

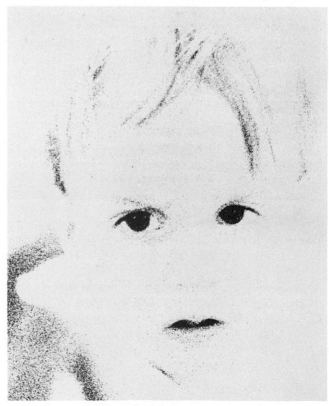

## THE COLOR PHOTOGRAPH

A color photograph can enhance the front page of a newspaper. But it is an expensive way to enhance the page and one which will work only when the colors come out with the sharpness and precision often found in magazines—but seldom in newspapers. Color photography and newsprint do not a good combination make! One newspaper, the *St. Petersburg* (Fla.) *Times,* has managed to perfect its color press and reproduces beautiful color photographs on its front page almost daily.

For the most part, newspapers can do very well without color photographs. It's better to have an all black and white newspaper than to print photos with "running colors" all over the page. Color is a luxury for newspapers, but it is a standard element for magazines, television, and film. The public is constantly exposed to color.

Based on the theory of opposites, it should be refreshing for readers to come to the black and white world of newspapers. The newspaper of the future will probably make less use of color photographs, capitalizing on what it can do best: black and white reproduction and spot color.

At this point, let us analyze the two basic methods for printing color, one of which is *spot* (or flat) *color*—used to color type, lines, art, or illustrations. The other is process color printing, the method used for reproducing an image that has a full range of colors, such as a color print or slide. Through this process the original photo is photographically separated into the four basic printing colors: yellow, magenta, cyan, and black.

## THE PHOTO PAGE

A typical, but now dated, study of newspaper readership revealed that 74.3 percent of all participants read picture pages. The figure would be higher if the same study were conducted today. We are more visually oriented. Today's reader expects photographs and tends to shy away from publications that do not offer him his share of visual gratification. Many newspapers devote an entire page to photographs; others, such as the *Des Moines* (Iowa) *Tribune,* publish a picture page weekly.

The successful picture page is based on *unity* and *cohesiveness*—the way in which photos relate to each other, to type, and to white space. Taking seven photographs off the wire machine and throwing them together onto a page does not make a unified picture page.

Here are some tips for making the picture page more pleasant to the eye:

1. Use one dominant photograph—call it the *parent* photograph—allowing the rest of the photos to play a supporting role.

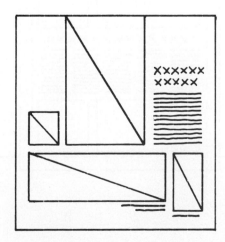

2. Combine horizontals and verticals for dramatic impact.

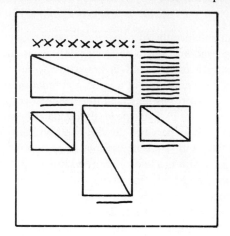

3. Inject a measure of white space on the outer areas of the page to emphasize the cluster approach given to the photographs.

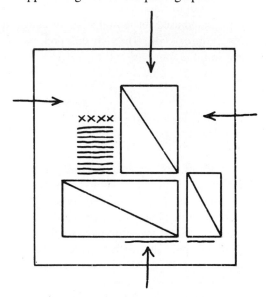

4. Avoid forming a perfect square of photos on the page.

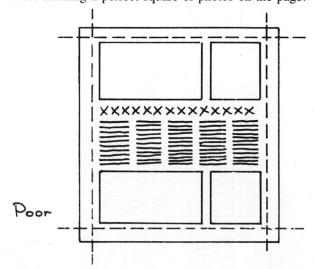

Poor

5. Let type be secondary, since the page is a *picture page,* but let photos lead reader to the copy areas.

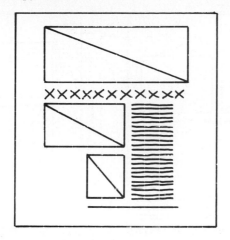

6. Avoid splitting the page into complete horizontal or vertical structures. Emphasize the contrast instead.

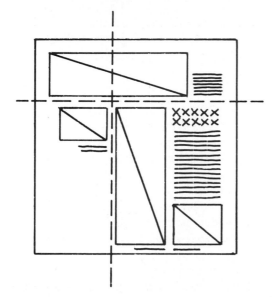

7. Do not trap white space between photographs.

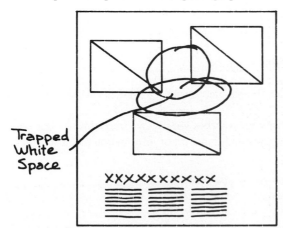

Trapped White Space

8. Do not use heavy borders when boxing the entire page but consider using thin lines to contain photos within a box when such treatment is needed.

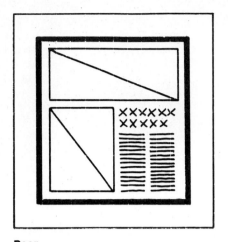

**Poor**

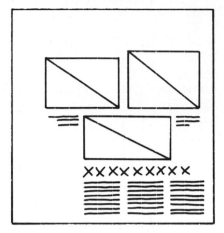

**Better**

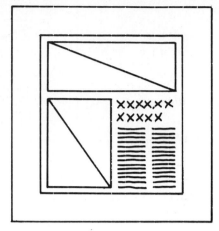

**Better**

## WRITING THE CUTLINE

Even a picture that is worth a million words should have a cutline.

Although often seen as necessary evils, cutlines are needed to complement every photograph. They identify persons in the photo, provide insight into the story, and sometimes offer background information about how the shot was taken.

Some people say that American newspaper readers are headline scanners. It is just as safe to say that they are also cutline readers.

Cutlines can be as simple as the mere identification of a person in a head shot. They may also describe what a person is doing, especially if it doesn't appear obvious to the reader. The best cutline is one that offers insight into the story behind the photograph, identifies the persons in the photo, and lures the reader to read the accompanying story.

Cutlines can also inform, which is the reason there is nothing wrong with using facts and figures when appropriate. For example, a lengthy in-depth piece on the status of local education may carry a photograph of a stack of textbooks. The cutline writer in a hurry may simply write

These are some of the texts used by local students.

A more informative cutline could be,

2.4 million textbooks are distributed annually to local students.

For head shots, many newspapers simply use the subject's last name or the full name, but readers also like the additional bit of information that a second line can offer:

Mary Jones

Mary Jones
. . . to visit China

A single line can carry both identification and additional information:

Mary Jones to China

Whether the cutline is used to identify, to expand, to inform, or simply to lure the reader, it must be present with every photograph.

Two daily newspapers that stand out for their use of photography and design are the *Allentown Morning Call* and the *Yakima Herald-Republic*.

## The *Morning Call*

The front page of the *Morning Call* uses a profile head shot as its sole photograph, creating dramatic impact.

The use of this dramatic photograph of a flood in the local area highlights the inside front page.

## The *Yakima Herald-Republic*

One of the first actions Stephen M. Kent took when he became managing editor of the *Herald-Republic* was to hire a director of photography to coordinate photo and design. Together, Kent and his photo director, Kurt Smith, redesigned the newspaper, basing their approach on the concept that photographs are just as important as words. They became convinced that to make the paper more readable and more exciting and to improve circulation, they had to place greater importance on photojournalism, and they did. Kent explains,

The idea was to make the paper easier for the readers. We have excellent offset reproduction, but layout was not taking full advantage of it. I felt that traditional headlines hampered communication with the reader, forcing him to puzzle out the message caused by the restricted space. I felt that in this day and age when the reader is assaulted thousands of times a day with visual messages, it is important that the headline communicate instantly. The format was arrived at by trying to make the pages and headlines more magazine-like in appearance.

The combination of a new headline style and large and dramatically cropped photographs makes the *Herald-Republic* a most attractive newspaper.

The newspaper of the future will make photography one of its indispensable graphic elements. The role of the photographer will change, placing him in a position of greater authority on matters pertaining to the visual presentation of news. The job of the editor will also undergo changes that will require him to be a more visual thinker. As we shall see in the next few chapters, all areas of newspaper design will be affected by the greater use of photography. In a sense, the 1980s will witness the rebirth of photojournalism as a widespread influence in American newspapers of all sizes—from the rural weekly to the small and large city dailies.

These pages from the *Yakima Herald-Republic* show the visual appeal which becomes possible when good photographs combine with well-organized design.

# Yakima Herald-Republic
a daily part of your life

## Retirement age
Bill raising mandatory age to 70 appears headed for early approval

## 4 dead
### Gunfire hits 6 in Seattle

**Prayers permitted**

The school day begins with a prayer at the Yakima Junior Academy, a school run by the Seventh-day Adventist Church. Boyd Smith and classmates shared a school day with the Herald-Republic recently, and the resulting picture story appears today on Page 17.

### Good Morning

*The weather*

**INDEX**

## Chinook Hotel
Convicted felon is one of two Californians interested in purchasing the 14-story hotel

## Test-tube babies
### A reality, says publishing firm

David Lygre checks test tube.

## Scientists on verge of creating human

---

## Panorama

# As American as apple pie

Bibles and schoolbooks go together in classroom at the Yakima Junior Academy.

Front page of the *Yakima Herald-Republic* (below, left) displays photo dominance. Headlines are used as indexing elements. Photo at the top is vertical, but page moves more horizontally at the bottom. Page on the right uses a large horizontal photo; rest of the page also uses horizontal structures.

Tuesday, September 20, 1977

# Yakima Herald-Republic
### a daily part of your life.

Granger teacher pickets school

## Strike
### Mediator arrives today
By DAVE LESTER

## Gov. Ray
### 'Bad times not yet over'
By JIM GARNEY

### Good Morning

**The weather** Partly cloudy today and Wednesday with scattered showers near the Cascades. Highs both days in the upper 60s. Lows tonight 35 to 40. Complete table on Page 11.

## Action wanted
A fired-up Rev. Joe Denman takes house case to Yakima City Council

### INDEX

## Pain in the side
### He's not taking it easy
By MARK NELSON

Attorney Fred Porter is ready for case

## Acre limit
### Strict irrigation enforcement ordered
By DAVE LESTER

Yakima Herald-Republic
Thursday, December 8, 1877—3

## The Local Scene

The picket fence

## Yakima Industrial sites
### Proposed pollution rules could limit city's growth

## Still stranded
### Snowmobiler planning appeal to Gov. Ray

# 10 editorial pages that convince the eye

Editorial pages are traditionally associated with a newspaper's sense of dignity and credibility. Some editors and publishers consider the editorial page the sanctuary of the publication—an area where little experimenting is permissible. And readers have grown to expect editorial pages that turn this dignity into visual dullness. So while the rest of the newspaper changes, sometimes drastically, the editorial page remains true to tradition.

Although the origins of such a tradition are unclear, one can't help wonder about the unwritten rules of editorial page design: (1) keep it vertical, (2) make it gray, (3) make it dignified through dull graphics, and (4) let it look the same day after day.

A quick and informal sampling of editorial pages from newspapers across the country shows that such tradition often remains virtually unchallenged. Fortunately, more editors and publishers are realizing the graphics potential in the variable content that is part of an editorial page, and changes are finally beginning to be made.

The nature of the contents makes the editorial page an ideal spot to lure readers through the use of graphics. The editorial page expresses a newspaper's opinion. It is its voice, and a strong one, for persuading the reader to take a course of action. On any given day it becomes the medium for a variety of opinions on timely or philosophical issues—most of which lend themselves to graphic communication through illustrations or photographs.

A graphics-oriented editorial page not only will make the content more visually appealing but also will lure new readers, particularly the young who may not be in the habit of reading editorial content.

Let us analyze five graphics strategies that are likely to make the editorial page more attractive and easier to read:

***1. Keep content unchangeable but allow for flexible design.*** The editorial page does not have to look the same from day to day. Graphic variety can be its strongest visual

147

characteristic. However, readers need a sense of reliability, which assures them they will find what they expect to find on a particular page. So the good designer places the editorials vertically on the left-hand side of the page (which is the traditional position for editorials) but keeps the option of using art, if available, for one of the editorials.

Content dictates the graphics for every page, and the editorial page is no exception. Through dependable content the page will derive its sense of continuity; through visual impact it will gain its graphics appeal.

An editor may decide that the editorial page will always carry editorials, a section of letters to the editor, one or more columns, and some art. Readers will become accustomed to such fare and will expect it on the page. Graphically, however, the editor may wish to use art with the letters to the editor one day or with a column the next. As long as graphics are used somewhere on the page, they no longer have to be in the same spot every time.

The editorial pages shown below, from the *Evansville* (Ind.) *Press,* illustrate how *organization of content* and *design flexibility* combine to create attractive and readable editorial/pages.

When a designer presents the same content on the editorial page every day, he keeps the reader comfortable. The reader knows that what he expects to be on the page will be there. However, if the designer honors flexibility, what the reader expects may not always be in the same spot. Because it isn't, the entire page will be more interesting to look at and easier for the designer to work with from day to day. Thus the best-designed editorial page provides the reader with familiar unchangeable content and surprises him with unfamiliar flexible design.

This is the most traditional of the three designs. The staff editorials appear at the left-hand side of the page. A cartoon dominates the top of the page, followed by a personal column, letters to the editor, and an Art Buchwald column, all in perfect structures. One of the columns is accompanied not only by a photograph of the writer but also by a two-column photo related to the content of the column.

The organization of this page tells at a glance that it is the *Evansville Press,* but its design provides a refreshing change. Instead of a cartoon, the designer has included a series of six photographs, in vertical fashion, to make a long column about a proposed ordinance more inviting to the reader. The George Will column, which appeared at the top in the previous illustration, is now at the bottom.

This third example offers even more graphic variety. The lead editorial is illustrated by a head shot. There are no cartoons or letters to the editor. Instead, the rest of the page is devoted to columns, except that the top is dominated by a "Speakout" feature.

The *Tribune*'s editorial page is clean and easy to read. Notice how a CVI is created by a large cartoon. Other points of interest around the page include the sole standing sig—"*Tribune* Editorial Page"—and the head shots used for columnists.

The *Miami News* labels its page "Opinion." Notice the use of unjustified type for the column of editorials and the use of column rules throughout. Most importantly, The *News*' masthead is economically placed as part of the page's sig at the top.

The *Free Press*' editorial page is one of the most graphic in the country. Notice how almost every item on the page is accompanied by a photograph, but the page looks pleasantly full, not overcrowded. The designer has capitalized on the use of bold type for a key word in each of the headlines, bringing the reader's attention to that nonpictorial section of the page.

*2. Create a pleasant environment around the page.* Other chapters have already emphasized the importance of a clean, easy-to-read, and uncongested page. For the editorial page this means an absence of heavy type, extremely bold lines, or other graphic gimmicks. To create a pleasant environment, an editorial page should be designed with some measure of white space and an easy-to-read typeface, which could actually be the same as that used for both body and display type in the rest of the newspaper.

Standing sigs for the editorial page should be clean, easy to read, and easy to use. Gimmicky sigs, such as gigantic illustrations of mailboxes for the letters to the editor section, or a well and bucket for the "in-depth" report, should be avoided. The sigs should harmonize with other sigs throughout the newspaper and say what they are meant to say, without congesting the page. Some newspapers label the entire editorial page "Opinion" or "Viewpoint," making an exception to differentiate "Our Opinion" from "Your Opinion." For letters to the editor, sometimes the word "Letters" will be enough. Phrases such as "Readers React" or "The People Speak" can help by telling readers that their opinions are welcome.

*3. Use photos—large and small—to make the editorial content more convincing.* Editorials that deal with traffic jams in the city, columns on the plight of senior citizens in the community, letters to the editor on topics ranging from alcoholism to malfunctioning traffic lights around a school—all present pictorial possibilities. Pictures can help the editorial page by creating initial interest. See *Detroit Free Press* (above, right) for effective use of photos throughout the editorial page.

*4. Use illustrations throughout the page.* The cartoon has always been a part of the editorial page; in fact, it's often the only graphic element. During the last few years cartoons have become larger; they have also been moved around the page, no longer permanently affixed to the top. But cartoons are only one of several graphics possibilities, as shown by the illustration below left.

Illustrations are not the only graphic devices available for designing the editorial page. *Borders* can be used to package stories, and *quotes* can be pulled from the copy and highlighted in larger sized type to break long masses of gray. Anything that will make editorial content more appealing and readable is worth considering as part of the design.

**5. Use the Op-Ed page to its full potential.** In his discussion of the *Washington Post*'s editorial page, editor J. W. Anderson refers to the Op-Ed page as ''that page to the right which, by its position and prominence, constitutes an invitation to further discussion.''

But while the invitation may always be there, it will take a dynamic graphics display of photographs, type, white space, and content organization to make the reader accept it. The Op-Ed page can be a catchall for any opinion content that didn't make the editorial page, or it can be an attractive page representing a variety of viewpoints other than those of the newspaper's editors and publishers. Personalized columns, background or in-depth reports, features, letters to the editor, and photo-essays are some of the possibilities.

Graphically, the Op-Ed page provides unlimited potential for magazine-style design, especially through the use of large photographs and illustrations.

The following Op-Ed pages have been selected for analysis here not only because of their effective use of typography and design but also because of the timeliness and relevance of their content.

While maintaining a strong vertical emphasis, this editorial page from the *Des Moines Tribune* introduces some noteworthy uses of graphics in the form of caricatures (top of page) and offers another alternative for the use of type: the large initial letters in the lead article. The two initials, plus the standing sig at the top of the page, appeared in spot color. As for the traditional cartoon, it can be found at the bottom of the page.

The *Chicago Tribune* labels its Op-Ed page "Perspective" and designs it in an organized structural manner, in this case following an L-shape. Notice the use of three columns as secondary elements on the page, while the "Course by Newspaper" feature dominates as the primary visual structure. More newspapers are using their Op-Ed page as an educational tool. Note the use of "Popular Culture" to identify the newspaper course.

The *Star's* editors receive more letters than can be handled in just a portion of the editorial page. As a result, a full Op-Ed page of letters appears from time to time. Notice the effective use of a large photograph to illustrate the lead letter at the top of the page. The distinctive sig identifies the page as one of the "Letters."

Advertisers seek—and often get—space on the editorial or Op-Ed pages. The *Herald American* has an ad at the bottom of the page. Notice the "Forum" feature, described as a free exchange of ideas on the issues of the day.

Indeed there is room for graphics experimentation in the editorial and Op-Ed pages. The editorial page of the future should include more of the well-written and relevant content that the reader expects, along with better typography and better use of photographs and illustrations.

It has been said that there is nothing more boring than tired opinion. We will add that there is nothing more boring than tired opinion presented in a dull visual manner.

# 11
# the graphics of sports coverage

Sports news and features take up more newspaper space than any other specialized topic. Most newspapers, from large to small dailies, suburban to rural weeklies, and student newspapers, devote a considerable amount of coverage to sports.

The sports section of the newspaper offers an opportunity to combine hard and soft news. Readers want to read play-by-play accounts of last night's game, but they also want some of the softer approach, such as a human interest feature on an injured player or the profile of a winning coach. Readers also seek interpretation and opinion to cover such diversified activities as player strikes, recruitment practices, the economics of professional teams, and the participation—or lack of participation—of women in sports.

Sports pages have always fascinated many newspaper readers, basically because sports coverage in its essence is based on two traditionally desirable news qualities: conflict and action. Every game or match becomes a *conflict,* a confrontation from which an individual or team emerges as the winner. Sports conflict is resolved through *action.* Athletes run, kick, jump, punch, or have a real-life argument with a disagreeable official.

Conflict and action translate into *movement*, which is the reason sports coverage is naturally visual and sports pages abound with design possibilities. Complete newspaper coverage of sports goes beyond the visual, however, to include detailed statistical information for the morning-after reader. Television networks cover any major sports event, and radio continues its traditional role as narrator of play-by-play accounts of significant games. Where does that leave the newspaper sports section? Because sports fans usually have an insatiable hunger for information about their favorite team or players, they will turn to the sports section even after they have watched an entire game on their television sets. When readers turn to the newspaper, however, they expect an interlacing of play-by-play accounts with a generous sprinkling of some behind-the-scenes information about pre- and postgame incidents. They look for explanations about a certain game strategy, or a human interest account of how a player accepted defeat. Most important, the readers will look for complete statistical information, and for *local coverage* of sports events not carried by the electronic media.

## CONTENT PRIORITIES

Today's sports section develops its content according to reader interest. Daily newspaper sports editors, however, usually distribute their available space as follows:

1. *Highly featurized coverage* of major athletic events already carried through the electronic media.

2. *Extensive local coverage* to include major and minor events, from college and high school activities to community table tennis tournaments and Little League competition. Local sports coverage is the area where the newspaper can offer the greatest service.

3. *Calendar information* of upcoming events at the national, state, and local level, including previews.

4. *Statistical information* with game results and team standing for all sports.

5. *People coverage*—through a column of briefs and through in-depth features about players, coaches, managers, and others involved in sports. Some newspapers, such as the *St. Petersburg Times,* use an economical approach by packaging people briefs and general sports briefs under the same heading.

6. *Reader participation* coverage through question-and-answer features. As participation sports become more popular, the newspaper can provide what the *Corpus Christi Times* calls "Sports Hot Line," sort of a Dear Abby for the reader who wants to know if he has what it takes to play professional baseball or the senior citizen who wishes to know where other seniors in the community gather to play table tennis.

7. *Consumer-related items* covering a variety of topics, such as what to look for when buying a pair of running shoes or, at a more local level, what the best spots are for fishing, skiing, or camping.

Effective packaging is one of the key elements in designing a readable calendar of events or weekend preview, as seen in this "NFL Weekend Preview" from the *Boston Herald American*. Notice how headlines pull the reader into tabulated material. The photos and standing sig also help the package graphically, so that the use of six-point body type does not offend the eye.

The *Tribune's* "Scoreboard" uses a simple standing sig that reflects the newspaper's primary graphic symbol—a three-dimensional box.

"Sports Hot Line" opens the sports pages to questions from readers.

Whether it is running, hiking, swimming, ice fishing, or skating, more Americans are participating in sports. The *Milwaukee Sentinel's* section on "Your Sports" is designed around participation sports. The lead story centers on runners trying to finish a marathon. The second story deals with kayaking.

Notice how various items in this package use small headlines, ragged right type, and boldface for names, facilitating eye movement on the page.

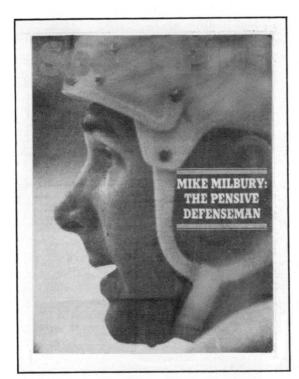

The sports supplement makes natural use of a double-truck spread to highlight a special feature. Notice the dominant use of photography and the effective placement of type.

8. *Health and physical fitness coverage* to inform an ever-increasing number of readers who are participating in sports and conditioning programs as part of their lifestyle. The best-sellers list abounds with titles dealing with health and the rewards of being physically fit. Newspaper sports sections must also deal with these subjects.

The *Boston Herald American* (left) recognizes readers' interest in physical fitness, particularly through running, and carried an entire series on what it termed ''The Running Rip-Off.'' Notice the effect sig used with type and art to identify the series.

9. *Radio and television schedules* of sports should be part of the daily coverage. Many newspapers use a short but easy-to-identify column to list the day's programs. For special events or for weekend coverage, a more prominent package may be used.

10. *Special supplements* to highlight features and to include such specialized areas as sports-related book reviews, sports medicine, things to do, and so on are becoming an important part of sports coverage, especially in large dailies. Supplements may become a regular part of the newspaper or they may be published as a bonus for sports readers, which is what the *Cincinnati* (Ohio) *Enquirer* did when it put out a special souvenir Pete Rose rotogravure magazine in 1978 to salute the Cincinnati Reds' star. The special Rose supplement included sixteen pages filled with stories and photos, in color and black and white.

The *Boston Globe* publishes a regular sports supplement on Fridays entitled ''Sports Plus'' (below). The *Globe*'s supplement is more than just sports features on famous stars. It also includes ''Sports Pulse'' (short takes about people, places, and events), ''Week's TV, radio schedule'' (informing readers when to tune in for sports events in the electronic media), ''Sports Fan-agram'' (for crossword puzzle enthusiasts), ''Things to do'' (a complete guide to a variety of activities from auto events to road running and squash), ''Sports Medicine'' (a question-and-answer forum about health and athletics).

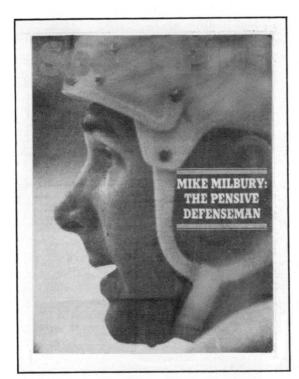

A color photo lures reader to the *Boston Globe*'s ''Sports Plus'' supplement.

Notice how type and graphics combine to direct readers to the inside content. Ads have been placed, in block style, at the bottom of the page.

## DESIGN STRATEGIES

It has already been mentioned that the sports page is based on naturally *visual* content. Effective design will enhance such visual content to lure the readers. The following design constants should be considered:

*Organization.* Organization, as discussed elsewhere in this book, gives each section a sense of direction. Sports page readers, who often pull the section out of the newspaper to read before they get to the front page or other content, like to find certain regular features, such as scoreboards, weekend roundups, sports columns, and calendar of events, in the same place all the time. Designing a sports section begins with a decision about the placement of these regular elements.

*Continuity.* The sports section is not an isolated unit within the newspaper. Standing sigs, the primary typeface used for headlines, cutlines, and bylines, and the basic design strategies should all be in harmony with the rest of the newspaper. Nothing can be more confusing than a sports page where each standing sig (for scoreboard, sports column, and so on) follows a completely different design.

*Readability.* Organization and continuity provide the major design blueprints, but readability makes the sports section easier to read. It also makes each page easier to index. A readable sports section will turn graphically dull information, such as scoreboards, into well-organized packages with the content arranged according to its importance. Typographically, these packages of tabulated material will emphasize the contrast between light and bold typefaces to provide comfort to the eyes and make the movement from one segment to another easier.

*Photographic impact.* Conflict, action, and the physical exuberance of athletics provide the photographic material. Even after we've watched the decisive moment that led to a spectacular touchdown during a televised game, it's interesting to see a photo of that same moment in the morning newspaper. Photos of faces showing agony and pain, or relief and happiness, photos of sweaty and bloody faces, of arms that reach or legs that kick—all are part of the standard sports photo fare that readers have come to expect. Sports pages should use large and dominant photos as an added visual invitation to the reader. Photographic impact is not limited to the section's first page; each inside page should also carry photos to attract the reader.

## SPORTS PAGE DESIGN: SOMETHING FOR EVERYONE

### Opening Page

This is the front page of the sports section, carrying the major stories of the day, the best photographs available, and an identifying sig, such as "Sports." Since sports coverage varies from season to season and even from day to day, alternatives are available to the designer, depending on the copy and photo art possibilities:

*Opening page with photo emphasis.* The sports opening page from *Today* (right) centers around two photographs, one a dominant facial shot of Coach Betty Jeffers as she addresses her players in a last-minute effort to win a basketball tournament. Notice the inset of Coach Jeffers, portraying her quiet mood after the team's loss. Other highlights of this page include the perfectly structured approach, with every item on the

page confined to a rectangular area. The sports column by the section editor appears on the left, and scores and standings receive unusually prominent display. Organization of content prevails. Notice "Today's Sports on Radio-TV" and "Today's Fishing Forecast" at the bottom of the page. In addition to the "Sports" sig, *Today*'s editors make effective use of space by including a "What's Inside" package.

The sports page from the *Miami Herald* (below left) shows the use of two contrasting photographs, a long vertical and a horizontal. Feature material prevails throughout the page. Notice the graphically illustrated index to the inside of the section. The package at the bottom of the page lures readers to that section.

The sports opening section from the *Morning Call* (center) uses a dramatic and dominant photo, surrounded by white space and bordered by tape. Notice the special type for headlines and the interesting display for the sports column at the bottom. Note also the close cropping for the columnist's head shot.

The *St. Petersburg Times* (below right) also emphasizes photos as its dominant graphic element. Here a large photograph attracts the reader into a structurally designed page, with effective positioning of photos throughout. Photos create interest for various areas on the page without producing a congested look.

***Opening page with art emphasis.*** The *Atlanta Constitution* (opposite page, top left) capitalizes on art and color as major design strategies on this opening sports page. Notice the effective use of packaging. The sports editor's column appears on the left. The page includes only four stories, the bottom one highlighted by an easy-to-read combination "inside box" and "scoreboard."

A full-color painting of O. J. Simpson dominates the opening page from the *St. Petersburg Evening Independent* (opposite page, top right). The staff artist has combined a portrait of the athlete with some action illustrations, plus the use of type for "San Francisco" and "49ers," creating tremendous visual impact for the page through the dominance of art. Notice that the entire page is based on feature material. Instead of bylines, each story carries an individual sig with a sketch of the writer, his name, and his staff position. The page is not only attractive and visually powerful, but also economical, considering that it includes three packages on "NCAA Soccer Playoffs," "Inside Content," and "Weekend Sports on the Air."

*Opening page with special coverage.* Many large and small dailies are beginning to carry special sports content at least once a week. The opening page usually identifies such coverage, as seen in the *Milwaukee Journal*'s "Sports Weekend" (below left), a complete guide to various weekend sports events. Notice how the page opens with an index on the inside, followed by two photographs and mostly feature material. Editor Mike Kupper runs his column at the bottom of the page. The illustration on the right shows an inside page from "Sports Weekend" devoted entirely to prep schools. Putting all related content into one package facilitates reading and makes editing and design easier.

It looks like a gigantic magazine page and has little resemblance to that newspaper's traditionally gray front page, but ''Sports Monday,'' the *New York Times'* graphically appealing sports section (top left), provides featurized and pictorial coverage of weekend sports while highlighting people features, participation, and ''Sports World Specials.'' Notice the pictorial index (top), use of typographic contrast for the ''SportsMonday'' sig—with an intentional lack of space between the two words—and dominance of photos throughout. The lead story uses a large capital letter for the opening paragraph.

Total packaging highlights the Friday ''Sports Plus'' section of the *Toronto Star* (above, center). Perfectly structural, this page moves the reader easily from item to item. The sports column appears at the top left, and a large photo dominates the main package on basketball. A pictorial index draws the readers' attention to the bottom of the page. The ''Sports Plus'' sig is printed in blue and as the only color used on the page, provides an interesting contrast. Continuity is achieved through use of the slanted sig (top right).

*Opening page with ads.* The demographics of the sports pages makes them an attractive target for advertisers. Some newspapers capitalize on such interest by selling space at the bottom of the opening page.

Three ads all the same size appear at the bottom of the opening page of the *Minneapolis Tribune* (left). A local hotel, a shirtmaker, and a lawnmower company managed to get their ads in this preferred spot, a practice which does not make the page look less attractive. The ads are blocked into the available space.

## Inside Pages

The inside page should be as graphically inviting as any other. This can be accomplished by using large photographs, convincing the advertising department to place ads in block style whenever possible, and packaging content and photographs.

The inside sports page of the *Toronto Star* (opposite page, top left) is dominated by a photo of a badminton player. Notice the six-column format, effective gradation of headline sizes, and an overall cleanliness that makes the page easy to follow. The

effective combination of photos and content is shown on this page. This is definitely a one-story page, dealing with a sports medicine center. The photographs are large enough to draw the readers' attention into the page. The long story is broken up by subheads.

The inside page can also be devoted to specialized topics. The *Milwaukee Journal* devotes one of its "Weekend" pages to prep schools.

More newspapers will devote more space to women's sports as equality becomes mandatory at all levels, from high school and college to professional athletics. The page from the *Boston Herald American* (above, right) shows how women's sports can be neatly arranged into a page.

## Photo Pages

Sometimes the sports editor will be hard pressed to decide which photo to choose from all that his photographer makes available. In such cases—and assuming that there is space available—a photo page can enhance the pictorial coverage of the sports section and create added visual appeal.

The *St. Louis Post-Dispatch* (right) devoted a full page to photo coverage of the NCAA Basketball Tournament. Notice the effective use of the identifying sig ("NCAA march to the finals") and placement of photos to allow for white space.

## Statistical Pages

Most of the conflict and action of sports events are summed up in graphically dull statistics. But readers seek such information, and designers have an obligation to make it more visually palatable. The following examples show that a scoreboard does not have to resemble a page from the telephone directory. Some small graphic symbol to identify each sports category, a bit of typographic contrast for light and bold, a sense of organization (what will the reader want to find first?), and a little design creativity can make a page of scores more attractive and readable.

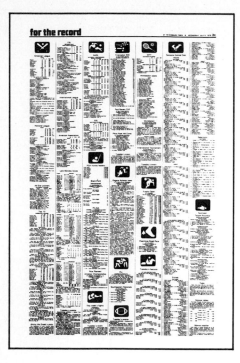

Notice how the *St. Petersburg Times* (top left) labels its statistical page "for the record" and underlines the sig with a bold rule. Individual sports categories are shown through basic drawings in black and white, bold enough to break gray areas without offending the eye. Column rules separate copy.

The *Miami News* (center) calls its page "Scoreboard" and includes more than just scores. Notice how the left side of the page is devoted to a local schedule of events, a column on horse racing, and even a sports wire story. The page is so economical that it even allows for an ad at the bottom. Individual sports categories are labeled through type, not art, but there is enough contrast to make the reader move easily from item to item.

The *Montreal Star* (top right) has a more pictorial approach to the score page. Notice the way head shots of players with major teams are used to break columns of gray matter. The page is also designed economically, with a column of sports briefs, a feature item, and even a regular feature on ski conditions—plus an ad—on one page.

Many design strategies can be used to enhance the appearance of a sports section, but they will prove effective only if combined with a reevaluation of content and how it has changed in the last few years. The next decade will probably bring even greater importance to the sports section, with spectator sports continuing as the country's favorite recreational activity and with more Americans discovering the personal satisfactions and physical rewards of participation.

# 12 the women's page goes unisex

Call it "Accent," "Modern Living," "Help for the Business of Living," "Family," or "Lifestyle." But don't dare refer to it as "The Women's Section," because it is not strictly for women anymore. In fact, it probably never was, considering the volume of letters that "Dear Abby" and "Ann Landers" have always received from male readers, even though their columns usually appear in the traditional "women's section."

Today the word *women* seldom appears as an identifying element on the page, and the content is strictly *unisex,* a result of the social awareness that developed in the 1960s and took firm hold during the 1970s. And although one still finds recipes, tips for needlepoint enthusiasts, and extensive coverage of gardening, these topics are no longer considered for women only.

The transition from a women's page to the unisex approach has not been an easy one for many editors. It was more convenient to label a page "for women" than to think of a title that would give it universal appeal. A sampling of several newspapers shows the work that some diligent editors must have gone through—with the aid of a thesaurus—to arrive at their adopted title. Participants in a newspaper workshop during the late 1970s were asked to pull out of the name-the-section trauma and concentrate more on content.

## THE NAME-THE-SECTION TRAUMA

Following are some of the titles adopted by several daily newspapers in their efforts to eliminate the "for women only" approach:

"Help for the Business of Living" *(Yakima Herald-Republic)*

The title "Help" inspires the content of this section, which opens with four columns: "Dear Abby," "Design," "At Large" (survival tips for busy city people), and "Health."

### "Family" (*Toronto Star*)

The *Star* centers its opening page around personality profiles of people in the community. Inside pages present the family approach through columns on child rearing, current events, and a special section for children.

### "Modern Living" (*Detroit Free Press*)

A typical lead story deals with the question of whether a family can be happy in a railway depot. The section deals with consumer-oriented tips, problem solving, and interior design.

### "Accent" (*Providence Journal*)

Columns on a variety of subjects dominate this section, with emphasis on needlepoint, consumer tips, health, recipes, and social news of the neighborhoods.

### "A.M." (Boston Herald-American)

Readers of the *Herald-American* wake up to a section full of features, with emphasis on consumer coverage, profiles of the well known, and a column on the Boston social scene.

### "Living Today" (*Miami Herald*)

The *Herald* publishes a colorful section daily, with emphasis on a major feature. Extensive coverage is given to social events around town, the social scene, consumer tips, and health columns. A special section deals with senior citizens in the community. The overall approach is people oriented.

## PLANNING THE SECTION

The content of this special section—we will call it "Lifestyle"—depends upon reader preference and will vary for each newspaper. A small daily may center its contents on club news, special events around the community, and other soft news. A large metropolitan daily, however, may concentrate on the "survival in the city" approach, offering consumer tips, complete calendars of events, and abundant feature coverage that will link the various lifestyles of the readers to articles of general interest.

Basically, the content of this section should be strictly soft news—a kind of daily textbook dealing with psychology, sociology, economics, personal care, home economics, recreation, religion, and public service. Add to that the localized element with a generous dose of names, and the section can become a source of reader service for the newspaper.

A successful section will inform the reader about social events taking place in the community, will teach him to cope with his problems, and will prepare him to be a better consumer. More important, the section will present him with summaries or sample chapters of new books, excerpts from timely speeches, and other materials that might prompt him to seek the originals.

If there is a part of the newspaper that will reflect the trends of the times, it should be the lifestyle section, and those in charge of selecting its content have a responsibility to keep well informed. Contemporary trends will give the editor many ideas for daily features, but editors must also be aware of the importance of club and social news. Although considered old-fashioned by some, both are an integral part of the section's coverage.

## ENGAGEMENT AND BRIDAL NEWS

Engagement and wedding announcements are part of the section, too, and an important one, at least to those involved. Many dailies now delegate the task of compiling and editing such information to clerical workers. It makes no difference who handles the material, as long as the announcements are there for the bride and her family to clip and save. Radical changes in the coverage of bridal news often bring stronger reader response; for example, a New York weekly decided to abandon the traditional oval-shaped photographs of brides, only to hear cries of protest from many irate brides—and their mothers—in the community. The oval-shaped photos were brought back in a short time.

Ironically, the content of a lifestyle section must deal with trends while preserving many of yesterday's traditions in the area of reader service. True, editors may tire of processing engagement and wedding news, but to the couple getting married for the first time, and to their families, such news is important. Features on getting a divorce, adapting to a single life, or having a first child may become repetitious to the staff but not to readers who are involved in such situations for the first time. It is for the readers that the section is ultimately prepared, and a happy balance of today's trends and yesterday's traditions should be part of the criteria for content selection.

## GRAPHICS AND ORGANIZATION

The graphics of this section can be as experimental as the designer wishes to make it; its organization, however, should follow the same standards of continuity and order outlined elsewhere in this book.

Graphically, the section should maintain its sense of continuity with the rest of the newspaper. For example, the opening section page should carry a title set in the same type used for standing sigs throughout the publication. The primary typeface used for headlines will be the same used through the rest of the newspaper. Standing sigs for columnists, and regular features will follow the same design as sigs in other sections.

Graphics experimentation will involve the use of *special type* to accommodate the mood of a certain feature. Different typefaces should be used, especially in the section's opening page, to grab the reader by surprise every day. Other areas of experimentation include the use of white space—there is normally a greater opportunity to work with white space in this section than in news pages; photography—photos can be large and dominant, in color, and may be used to illustrate the point of a story; and art or illustrations. When photos are not available, and a staff artist is, illustrations can create instant graphic appeal.

The illustrations that follow show several graphics approaches to designing a section opener in which the front page varies from day to day, according to available content, both pictorial and nonpictorial.

The section opener for the *Miami Herald*'s "Living Today" uses color to lure readers to the page. Dominant feature on "Mothers and Daughters" uses a feminine-looking typeface. The photograph was set up for the special content here, a practice made popular by magazines and now used by many newspapers. Note the use of white space and the gradation of type sizes to lure readers into a lengthy article, another practice brought over from magazine design.

The *St. Petersburg Times'* section opener is dominated by two structures: one dealing with the immortality of flowers and one dealing with an index to inside content. The flower illustration was done through color process. Notice the effective packaging—the use of thin borders in order not to create excessive boldness that otherwise could have competed with the flower illustration. The inside content is highlighted by ragged right copy, sans serif bold type, and plenty of white space.

Photos do not have to be in color to create instant appeal, as seen in the black and white photo arrangement used by the "A.M." section of the *Boston Herald American*. The lead feature deals with buying toys, so the illustration shows a series of toys. The background has been dropped to create movement around the toys. Notice how the copy wraps around the photograph, creating an effective CVI. The bottom of the page uses a horizontal structure, with an interesting treatment for a head shot of Rod McKuen. Here is an attractive but economical section opener.

Some section openers, however, are designed around a standard pattern. Readers know exactly what to expect when they turn to the front of the section. This does not necessarily mean that the section opener will be graphically dull, as illustrated by the sections shown at the top of the opposite page.

## INSIDE PAGES

The section's inside pages (as shown opposite) will also require graphic impact and organization of content. The former may be achieved by the use of at least one dominant photograph or package. The latter depends on the placement of various elements around the page, especially the effective use of standing sigs to separate stories and permit faster reading.

"Accent" capitalizes on content organization. Notice how various vertical structures present familiar material to the reader: "Dear Ann," "Needleplay," "Good Health," "For the Consumer." These are regular features which the editors consider their most enticing material. The fashion photograph and column dominate the center of the page. Notice that there is also a fashion column for men.

Four regular columns dominate this section opener. Notice the use of structural design and the placement of the ad at the bottom of the page. This newspaper uses another section, "Valley Life," for fashion, personal care, and other related coverage.

In this section opener, dominated by large photographs, the editors have minimized copy. Notice the special use of type for the words "foxes and furs."

This inside page is built around the picture at top. Notice how continuity is achieved through standing sigs.

At least one of the section's inside pages will be used to jump copy from the section opener. In this case, notice how the *Miami Herald* uses effective vertical blocking for ads (right) and still produces an attractive area for copy and photographs. Often, the manner in which ads are placed makes the difference between a crowded page and one with graphic appeal.

The indentation of white space at the top of this inside page leads the reader into the story about beer. The effective contrast of bold and light typefaces and the use of a large photograph make the page look almost as attractive as a section opener. Notice the effective placement of ads at the bottom of the page.

# Pages of Tabulated Material

This page, labeled "Datebook," tells readers about activities in the local community. Notice the dominant use of bold type for the name. The only other graphic breakers throughout the page are the small illustrations to designate categories of special events.

Engagement news is simply packaged into a structure at the top of the page. Notice the small label for "Engagements," accompanied by one-paragraph items and headlined with a light typeface.

For one of its Sunday bridal pages, the *Yakima Herald-Republic* divides the page into weddings, engagements, and anniversaries. The page is well organized through the use of bold headlines for individual sections. The light typeface is used to identify couples married or engaged. Notice the use of couples in wedding pictures. (After all, the page is now unisex, so why just have photos of the bride?)

## Standing Sigs

The type selected for standing sigs and their design establish graphic continuity for the section. The illustrations below and opposite show how various newspapers identify their section.

The two opening page labels are graphically appealing, but also economical, as they allow for teasers inside the section.

The *Toronto Star's* sigs use a bold rule at the top, a thin (hairline) border at the bottom, a closely cropped photograph of the columnist, and the name of the columnist plus the title of the column.

Some newspapers, like the *Minneapolis Tribune,* carry occasional items to involve their readers. The sig is used to accompany a column dealing with community agencies that use volunteers to provide different services.

Not all sigs need lines or boxes to make them attractive. The illustrations from the *Boston Herald American* are simple kickers, set in italic and underlined by double rule. Notice how consistent style is maintained when the sig includes a photograph of the columnist.

These standing sigs for "Family/Part 2," "Weddings," and "School Lunch Menus" from the *Minneapolis Tribune* illustrate the three-dimensional design that has become that newspaper's graphic trademark. No matter how large (opening page sig) or small (for individual columns and regular sections), the design remains consistent throughout, even when a photograph is used.

## SPECIAL TOPICS

The staff of the lifestyle section is often in charge of producing pages or entire sections devoted to such specialized topics as food, travel, and religion. The same graphics and design guidelines that apply to the lifestyle section are in order for specialized sections. In all cases, there is more use of photography and illustrations.

### Food Section

The newspaper's food section was probably the forerunner in what we now refer to as consumer journalism. Traditionally, it was this section that reminded readers how to choose meat, what to look for in food packaging, and where to go for the best wine buys in town. Today's food sections continue the tradition. Recipes rate higher than ever with readers, and the cooking craze in America gained enough importance to become the cover story in *Time* magazine.

The food section, too, has been affected by some of the lifestyle changes of the 1970s. Typical coverage today includes regular sections on cooking for two (or for one), recipes for dieters and vegetarians, easy-to-cook meals for the working woman (or man), and features on how to buy and use many of the new tools that make cooking easier, quicker, and more fun.

Today's food section not only instructs its readers on the art of cooking but also directs them to good restaurants. The content of the food section deals primarily with four areas: taste, technique, economics, and nutrition. Let's analyze the way one newspaper, the *Minneapolis Tribune,* accommodates these areas:

*Taste.* The section selected for analysis here carries recipes for barbecued ribs (picnic style), organic soups (accompanied by a personality profile of an organic food advocate), raddison cornbread, baking soda biscuits, and breakfast muffins.

*Technique.* Features deal with blenders, processors, microwave ovens, and the element of timing.

*Economics.* The lead article deals with good places locally for outdoor eating. A column presents price comparisons for beef and pork.

*Nutrition.* A column on special diets examines how little most people know about their bodies, especially their digestive systems. A short item outlines and reviews a natural food cookbook for children.

The *Tribune*'s food section also includes a short column, "Ahead," dealing with news and events of special interest, a lecture on nutrition awareness, a Renaissance dinner, and so forth.

The front page of this food section uses illustrations, ragged type, and lines to highlight content. A food section no longer needs splashy color photographs of elegantly set tables and mouth-watering dishes to attract the reader's attention.

This sig is used for a special question-and-answer feature which aims at reader participation. When the columnist does not have an answer, she poses the question to her readers.

The topic varies from week to week in this "Special Diets" section. Notice the three-dimensional sig and the polarized photograph of the columnist.

Here's how some recipes are presented, packaged in a simulation of a recipe card for easy cutting and filing.

A dollar sign identifies this section on consumer tips.

## Religion Section

Religion pages can be as matter-of-fact and informative as a bulletin board of church events, or they can be provocative and interesting. Ideally, the content of today's religion section will perform both functions, while displaying attractive design through photographs and illustrations. Graphics can be used to convey clear messages to the reader, and religious messages are no exception.

The illustration at left shows how the *Toronto Star* uses an interesting and economical page to include a "Religion Roundup," an opinion column illustrated by photos and art, and a second column of opinion at the bottom of the page. Notice the outline type for the "Religion" label.

## Fashion Section

Many newspapers incorporate a showcase of design and color into their newly created fashion sections. We have already seen sample pages of "Fashion! Dallas" (Dallas *Morning News*) and section openers from the fashion section of the *Washington Star*. These newspapers have created a standard format, somewhat different from the rest of the publication, to introduce readers to fashion and related subjects. One of the most lavishly designed fashion sections appears weekly in the *Toronto Star*. "Fashion/80," designed by Jim Harrison, shows what a well-packaged section should be like: discreet but effective use of color photos; a distinctive section opener; an index to guide the reader through inside content; and the use of one topic (or story) as Center of Visual Impact on the opening page. The following section openers from "Fashion/80" display these qualities.

Thursday, July 24, 1980, Section B, pages B1-B8

# Fashion/80

Toronto Star

## Shades of fall

**By Bonnie Hurowitz Star fashion writer**

Metro's top designers are painting a bright, classic picture for fall. Brilliant tartans, deep colors and new silhouettes are at the forefront of fall collections. Designers are keeping a close eye on today's tight economy and on fabric and manufacturing costs, as well as on the needs of their customers. The result: An emphasis on classic pieces, femininity and versatility, with flair in detailing and accessorizing. The Star asked designers to preview their most exciting new looks for autumn.

**Alfred Sung:** With the young working woman in mind, 32-year-old Sung sees fall as a time for unexaggerated co-ordinates with a long, long fashion life.

Admittedly influenced by the popular "prep" look, the standouts in Sung's line for Ms. Originals are pleated, often plaid, skirts matched with close-fitting but boxy blazers. Jackets are squared and only slightly padded.

An interesting touch in Sung's look is the blending of traditional and very modern elements, as in his traditional, knife-pleated, orange plaid skirt, worn with a matching but modern, asymmetrically-buttoned blouse with side ruffle.

Asymmetric details are a favorite for fall, says Sung.

Rich fall colors — eggplant, deep burgundy and rust — form the basis of his line. His hemlength is about three inches below the knee — a bit conservative, but practical. "Length is important for our Canadian winters, which are so cold," he says. "A longer length is better with high boots. You don't want to have skin showing between your boot and skirt, it's so ugly. This way, also, women have the option of shortening their skirts."

Alfred Sung's clothing is available in Metro at Simpsons, The Bay, Eaton's, Harridge's, Holt Renfrew and other stores.

**Shelley Wickabrod:** Well known for their very tailored style, Shelley Wickabrod, 28, and her husband and design partner, Bernard McGee, 27, once again have taken the classic approach in their fall collection for Clotheslines.

But this year, their man-tailored line has been infused with the brightest colors the couple has ever used. Wickabrod has turned bright red plaid into a simple, chemise-like dress with an elaborate detachable pierrot collar and bowed tie.

The red plaid also shows up as walking shorts; and a whole range of purples, from dusky rose to the hottest shade, have been incorporated into the line. "Usually we despise hot colors," says Wickabrod, "but we bumped into some fabulous fabric and we had a good muted range to go with the brights."

The most important suit for the Wickabrod-McGee design team is the asymmetrically closed or one-lapel suit. Generally, the couple's fall jackets are more fitted and skirts are fuller than last year.

Mid-calf length Zouave pants and jodhpurs are new pant looks, and skirts are still shown fairly long — about four inches below the knee — in deference to Clotheslines' generally tall clientele.

Clothing by Shelley Wickabrod and Bernard McGee is sold at their boutique, Clotheslines.

□ **Designer Colin Watson goes romantic and Debbie Shuchat stresses soft fall looks/See page B1**

Photograph by Bob Olsen

**Fall sunshine:** Alfred Sung's traditional knife-pleated skirt, far left, is a snappy orange plaid, $120, to match asymmetrically buttoned blouse with ruffle, $100.

**Bright brilliance:** Straight plaid dress by Shelley Wickabrod, left, features detachable pierrot collar and bowed tie, $200. It's worn with navy flannel blazer, also $200.

Shoes and purses from Town Shoes; earrings from Fusion; other accessories by Buch & Deichmann.

For fine fall blouses, put the spotlight on white. All the rage/**B3**

Men's stores' summer sales mean hot bargains on bright accessories/**B6**

Montreal's boutiques bouncing back as summer works its fashion magic/**B8**

Notice effective silhouetting of photograph. Copy block is set ragged right, with large initial to indicate beginning of copy; a boxed index appears at bottom of page. This is a clean, easy-to-follow design. (Designed by Jim Harrison for the *Toronto Star*)

# Fashion/80

Toronto Star, Thursday, June 19, 1980, Section B, pages B1-B8

Few readers will be able to resist the visual attractiveness of this "Fashion/80" section opener. There is less copy than in the other examples shown here, but the placement is just as effective. Notice dramatic interruption of index box by model's hand. Although more than one photograph appears here, the dominance of the top silhouetted photograph paves the way visually for the rest of the elements on the page. (Designed by Jim Harrison for the *Toronto Star*)

## Baubles & bangles

By **Marina Sturdza** *Toronto Star*

Summertime accessories are bright and fanciful; definitely not meant to be taken too seriously. Match or contrast your bright cottons with an armful of plastic bangles; wear real or frankly fake flowers in your hair or anywhere. Gleaming brass, copper or silver cuff bracelets (try them on the upper arm for a change), and earrings look wonderful against bare, tanned skin. Fabric, beads, plastics, glass and enamel — all make great summertime jewelry. And think bold; better one really stunning item worn with confidence than a handful of lesser pieces. Plastic is the big news this year, used in crystal-like transparencies or in brilliant colors ranging from the primary colors to fuchsia, lime and orange. Think big when it comes to the best of these plastics, and try geometric shapes or an original, fun-to-wear free form. Leaf and flower motifs are new-looking; beaded lariats with decorative ends are a novelty.

**Big and bold:** This year's bright bracelets are better by the armful. On arm at right, from top: Wide yellow plastic; transparent pink round band; yellow carved geometric relief; transparent yellow circle band, all from Fabrice. Narrow bright pink plastic, Finishing Touches; yellow bangle, Fabrice; carved red plastic, KSP; oversize bracelet, T.J. Anemone; pink plastic, Fabrice; wide yellow disc, Creeds. On arm at top of page: Purple plastic disc, Creeds; orange swirl pattern bracelet, narrow purple band, Finishing Touches; clear plastic tubing with licorice candy enclosed, Fabrice; orange leather bangle, T. J. Anemone; more candies from Fabrice; clear purple bracelet, wide lilac shape, transparent purple, all from Fabrice.

Photographs by Erin Combs

**Creative plastics:** Nobody handles plastic better than Vancouver's Martha Sturdy. From her summer collection: Big disc necklace and dangle earrings with color-slice bracelets. At Art Gallery of Ontario and KSP. Leotards by Danskin at Capezio.

The best hairstyles for warm weather? We went to the experts and got six sharp ideas/**B2**

Summery sweaters add a cool and classy touch/**B5**

Peek into sexy Tina Turner's book of dreams/**B8**

The section's name has been moved to the right in this example, a practice made popular by designers at the *Toronto Star*, who refer to their folios and standing sigs as "flirting" elements, open to flexibility and movement. Four small head shots dress the index at bottom of page. The rest of the page is well organized and visually appealing.
(Designed by Jim Harrison for the *Toronto Star*)

Toronto Star, Thursday, July 3, 1980, Section B, pages B1-B8

**Toronto Star**

# Fashion/80

## Cool times in hot colors

By **Bonnie Hurwitz** Star fashion writer

T-shirts and jeans. They're the soup and sandwich combination of the fashion industry, the mainstay of casual wardrobes — and this summer they're packed with more pizzaz than ever. T-shirts are bright and festive, covered with a dazzling array of stripes, bold geometrics and large animal prints. Basic round- and V-necks are shot full of life with the infusion of summer color. The brights — yellow, fuchsia, turquoise and purple — are by far the most plentiful, but Ts are also widely available in soft pastels and white. The newest T-shirt basic is the traditional Lacoste style with a knitted collar. Inspired by the preppy look, manufacturers have come up with brightly striped summer versions with knitted collars and cuffs and snap closings at the neck. The impact of the fashion sweatshirt is seen in T-shirts — round necks, dropped shoulders and elasticized waists. One-shoulder styles, strapless Ts and tanktops are also immensely popular this year. Below the belt this summer, jeans are as bright as their T-shirt partners. Lightweight cotton pants in fuchsia, purple, red and blue have been hot sellers this summer, according to Sally Firth, a buyer for Thrifty's and Joel Carman, owner of Rainbow. Jeans in pastel pink and mauve shades have also begun to take off. While the straight leg jean remains the basic and most important style, the "slouch" or "baggy" has been a strong contender on the summer scene. The new "slouch" has a cleaner front and a modified silhouette. There are no pleats, the fit is tight across the hips, the legs are roomy but not extremely baggy, and the pant tapers below the knee to a 14-inch ankle. This modified slouch promises to become a fall basic, re-christened the "trouser pant."

**Summer whimsy:** This season's T-shirts are bright and stunning — and sometimes boldly striped, left, in one-shoulder cotton styles, $16. Slouch jeans, $34. Comical cotton T-shirts add to summer fun, $14. Above right, one-shoulder T-shirt in two colors sets off tan. T is $20, straight-leg jeans, $30. All T-shirts from Seesaw; jeans from Rainbow; shoes from Capezio; hair accessories, from The Scarf Shop.

Photographs by Bob Olsen

Winston Kong wins with styles that inspire loyalty/**B3**

East meets West as cowboy look rides into Beaches/**B6**

Inspiration comes out of closet for Algicyruss owner/**B5**

Makeover: Jobhunting grad puts best face forward/**B8**

## Travel Section

More Americans are traveling than ever before. One could also add that more younger Americans are taking to the roads, skies, and oceans. Travel sections are the ideal place for displaying large photographs and consumer-related content. Opening section pages usually center on one story, highlighting a place which is presented as pictorially as possible. Other content may include tips on low-cost traveling, accommodations, preparing for a trip, news of the airlines, travel questions and answers, and special columns for young travelers.

## Leisure Section

The *Star* includes two pages of leisure coverage as part of its travel section. These pages include columns on stamps, antiques, handicrafts, chess, car problems, birds, wine, and coins. With readers enjoying more leisure time, at least a weekly page in this area may be recommended.

The family or lifestyle section has evolved tremendously since the ''for-women-only'' days. Although the content has become more general in terms of reader appeal, the graphics of the section offers unlimited possibilities for the designer who likes to combine the security of an organized format with the creativity and experimentation made possible by the changing nature of its content.

# business and classified pages

The business and classified pages of the newspaper become the reader's marketplace. They also become the designer's graphic puzzle, one in which the pieces are many and varied, and the result is usually long and visually unpalatable.

But the pages are necessary because the information ordinarily included is timely, vital, and not easily found elsewhere. In a sense, the business and classified pages of the newspaper remain about the only territory unchallenged by the electronic media.

Television news coverage of business is scanty when compared to the thorough and highly departmentalized financial information carried by newspapers. Although some local television stations run ''bulletin boards'' of announcements, especially classifieds, the screen does not offer the necessary qualities of indexing and permanence available through the newspaper.

Obviously, when a reader turns to the business page he is seeking information that is not available elsewhere, and he will struggle with a page that is difficult to read *if he has to*. We all struggle with the telephone directory—by no means exemplary in its use of graphics—simply because we are seeking information that we need and we will endure graphic noise to get it.

Likewise, a person looking for a job or a house will comb through the classified page, in spite of the small type and crowded columns.

The most complete financial newspaper in the country is no example of graphic innovation, but the *Wall Street Journal* continues to attract readers who appreciate its timely and relevant content and the organized manner in which it is presented.

Fortunately, some newspapers, such as the *New York Times* and the *Chicago Tribune*, demonstrate that it is possible to package timely and relevant business content into well-organized and graphically attractive pages.

Both newspapers reorganized and redesigned their business sections in the late 1970s. The *Chicago Tribune* created what it calls its ''Midwest Business Report,'' a section published on Thursdays, to include analyses of business trends, expanded stock market listings, commodities coverage, and a generous dose of features about business and industry and the people, places, and events that create financial news. Regular features of this section include ''Business Ticker'' (a summary of business news updates), ''Spotlight'' (a local feature), ''People/Places,'' ''Labor/Jobs,'' ''On the Farm,'' ''Financial Planning,'' and ''After Hours'' (a section suggesting leisure activities for busy business people).

''Midweek Business Report'' is designed structurally. The opening page includes an illustrated index at the top, and most news items carry illustrations, such as charts. Since most items are regular features, designers have labeled the various columns ''Stock market,'' ''Spotlight,'' ''Chicago indicators,'' and so on.

One of the best examples of page organization is found in the *Tribune*'s ''Monday a.m. business report,'' a vertically designed five-column page which provides a wrap-up of business news. ''Nobody's time is more precious than that of the business person,'' states the *Tribune*'s promotional campaign for its business report.

At the *New York Times* a complete business section, ''Business Day,'' appears Monday through Friday as a separate, fourth part of the newspaper. Like the *Tribune*'s business section, ''Business Day'' provides regular coverage of financial news plus extensive feature coverage. The *Times*' section entices the reader through large photos and charts that begin to tell the business story of the day long before the reader gets to the copy.

## ORGANIZATION COMES FIRST

Organization is most important to the business and classified pages. It precedes attractiveness, a statement that could not be true in other sections of the newspaper where reader impulse rather than habit are important determinants of audience.

The business page reader—and there are roughly thirty million stockholders in the United States who turn to the business page at one point or another, if not daily—knows exactly what information he wants and does not have much time to search for it.

He does not want regular features switched around the page from day to day. A stationary and well-organized design is more functional.

Thus the designer should assign certain areas of the page to regular columns and features, while allowing space for spot news, timely features, and of course, photographs and art.

## THE BUSINESS PAGE

Many newspapers devote one page to business news; others use three or four pages daily, plus an entire section on Sunday. Regardless of how much financial coverage appears in the newspaper, chances are that there will be at least one page. This page can be inside another section of the newspaper or it can be the section opener. In either case a page identification label usually lets readers know that the page or section is devoted entirely to business news.

The illustration from *Today* shows that a business page does not have to be gray. A color photograph draws the reader into the page, and there is enough other photographic impact to keep his interest. In terms of content, this business page leads with a human interest feature about a local entrepreneur who parlayed a $500 investment into a million-dollar paint company. The page includes a regular column, "The Ledger," dealing with short items from the news wires. The bottom of the page is highlighted by a column of economic analysis.

The *St. Petersburg Times'* page is completely structural, and also very economical. A photograph highlights the bottom of the page, along with a column by a question-and-answer expert. Headlines are small, and the page identification label is simple enough to provide continuity with the rest of the newspaper as well as inject white space into the page.

This section opener from *Today* (Cocoa Beach, Florida) uses its space economically. Notice the page identification label at the top, which is also used as an index to the inside coverage of stocks and financial news.

This business page from the *St. Petersburg Times* relies on graphic symbols to tell one of its business stories. Note the use of arrows for Dow Jones averages, a practice that provides instant information for the reader who might be too hurried to read the entire article.

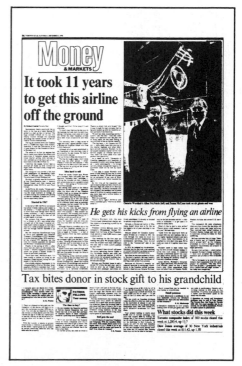

The *Toronto Star* labels its financial section "Money" and uses packaging as a means of graphic organization.

The "Money" section of the *Toronto Star* capitalizes on features and columns, a winning combination. Notice how the lead feature about an airline that took eleven years to get off the ground is packaged to include page identification, a large photograph, and a sidebar (related story). The bottom of the page is devoted to a column about "Your Money," a consumer-oriented feature in which readers are given a chance to present their problems or questions.

The *Journal*'s business and financial page opens with a package of tabulated information on how local stocks performed the previous week. Wire copy, a syndicated column, and advertising take up the rest of the page.

## STOCK MARKET REPORTS

It has been said that many readers buy an afternoon newspaper simply to check on the stock market, since this information cannot be obtained from broadcast news. What can the designer do to make these reports more attractive and easier to read?

*Alphabetical breakers.* Contrast of bold and light type will make stock market reports more visually appealing. Notice how the *Midland* (Texas) *Reporter-Telegram* (below left) provides some contrast and produces readability by using bold letters to separate stock listings alphabetically.

*Lines and rules.* The *Toronto Star* (below right) uses bold lines and rules to separate stock listings, but it also helps the reader who is in a hurry by classifying certain information, such as "Most active stocks," or "N.Y. big movers."

The *Providence Journal*'s business page appears as an inside page in Section A of the newspaper. Notice the effective use of ads at the bottom of the page.

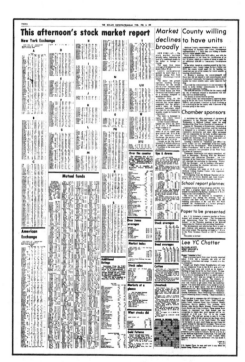

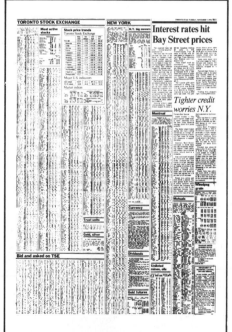

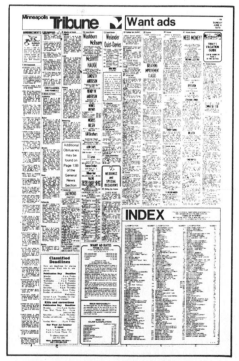

The *Minneapolis Tribune*'s classified page uses graphic breakers to guide the reader. Notice the use of bold squares to classify information and to move the reader through the page.

## THE CLASSIFIED PAGES

Space becomes money in the classified pages, which is the reason many newspapers that use a six-column format throughout their news pages suddenly present the reader with a nine- or ten-column classified page. Although definitely more profitable, these narrow-column pages are more difficult to read and to follow.

The classified page is not one that we read thoroughly. It is a page that most readers *scan*, making stops to read brief items of interest. Pages that are meant to be scanned require points of direction, not only as graphic elements to break up the gray matter but also to guide the reader who might be interested in "furniture for sale" but who could not care less about the rest of the sections on the page.

Graphically, then, the classified page should offer the following:

1. Contrast of bold and light areas on the page.
2. Points of direction through key words or graphic elements that help identify content.
3. A good index, especially in Sunday classified sections, so that readers will know where to turn for specific information.

## DESIGNING GRAPHIC BREAKERS

The graphic breakers that will separate information in a classified page should be designed around *type only* or they should be *symbols*. In either case simplicity of design is in order.

### Type-Only Breakers

This is one case where the use of white letters on a black background may be justifiable. Caps are also recommended since in most instances the designer is dealing with one key word: for example, pets, furniture, antiques.

### Symbols

Sometimes a graphic symbol, accompanied by a key word, will speed the reader's journey through the classified page. Most of the symbols required can be cut out from one of the many clip books available to editors and designers. What the designer should do is to clip the symbol he needs and then try to design the breaker so that it is used as attractively and as simply as possible.

Although the business and classified pages may not be the newspaper's graphic showcase, they offer the designer an opportunity to apply typographic strategies that will organize content for the reader. And there is always the creative challenge facing any designer who wants to make a page of stock listings or classified ads more attractive and easier to read.

# entertainment pages

Entertainment pages are probably among the most popular pages in the newspaper today. Americans are spending more time and money on entertainment and leisure activities than ever. Today's readers expect the newspaper to offer a guide to those activities, preferably with a consumer perspective.

A well-planned entertainment page or section may be described as a service area of the newspaper, offering coverage of immediate activities (movie schedules; television listings; calendars of events for plays, recitals, concerts, lectures, and exhibits) and *advance* notice of coming events. But the reader expects more than a printed bulletin board; he also wants reviews, photos, and extensive feature coverage of personalities, places, and events in the arts.

To a certain degree, the content of an entertainment page or section depends on local interest. Restaurant guides may be necessary for some newspapers, while others will emphasize television coverage or art or drama. The best evaluative criterion to use for the content of an entertainment page or section should be that it serve the information and cultural needs of its readership adequately and thoroughly.

Graphically, the entertainment page presents some of the problems discussed in relation to the sports and business pages. Entertainment pages must include some tabulated material as part of the coverage; for example, movie times, television listings, and calendars of events. And because of the service nature of the entertainment page, readers expect to find specific information in a set place.

The designer's job is to highlight the page with a large photograph or illustration and a new feature article that will serve as a frame for the regular features the reader expects to find. Many design possibilities exist to create an attractive display of photo and copy. Also the designer will be able to make use of the many photographs he receives from movie companies, theaters, and television networks. Here's one section of the newspaper where the visual content is almost always going to be readily available.

## PLANNING THE ENTERTAINMENT PAGE

First, the designer should decide on the number of regular features that are to appear. For example, it may be wise to include a daily listing of "what to do today (or tonight)" on the opening page to give the reader a quick reference to the available activities. The *Miami News* does this successfully, including a daily column of activities that begins with "On TV Tonight" and ends with "Elsewhere," for those readers who won't be staying home watching television. The *Toronto Star* also carries a column of "TV Highlights" on its entertainment front page and then lists highlights of the local entertainment scene.

Second, the designer should establish individualized standing sigs for each of the regular sections, making sure that they follow the same format as the rest of the sigs in the newspaper.

In terms of position, once the designer knows what his regular standing features will be, it may help to place them where they will be most accessible to the reader, but also where they will allow ample space to cover spot news and features of the entertainment world.

For example, the L-shaped structure (discussed in Chapter 4) may be convenient for structuring the front page of the entertainment section.

An inside page can also be designed with a column of movie times (left) in a stationary position, allowing the rest of the page for news and features and for ads at the bottom.

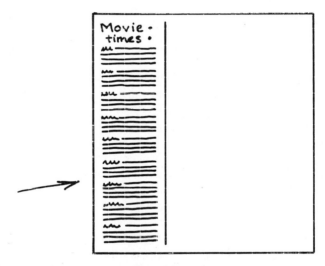

The designer may wish to use the horizontal top section of the page for a regular section, such as television listings; these rate high with the reader and therefore should be placed in a prominent, easy-to-locate area of the page.

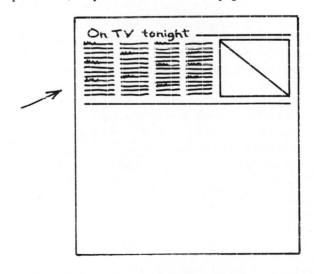

Packaging is probably the most desirable design strategy to use for the entertainment page, where organization of content is paramount. The designer will create structures for all content, emphasizing one large and dominant package per page, as illustrated below:

The *Star*'s opening page includes the page identification label at the top ("Entertainment/ Classified"). Notice the column of "TV Highlights" left and the entire package of features on the right. The border used to package the content is the same point size throughout, avoiding visual competition. What the packaging does here is to organize the content and give the page a sense of order. Photos are distributed throughout the page, with emphasis on head shots.

The inside page of the *Star* follows a structural pattern, in this case an inverted L-shape. Three columnists ("On and Off the Air," "Soap Opera Scene," and "Opera") cut horizontally across the page. The rest of the available space is devoted to a "Toronto Theatre Guide," "Tonight's Television Listings," and ads.

## ENTERTAINMENT SPECIALS

The weekend is when most people have leisure time available, which is why many editors publish weekend guides to entertainment and leisure in their Friday editions.

The *St. Petersburg Times* calls its section "Friday/the Weekend," and opens with various features, accompanied with a column entitled "TGIF," to highlight weekend activities.

Color is an important part of the overall design of this page, but organization and the structural approach also help to make it more attractive. Notice the use of lines and rules for "TGIF" at the bottom of the page.

One of the most functional aspects of the *St. Petersburg Times'* weekend entertainment section is its "Pullout," a double-page spread designed structurally to include an easy-to-follow guide to dining, nightlife, theater, and movies. Generous space is also given to advertising.

The pullout section is a double-page spread separated into four structures. The top three structures are vertical and carry entertainment guides. The horizontal structure at the bottom is used for advertising.

## ENTERTAINMENT AND THE SMALL DAILY

Not every newspaper has the resources—or the need—to include such extensive entertainment coverage as in the previous examples. Many small dailies serve the needs of their readers by including a single page for weekend activities. The key element is to design a page structurally with a place for everything and everything in its place.

It is also possible for a small daily to combine entertainment news with other leisure-related coverage, such as comic strips, advice columns, and so on.

## THE TABLOID ENTERTAINMENT SECTION

Practicality should be a design criterion in preparing an entertainment section. Some newspaper editors realize that their readers will use the week-long television listing, in which case the full-size page may be too large and cumbersome to keep around for seven days.

The *Syracuse Herald-Journal* publishes a Sunday tabloid section called "Stars" with full listings of television programs for the week, plus extensive feature coverage of the arts, theater, cinema, stamp collecting, and regular columns and reviews. The section is full of photographs and copy. It is easy to read, and to keep.

Newspapers are also experimenting graphically with sections of television listings that resemble miniature magazines but which are easy to read and to keep for further reference. One such section is the *Miami Herald's* "TV," published every Sunday and compiled by a five-member staff under the direction of a television magazine editor.

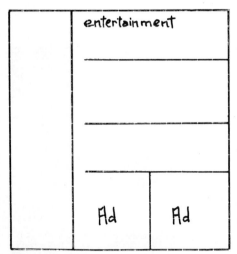

Notice how this page has been used economically, with three horizontal structures at the top of the page, one vertical structure on the right, and some space available for horizontal blocking of entertainment-related ads at the bottom.

The content of "TV" is distributed and labeled effectively throughout. Sections deal with the television set, movies, sports, serious programming, programs for children, daily programming, and top choices; a box breaks up the tabulated material to highlight one special and recommended program.

## STRATEGIES TO MAKE TABULATED MATERIAL EASIER TO READ

1. The contrast of light and bold typefaces will help the reader who is trying to find out what time a movie will begin and at what theater; bold type for the name of the theater ensures easier reading.

2. Some newspapers highlight the name of the film in boldface and use a light or regular typeface for the name of the movie house and the times the film will be shown.

3. Indentations help to make tabulated material easier to find. A 3- to 5-pica indentation will help the reader find what she is looking for.

4. Photographs to highlight a movie (perhaps a new one on the schedule) will also help make the movie listings and the page more readable.

5. Lines to separate various sections of a television listing will help the reader. The *Toronto Star* uses thin lines to separate information for different networks.

6. One of the most important design strategies for tabulated content is to keep it as well packaged as possible, preferably within structural patterns, even when borders or lines are not used, as in the *Providence Journal's* entertainment page.

The cover of "TV" uses an illustration to alert the reader to the lead feature story inside.

It matters little whether a newspaper publishes one page or an entire section of entertainment news and features; the possibilities for creating well-organized and attractively designed pages are unlimited.

# 15 designing tabloids

Although it has been many years since the *New York Daily News* published its first issue in 1919, becoming the first modern American tabloid-sized newspaper, the term *tabloid* continues to remind some people of the splashy front pages packed with sex and crime news that made that publication—and other tabloids—popular.

However, editors and designers are beginning to recognize those qualities of the smaller publication that make it desirable:

1. *Manageability*. It is easier for the reader to handle a tabloid-sized newspaper than a broadsheet.
2. *Design possibilities*. The smaller pages make it possible to create more attractive pages and to experiment with a more unified design.
3. *Advertising potential*. Many editors have found it profitable to use this format because advertisers are more willing to buy full-page ads.
4. *Departmentalizing*. Newspaper designers trying to incorporate ideas from magazines will find that the tabloid format offers a more practical approach to separating news and features into departmentalized pages.

## NEW STATUS

When the *Christian Science Monitor* changed its format from broadsheet to tabloid in 1974, tabloids immediately gained a higher status. The *Monitor*'s front page is newsy and follows a four-column format. It includes an easy-to-read nameplate, an inside-

An easy-to-read newspaper, the *Monitor* displays several stories on its front page. Notice the small headlines and photographs. A four-column format allows a readable page.

The *Monitor*'s double truck is devoted to a single story, designed as if it were for the pages of a magazine and illustrated with dominant art or photograph. This example shows special treatment of the feature, "The Cosmic Cradle."

Notice that "arts/entertainment" is set in bold type, all lower case, at the top of the page. One photograph suffices to make this page attractive and easy to follow.

The *Monitor* devotes all of page two to "inside the news—briefly," a section for which it uses ragged right type and column rules. Notice the major feature, "Focus," at the top of the page.

contents box, and at least four news stories—thus destroying the myth of the stereotypical tabloid front page: a 196-point headline and a large photograph. But the *Monitor*'s new format did more than simply demonstrate what was possible through the use of readable type and good story organization on the front page. It also included excellent content organization throughout the publication, including attractively designed standing sigs, effective departmentalizing, a magazine-design approach to its double truck (centerspread), and attractive and readable typography throughout.

Notice the effective framing with white space around this page. The photographs are a CVI but do not compete with the type packages. The entire page is structurally designed.

*Newsday* devotes page two to an index to the inside of the bulky publication. The space at the bottom is used to promote content of the Sunday newspaper.

"Part II" of *Newsday* includes comics, advice, interior decorating, the arts, television, and movies.

Editorial and opinion content are distributed over a two-page spread. Notice that there are no photographs or illustrations, but the two pages appear unified and easy to read, mainly because of the effective use of bold and light typefaces.

## *NEWSDAY* PIONEERS STYLE

One of the best-designed tabloid newspapers in the country, and a pioneer in the concept of the daily news magazine, is *Newsday,* the Long Island newspaper. *Newsday*'s designers were using white space effectively—and generously—many years before it became a common design tool. *Newsday*'s front page is typical of the traditional tabloid in its use of large and dominant photographs, but the newspaper rarely uses a full photo page. Instead, its front page combines display type, small amounts of body type, and one or more photos to create what may be described as a *partial cover*. We say *partial* because the page capitalizes on photography but includes sufficient type and white space to create a clean environment.

The front page of *Newsday* typifies what all tabloid pages should be like: attractive, clean, readable, and economical.

One of the often-mentioned disadvantages of the tabloid format is that the newspaper can't ordinarily be shared by two readers. *Newsday* solves the problem by incorporating a "Part II" inside the newspaper that can be pulled out and read separately from the rest.

## INNOVATION AT THE *DAILY NEWS*

The *New York Daily News* continues to carry dominant photos with a large two-line headline that is visible to commuters in a hurry during the rush hours. But sex and crime are no longer the standard news fare. The inside pages of the *News* are designed in magazine style, emphasizing wider columns, smaller photographs, and the use of lines as design tools. Phillip Ritzenberg, assistant managing editor for design and production, describes the *News'* inside sections as "unique black and white magazines."

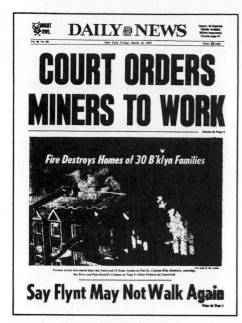

Although the front page of the *New York Daily News* has not changed much through the years (a large headline and large photograph are dominant graphic elements), the inside pages show graphic order and emphasis on design. Notice the effective positioning of photographs and the use of rules and initial letter.

## TABLOID DESIGN STRATEGIES

Most of the graphic strategies mentioned in this book so far apply to the tabloid format as well as to broadsheets. A few special suggestions are in order, however, to avoid the pitfalls inherent when working with the smaller page:

### Column Format

The most important decision the designer has to make is the number of columns per page. Most tabloids today adhere to the easy-to-read four-column format, but some editors prefer three or five columns—and the most economy-minded even force their readers to struggle through six columns.

*Three-column format.* This format is not the most functional because it lends itself to long articles. When a four-paragraph item is set in the wider measurement, it looks even shorter set in type and detracts from the overall look of the page. Some tabloids use three columns on the front page but return to four columns for inside pages, to stretch their space and make it more attractive and economical to advertisers.

The three-column format works best when used for a special full-page treatment of a story and pictures, particularly long pieces that will become more readable set in wider columns, or for full-page packages that require space for borders around the page.

*Four-column format.* This is the most widely used, most readable, and usually most attractive format, but it is not necessarily the easiest way to design the page. Faced with an even number of columns, the designer may tend to split up the page into equal units. For example, if the designer sets aside two columns on the left for a story, he ends up with two columns of equal size on the right. But this problem may be overcome by exercising care and proper planning and by establishing a sense of structural contrast.

Let us analyze the following sketches made by a designer at work:

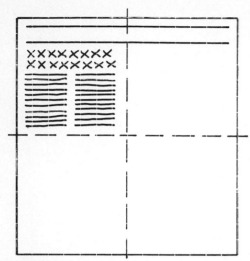

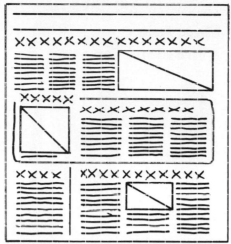

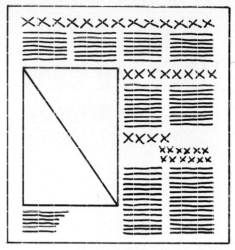

The designer places a two-column structure on the left, then faces three equally sized structures through the rest of the page. Notice the dotted line, indicating perfect symmetry for this page—which must be altered as indicated in the next sketch.

The space to the right of the copy block is now occupied by a photograph, sized as deep as its adjoining copy block. The bottom of the page moves horizontally, to create contrast.

The horizontal structure at the top allows for two large verticals at the bottom. Notice use of the reverse kicker for the lower story to avoid monotony and bring graphic interest to that area.

The four-column format also makes it easy to block ads into the available space, either on one side or at the bottom, as shown:

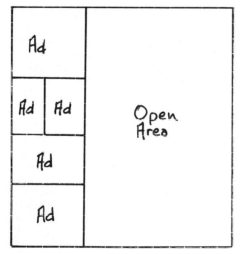

This is an all-horizontal page, with graphic variations to avoid monotony. For example, the second horizontal package (from top) is boxed. The bottom package is divided into two unequally sized structures.

*Five- and six-column formats.* Extremely narrow columns, as found in a five- or six-column tabloid format, are difficult to read and even more difficult to make into attractive pages. But they are economical, which is why some newspapers—especially shoppers—continue to use them.

## Style

Because of its size, a tabloid newspaper affords the designer some choices in graphic styles. For example, a tabloid may follow a regular newspaper style, as does the *Christian Science Monitor,* whose front page is based on news content. Other tabloids may be designed as "newsmagazines," emphasizing photography or illustration on the cover.

Designing in the latter style includes selecting one top story or photograph for display on the front page. In some cases photo and story may combine for an attractive page, but designers should be careful not to create typographic congestion. If a photo is the dominant element, type should take a back seat. However, if copy is what's important, photos should be small and secondary. The following sketches illustrate the point:

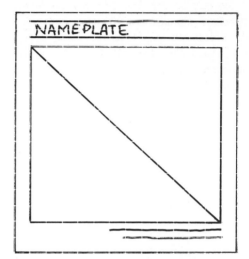

A newsmagazine's front page is based exclusively on a photograph. Type at the bottom leads the reader to the related story inside.

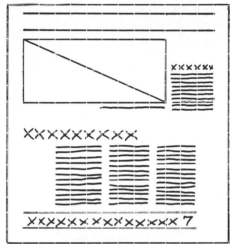

The partial cover has a large and dominant photograph but also includes its accompanying story. Notice that there is still space left for a teaser headline at the bottom of the page.

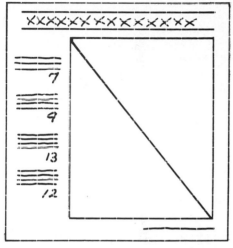

This is an *index* front page, in which a photo serves as a target spot to attract readers. The column on the left of the photo serves as an index, in the same manner in which magazines display content on their covers. Special typographic effect for page numbers will offer visual impact.

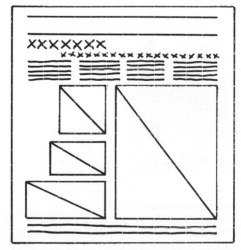

When photos are secondary to copy, the designer places the article at top, the photos at bottom, of the page.

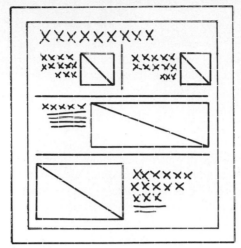

The newsmagazine's front page is a photographic index. Notice the use of boxes to include a teaser and miniature photograph. The page is designed structurally, emphasizing unequally sized boxes.

Art and illustrations can become effective graphic tools on the front page, as long as the reader has a clue to their content, as indicated through the headline.

The newsmagazine style enjoyed tremendous popularity with high school and college newspapers during the 1970s. Several student newspapers perfected the style, among them *West Side Story* (West High School, Iowa City, Iowa) and *Shield* (Austin McCallum High School, Austin, Texas). Some professional newspapers are experimenting with the format through the publication of special sections and supplements (Chapter 16) and Saturday or Sunday editions.

Newsmagazines display their best art on the cover and then usually devote one or two inside pages to news copy. The pages are designed in an open format, with an abundance of white space, vertical and horizontal column rules, and a strong emphasis on graphic design.

One of the main characteristics of the newsmagazine is the use of the cover front page. This issue uses large art of a motorcyclist to attract readers to the inside story on the subject.

This open feature page capitalizes on large type and vertical placement of copy and photos. Notice the use of white space at the top of the page.

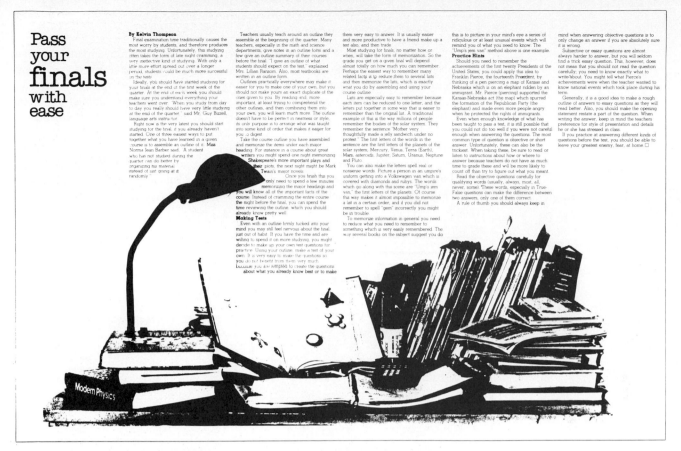

## Pass your finals with ease

By Kelvin Thompson

Final examination time traditionally causes the most worry among students, and therefore produces the most studying. Unfortunately, this studying often takes the form of late night cramming, a very ineffective kind of studying. With only a little more effort spread out over a longer period, students could be much more successful on the tests.

Ideally, you should have started studying for your finals at the end of the first week of the quarter. At the end of each week you should make sure you understand everything your teachers went over. "When you study from day to day you really should have very little studying at the end of the quarter," said Mr. Guy Bizzell, language arts instructor.

Right now is the very latest you should start studying for the final, if you already haven't started. One of three easiest ways to put together what you have learned in a given course is to assemble an outline of it. Miss Norma Jean Barber said, "A student who has not studied during the quarter can do better by organizing his material instead of just going at it randomly."

Teachers usually teach around an outline they assemble at the beginning of the quarter. Many teachers, especially in the math and science departments, give notes in an outline form and a few give an outline summary of their courses before the final. "I give an outline of what students should expect on the test," explained Mrs. Lillian Ransom. Also, most textbooks are written in an outline form.

Outlines practically everywhere may make it easier for you to make one of your own, but you should not make yours an exact duplicate of the ones given to you. By reading and, more important, at least trying to comprehend the other outlines, and then combining them into your own, you will learn much more. The outline doesn't have to be perfect in neatness or style; its only purpose is to arrange what was taught into some kind of order that makes it easier for you to digest.

Take the course outline you have assembled and memorize the items under each major heading. For instance in a course about great writers you might spend one night memorizing Shakespeare's more important plays and their plots, the next night might be Mark Twain's major novels.

Once you finish this you only need to spend a few minutes memorizing the major headings and you will know all of the important facts of the course. Instead of cramming the entire course the night before the final, you can spend the time reviewing the outline, which you should already know pretty well.

**Making Tests**

Even with an outline firmly tucked into your mind you may still feel nervous about the final, just out of habit. If you have the time and are willing to spend it on more studying, you might decide to make up your own test questions for practice. Using your outline, make a test of your own. It is very easy to make the questions so you do not benefit from them very much, because you are tempted to create the questions about what you already know best or to make

them very easy to answer. It is usually easier and more productive to have a friend make up a test also, and then trade.

Most studying for finals, no matter how or when, will take the form of memorization. So the grade you get on a given final will depend almost totally on how much you can remember. Perhaps the easiest way to remember many related facts is to reduce them to several lists and then memorize the lists, which is exactly what you do by assembling and using your course outline.

Lists are especially easy to remember because each item can be reduced to one letter, and the letters put together in some way that is easier to remember than the original list. A traditional example of this is the way millions of people remember the bodies of the solar system. They remember the sentence "Mother very thoughtfully made a jelly sandwich under no protest." The first letters of the words in the sentence are the first letters of the planets of the solar system, Mercury, Venus, Terra (Earth), Mars, asteroids, Jupiter, Saturn, Uranus, Neptune and Pluto.

You can also make the letters spell real or nonsense words. Picture a person in an umpire's uniform getting into a Volkswagen van which is covered with diamonds and rubys. The words which go along with this scene are "Ump's jem van," the first letters of the planets. Of course this way makes it almost impossible to memorize a list in a certain order, and if you did not remember to spell "gem" incorrectly you might be in trouble.

To memorize information in general you need to reduce what you need to remember to something which is very easily remembered. The way several books on the subject suggest you do

this is to picture in your mind's eye a series of ridiculous or at least unusual events which will remind you of what you need to know.

**Practice Hints**

Should you need to remember the achievements of the first twenty Presidents of the United States, you could apply this idea to Franklin Pierce, the fourteenth President, by thinking of a pen piercing a map of Kansas and Nebraska which is on an elephant ridden by an immigrant. Mr. Pierce (piercing) supported the Kansas-Nebraska act (the map) which spurred the formation of the Republican Party (the elephant) and made even more people angry when he protected the rights of immigrants.

Even when enough knowledge of what has been taught to pass a test, it is still possible that you could not do too well if you were not careful enough when answering the questions. The most common type of question is objective or short answer. Unfortunately, these can also be the trickiest. When taking these, be sure to read or listen to instructions about how or where to answer because teachers do not have as much time to grade these and will be more likely to count off than try to figure out what you meant.

Read the objective questions carefully for qualifying words (usually, always, most, all, never, some). These words, especially in True-False questions can make the difference between two answers, only one of them correct.

A rule of thumb you should always keep in mind when answering objective questions is to only change an answer if you are absolutely sure it is wrong.

Subjective or essay questions are almost always harder to answer, but you will seldom find a trick essay question. This, however, does not mean that you should not read the question carefully; you need to know exactly what to write about. You might tell what Pierce's achievements were when the teacher wanted to know national events which took place during his term.

Generally, it is a good idea to make a rough outline of answers to essay questions as they will read better. Also, you should make the opening statement restate a part of the question. When writing the answer, keep in mind the teachers preference for style of presentation and details he or she has stressed in class.

If you practice at answering different kinds of questions before the test, you should be able to leave your greatest enemy, fear, at home. □

This double truck from *Shield* shows the proper use of type, white space, and illustration to create a unified and graphically appealing spread.

*West Side Story* pioneered in the somewhat controversial style of devoting entire pages to advertising. Those who believe that ads and copy should blend as much as possible oppose this treatment, but the *West Side Story* staff considers it a most successful approach.

This cover page from *Our Sunday Visitor,* a Catholic newsmagazine, creates photographic impact while using the bottom of the page to display headlines and short summaries of inside stories.

The *Allentown (Pa.) Morning Call* reversed its sliding Saturday circulation when it created *Weekender,* a tabloid newsmagazine which runs thirty to forty-two pages and has received wide acceptance.

*Weekender* contains two sections, one devoted to local and national news, the other to features, sports, lifestyle, astrology, entertainment, and a weekend calendar of events. The design is strictly magazine-oriented, and the nameplate calls attention to *Weekender,* not to the *Allentown Morning Call*.

Another newspaper that has capitalized on a once-a-week newsmagazine is the *Willoughby (Ohio) News-Herald,* which converted its Saturday morning edition into a tabloid to increase circulation and to boost advertising revenue. It accomplished both goals.

*Old Pueblo,* the newsmagazine published by the *Tucson Citizen,* includes a photo and story on its cover.

## Double Trucks

Tabloid newspapers offer the designer a bonus through the double truck (center spread), the natural centerfold of the publication. Some newspapers use the space for advertising in part or completely. When the space is available for news and features, however, the possibilities are unlimited for creating a magazine-style design. The double truck may become the publication's design showcase, a visual treat for the reader.

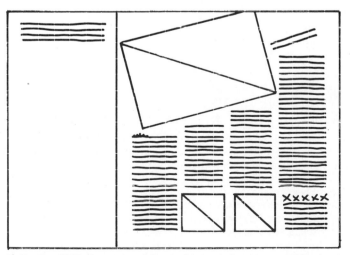

Notice the CVI in the center of the double truck, leaving unequal column space on both sides.

The basic rule in designing a double truck is that *it should be treated as a single page,* not as two pages. The designer should begin by placing a Center of Visual Impact as close to the center of the spread as possible, but without "centering" it. That is, there will be unequal column space around the CVI.

Double trucks may center around photography, art, or type. Rarely should all three elements be used as primary visual tools on the page.

A double truck does not have to be devoted to a single story. In fact, many newspapers use the space for several items, but they concentrate on one major graphic element to attract the reader.

The *Toronto Star*'s "Street Talk" displays artwork as a CVI.

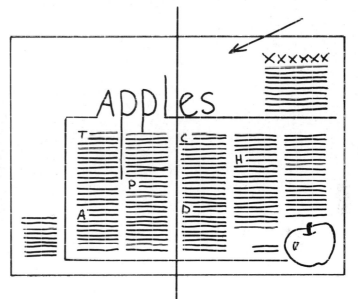

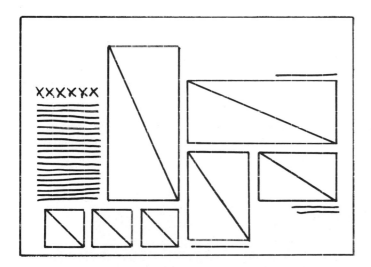

Tabloids are enjoying a new status and becoming useful in attracting new readers. Ironically, the early tabloid press in America had a similar purpose. At the turn of the century, tabloids splashed sex and crime on their front page to attract the nonreader—primarily immigrants and blue-collar workers. Today's colorful newsmagazines and special sections still use the tabloid format to attract the nonreader, except that the category now includes white-collar executives, sophisticated suburbanites, and the young.

# 16
## special sections and supplements

They used to be part of the Sunday edition of the newspaper, those colorful, tabloid-sized special sections on gardening, hunting, football, or car care. Editors and readers considered these special sections a bonus, which added to the content—and weight—of the Sunday newspaper.

Special sections are more popular than ever and are no longer restricted to Sunday editions. Graphically, they allow designers freedom to experiment with type, color, black and white, and illustrations. Although most special sections are tabloid size, others are broadsheets.

The content of the special section is not limited to consumer-oriented or seasonal events. Special sections include in-depth coverage of news, features, trends, and controversial issues. Some special sections are based entirely on photography, and a few deal with specialized topics such as sports, food, or entertainment.

## REGULAR "SPECIAL" SECTIONS

The popularity of special sections is probably an outgrowth of what John McMullen of the *Miami Herald* describes as "the need for newspapers to offer something more than just the traditional news in the traditional format day after day." In many cases, what started as special sections have developed into regular features in some newspapers.

*The New York Times.* "As far as the *Times* is concerned, you can't really separate the special sections from the whole plan of putting out a four-part newspaper daily; they all go together," says Abe Rosenthal, executive editor. The *Times* is designed as a four-section newspaper five days a week. The first two sections are devoted to the extensive and thorough news coverage that has made the *Times* famous—foreign news, national news, metropolitan news, cultural news, and so on. The third section is a magazine-type special produced four days a week. Section four is a strong financial section called "Business Day" (see Chapter 13). Overall, the *Times* offers its readers a general newspaper, a magazine-type special section, and a business section daily.

*The Chicago Tribune*. The *Tribune* runs the following regular sections: "Feminique" on Monday, "Taste" on Thursday, "Sports Week" and "Weekend" on Friday, and "Home Section" on Saturday. In addition, it includes the "Midwest Business Week" on Thursday (see Chapter 13).

*The Minneapolis Tribune*. The *Tribune*'s regular sections include "Food," a Friday special called "Lifestyle," "Neighbors" on Saturday, and "Shelter," a real-estate section.

*The Boston Globe*. The *Globe* publishes "Sports Plus," "Calendar," and special magazine sections on Sunday ("The Boston Tea Party," "Lexington and Concord," "Bunker Hill Section," "The Bicentennial Section," "Treasures of New England," and "The Constitution"). Robert L. Healy, executive editor of the *Globe,* says that since the 1960s, when the newspaper started running special sections like the ones described, his newspaper has increased Sunday circulation from 400,000 to 650,000 copies: "The impact has been tremendous, not only from our readers, but also for our advertisers."

*The Toronto Star*. Following its redesign in 1978, the *Star* instituted two special sections as regular fare: "Sports Plus" and "Street Talk," a tabloid written and designed to appeal to young readers.

## ANALYZING A SPECIAL SECTION

The tabloid format offers the most practical and manageable size for a special section which is meant to be something extra—and the reader gets a feeling that he is getting something extra when he is able to *pull out* the entire section from his newspaper.

In terms of design, tabloids also offer a more limited area with which to work, contributing to more effective packaging and distribution of content.

The format of a tabloid section varies from one newspaper to another (see Chapter 15). Some tabloids use a four-column format, whereas others have three or five columns. The four-column format is the most adequate, since it allows an appropriate line length—not too narrow and not too wide. The pages analyzed at right and at the top of the next page are from an edition of "Calendar," The *Boston Globe's* special section.

The cover of most special sections, like those of magazines, is used to highlight the inside content through photography or, as in this sample, illustration. The most functional cover pages will also include headlines about stories found on the inside. Notice how the entire section is packaged. A miniature nameplate of the *Boston Globe* appears at the top, since readers should be reminded that the special section is an integral part of the parent publication.

One of the most functional and important pages of a special section is the index page. "Calendar" has also used the index page for advertising. Notice how the page is split into two structures. The index combines bold and light typefaces.

The double truck, a two-page spread in the center of the tabloid, offers the designer unlimited possibilities for the display of large and prominent photos and interesting type. Notice the numbers in bold type, in addition to the column rules and photos.

Regular features of "Calendar" are usually carried as horizontal structures at the top of the page, with an ad at the bottom. Notice the special typeface for the title of the regular feature ("Nightlife") and the double lines for placing the headline in bold type.

So far we have seen how special sections can become a regular part of the newspaper's coverage mainly because of the added perspective they offer for the reader, bringing magazine-like material into the home every day. Special sections also boost circulation and provide the much-desired quality of accessibility—the reader pulls the section out of his newspaper and finds twelve, sixteen, or more pages about a topic neatly packaged for easy reading.

But many newspaper editors today say they produce special sections as a *service to their readers*, which is why we can separate them into two categories: those that provide *reader service* and those designed to bring in *advertising revenue*.

## READER SERVICE

Newspapers may provide service to their readers through the publication of a special section, as illustrated by the following examples.

*News-oriented special sections.* The *Sarasota Herald-Tribune* published a twenty-page, full-size special section to examine in detail the phosphate industry in Florida, its effect on people, the economy, and the ecology of the region.

When the *Fort Worth Star-Telegram* published its sixteen-page special section, a tab, it did so to explore in detail one of Texas' most sensational murder trials, which had been front-page news for weeks. The section pulled all the material together, offering the reader a complete, in-depth analysis of the story in which a millionaire spent $3.5 million for a defense and finally won acquittal.

*Trends.* A special section can be devoted to local or national trends. When the editors of the *Seattle Times* realized the widespread problem of minority unemployment, they decided to inquire into the situation and found that it would have been difficult to report all the detailed aspects of their findings in several installments in the regular newspaper. Instead, they ran a special section, a twelve-page tab with a photo cover and interesting magazine-style layout throughout.

*Personality.* Americans worship their heroes, which is one reason readers of the *Sioux Falls* (S.D.) *Argus-Leader* enjoyed their newspaper's ten-page tab section on "Hubert H. Humphrey: South Dakota Remembers." The late senator from Minnesota was born in South Dakota. Because editors of the *Argus-Leader* knew that other newspapers and television obituary writers would mention that fact only in passing, they decided to highlight the life, career, and accomplishments of the man executive editor Larry Fuller described as "one of us." The special biographical section did not sell ad space. It was strictly a publication to serve the readers.

Supplement To THE CINCINNATI ENQUIRER

The *Cincinnati Enquirer* also capitalized on hero worship when it published its special section, ''Rose: 3,000,'' following Pete Rose's three-thousandth hit. As with the HHH special, there were no advertisements, although the section cost the *Enquirer* $12,000 in production costs alone. The cover of the special section carried a dramatic color photograph of Rose actually hitting number 3,000.

**Issues.** Some of the issues that would traditionally have been the exclusive property of editorial and opinion pages have now become ideal material for special sections. Editors find that serializing an important group of articles on a given issue tends to break the continuity. Putting all the material together in one pull-out section makes it more useful as a reference tool.

The *Camden* (N.J.) *Courier-Post* staff tackled what should be a complicated and controversial issue in any community, rating the performance of judges. Editors asked about one thousand lawyers to rate the judges in the area, and the *Courier-Post* ran an extensive daily series examining the municipal court system in its New Jersey region. A special section, ''A Report Card on the Judges,'' was published to highlight the series. The result? The New Jersey Supreme Court, the governor, and the state bar association have instituted reform studies because of the report.

**Photo essay.** A good photo story that is too important or extensive to include in a photo page may be planned as a special section. The *Topeka Capital-Journal* tried it successfully. Its staff photographer, Jim Richardson, was traveling around the state on assignment and kept taking photographs of the rural scenes he passed. Eventually enough good photographs were available for a special section on ''The rural life of Kansas,'' an ad-free tabloid where photos and white space provided easy-to-follow pages (next page, top).

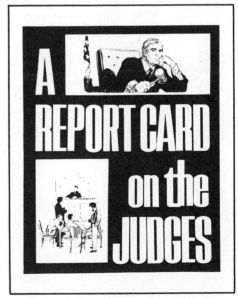

The cover of this special section may be described as a typographic front page, relying on type more than on illustrations.

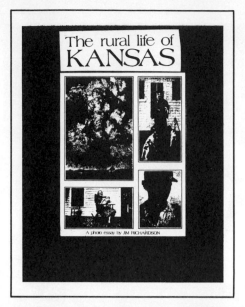

The rural life of
KANSAS

A photo essay by JIM RICHARDSON

Fort Lauderdale News

Thursday
March 2, 1978

**west**

Young Blind Skier
On Denver Special
Page 2

Plantation Retains
Controversial Zoning
Page 3

'Town Meeting' Called
In Coconut Creek
Page 14

Secret Influence
Swaying Voters?
WEST/Politics
Page 34

Davie Rodeo Gates
Swing Open Saturday
Page 36

Lakes Condo Residents
Want Traffic Lights
Page 37

Dedications Saturday
In Coral Springs
Page 40

Piper High Students
Seek Radio Funding
Page 41

Air Pioneer To Leather Artist
Page 16

*Regional coverage.* Special supplements have been used for regional coverage for many years. The *Orlando* (Fla.) *Sentinel* pioneered in this field twenty-five years ago, but it has most recently developed a vigorous campaign to amplify regionalization. Special tab sections, called "Little Sentinels," have been produced for the ten regions covered by the newspaper. Neighborhood news becomes the major target for the supplements. Everything from Little League baseball scores and junior high track results to local gossip and features are attractively packaged within a modern newsmagazine format. The front page of the "Little Sentinel" uses effective graphic display to tie in with the lead story; the logo is easy to read and is set in all lowercase type; and teasers leading to inside items accompany the logo.

Another example of a newspaper reaching out for neighborhood readership through a special supplement is the *Fort Lauderdale* (Fla.) *News*, which publishes a semiweekly tabloid section with a newsmagazine format. "West," as the section has been named, is geared toward a specific circulation area west of Fort Lauderdale, focusing on its people and activities. The section's front page capitalizes on a large photograph, usually in color, adequate use of white space, and a well-displayed index of inside stories. Highly localized coverage of one typical issue may include such stories as the following: Lake Condo residents want traffic lights; Piper High students seek radio funding; and a town meeting is called in Coconut Creek.

*Experimental sections.* Special sections are often published for experimental purposes and to test reader reaction and interest. At the *Louisville Courier Journal* and *Louisville Times*, editors have experimented with what they describe as the *tailored newspaper* concept. The brainchild of the staff, particularly Carol Sutton, the tailored newspaper is designed for readers who do not wish to read every section a newspaper carries every day. As the name implies, the tailored newspaper would accommodate the needs of its readers in a practical and economical manner: readers would buy only the section or sections of the newspaper of interest to them. The core section (or front-page section) would always be included, but anything else would be optional.

Ms. Sutton's initial exploration of this concept in Louisville started in 1978 with the publication of eight issues of the *Consumer Extra*, a four-column tabloid without ads, sold for 25 cents and devoted to major articles on such topics as "Repairing Winter's Damage," "Groceries Carry Clues to Unit Cost and Freshness," "Should Trees Be Topped?" "Reading Utility Meter Is Simple," and "Gardens for City Folks."

Regular features of the *Consumer Extra* include "Hand Around the House," "The Wary Buyer," "Waste Not . . .," "The Butcher," "$avvy: The Adventures of a Louisville Shopper," and "Mind your Money."

Ms. Sutton's staff was encouraged by the initial reaction to its publication, and she remarks:

Ideally, ultimately, we would have an entire "menu" of special interest publications to offer our readers along with the "general" or core newspaper, much as it is now. The experience of our circulation department in delivering *Time* and *Newsweek* magazines on newspaper routes and the development of computerized subscriber and non-subscriber lists convince us that we will one day be able to deliver the "tailored newspaper" on an individual subscriber basis. The general newspaper to one house, the general plus arts and consumer supplements to the next, the general plus business and super-sports to the next, etc.

Ms. Sutton also mentions the possibility of someday being able to press-deliver an individual newspaper for everyone in the subscriber's household.

At a time when conservation of resources has never been so vital, the tailored newspaper concept appears an attractive proposal. Practically speaking, why should readers who do not desire a sixteen-page section on home furnishings, real estate, or travel be forced to receive them as part of their Sunday newspaper?

On the other hand, many readers do not know exactly what they prefer to read until a catchy headline, photo, or graphic display attracts their attention. Impulse reading—like impulse shopping at the supermarket—often turns up some delicious discoveries which the tailored newspaper unfortunately may keep the reader from sampling. Perhaps this is the reason why Ms. Sutton and her staff concluded their experiment with *Consumer Extra* but postponed plans to make it a regular part of their content.

Double truck moves the reader horizontally through the large photograph, white space, and effective packaging.

Front page of the *Consumer Extra,* the nation's first attempt at the tailored newspaper, has a four-column format, a one-story front page, and an index. Simple design characterizes this easy-to-read tabloid.

## ADVERTISING SECTIONS

Long before the other special sections became fashionable, those made up of advertising had become profitable. Although advertising and promotional sections on cars, brides, gardening, and seasonal events are a source of revenue to the newspaper, editors often try to deal with them as little as possible, using free-lance workers to handle them instead of regular staff.

However, an advertising special section can be readable; it can also look attractive and give the reader consumer-oriented coverage.

When the *Providence Journal* published a fourteen-page full-size section on cars, "Automobiles '78," it combined photographs, illustrations, and feature copy to make the section more appealing. The front page carried a lead article on car inspection, written by the staff's automotive writer. It also included syndicated material of consumer interest to prospective car buyers. Every page of the section included at least one story related to buying, maintaining, selling, or driving cars.

The popularity of special sections as part of today's newspaper confirms the belief that what is only a bonus for the reader now—the icing on the cake—may soon become a daily part of the publication, another reason many nonreaders might want to buy a newspaper.

Photographs dominate this front page, but its contents do not reveal the fact that this is an advertising section on cars. Packaging, the size of the photographs, and the use of two articles attract readers to the page.

# 17 community newspapers

Community newspapers have always served an important purpose by concentrating their coverage on specific areas, localizing the news, and in the case of suburban newspapers within large metropolitan areas, creating a sense of community awareness.

Today's community newspaper continues to serve that purpose, but it faces a new challenge: the expanded coverage of daily newspapers into its territory. Alert community newspaper editors are examining their product closely, finding new ways to create a more readable newspaper and packaging content in more graphically appealing pages.

In Chapter 2 of this book we noted the trend of major city newspapers to expand into the suburbs, reaching out for readers who have moved to neighborhoods surrounding the metropolitan areas. Daily newspapers such as the *Miami Herald,* the *Seattle Times, Louisville Times,* and *Orlando Sentinel* prepare weekly editions specifically patterned to cater to the informational needs of readers in the suburbs and surrounding municipalities. Often, these newspapers have the resources and technical capabilities to publish high-quality editions that compete with the community newspaper.

However, the community newspaper editor who has earned the loyalty and trust of readers in his community will probably be able to continue publishing a weekly newspaper as long as he becomes aware of what the competition has to offer and attempts to improve his own publication. The community editor who lives in the community served by his newspaper is more apt to know the inner workings of that community than the editor of a suburban section who operates from the newsroom of the metropolitan newspaper. Although the large city daily can probably send an army of reporters and photographers to cover the suburb or small community, the editor of the community newspaper is more likely to get news tips from the president of the chamber of commerce or the school superintendent. It is also the community newspaper editor who probably serves as coach with the community's Little League team. And

one is more likely to find the community newspaper editor enjoying a backyard bar-
beque with a group from the local high school swimming team than his daily newspaper counterpart.

## EMPHASIS ON PEOPLE

Probably the best suggestion for community newspaper editors is to emphasize *coverage of people*. We have already explained that the staffers of community newspapers
usually have the loyalty and trust of people in their communities. The community
newspaper of the 1980s must center its coverage around people, making every effort to
profile the community's prominent citizens, as well as the less well known, the old,
and the young.

Geoffrey Edwards, general manager of the Journal Newspapers, a group of five
suburban newspapers in the Washington, D.C., area which publish twice weekly,
attributes the success of his community newspapers to the emphasis on people.

> The Journal Papers mirror on the community level what the metropolitan
> dailies cover on the national scale. Journal sports pages, for example, are
> as professional as the (Washington) *Post* and the (Washington) *Star*. The
> big difference is that the names are those of the boy next door and the
> neighbor across the street; people you know—the little leaguers, the high
> school football coach assessing his team's chances. . . . There is also
> appeal for businessmen who want to advertise in a medium that is efficient
> in reaching a particular audience.

Edwards introduced his newspapers to the highly competitive capital-area audience through a vigorous campaign emphasizing this same concept of human involvement. With the slogan, "At the Journal, Community Service is our day-to-day business," Edwards managed to build up the newspapers' circulation from 2,000 to
110,000 paid subscribers throughout the northern Virginia and Maryland suburbs.

These two suburban sections from the *Seattle
Times* exemplify the trend for daily newspapers
to increase coverage of the suburbs.

In Miami, suburban readers receive a copy of
"Neighbors" as part of their regular newspaper
fare when subscribing to the *Miami Herald*.
"Neighbors" covers the neighborhoods like a
blanket.

The *St. Paul Dispatch* treats its suburban
readers to this "Extra" edition, with large
photographs and thorough news-feature
coverage of the community.

It is true that not every community newspaper editor has to compete with the *Washington Post* and the *Washington Star,* but it is nonetheless important to use promotional campaigns to remind readers that the community newspaper knows the community best and served it long before other publications discovered the territory. The community newspaper that does not promote itself runs the risk of being taken for granted.

## GRAPHIC AWARENESS

Community newspaper editors are developing a sense of graphic awareness which becomes obvious at their national gatherings. More sessions in the program are being devoted to newspaper design. In many cases, editors seek assistance from consultants to redesign their newspapers and create more attractive pages.

Although many of the graphic problems faced by community newspapers are not too different from those presented in other chapters of this book, the community newspaper editor is also affected by a lack of skilled personnel to help him carry out the design aspects of production and by a lack of training in typography and design.

Many community newspaper editors play several roles: reporter, photographer, designer, paste-up artist, and bookkeeper. It is not unusual to meet an editor who confesses he is dissatisfied with the way his newspaper looks, but who also admits he does not have the time, nor the training, to improve upon it.

Basic training in typography and design is not difficult to obtain, either by reading material on the subject or by attending annual seminars and workshops. The time element is more difficult to overcome, especially when the editor and an assistant handle all production. This doubling of assignments is the reason for emphasizing simplicity of design, continuity, and order in format.

The community newspaper of the 1980s should look clean, orderly, and easy to read. It should also be easy to put together, which means that those in charge of production should follow a prescribed style for its design. Chapters 6 and 7 of this book deal with continuity and order (a basic criterion for all newspapers) and graphic strategies (techniques that can make the newspaper look more attractive).

Let us analyze some recently redesigned community newspapers, emphasizing the reason for the various changes.

### *Review* (Liverpool, N.Y.)

*Review* is a tabloid-sized community newspaper published in Liverpool, a Syracuse suburb. The editors wanted to emphasize people throughout but somehow kept such coverage off the front page. Instead, they usually carried a news story and a photograph on page one. The nameplate was overpowering, usually with a dark background color. The newspaper lacked continuity and order. The front page was often gray, the editorial page followed a vertical pattern, and there were at least forty different styles for standing sigs throughout the newspaper.

The first step in the redesign process was to seek a sense of identity for the newspaper. The editors decided that they wanted to emphasize a photo cover, but they also wanted to have the option of including copy when the news deserved front-page treatment. Two prototypes were created to allow for such flexibility. A different nameplate was designed, eliminating the word *The* and highlighting *Review* and listing the three small communities served by the newspaper. The front page was highlighted through an index called "pReview," in which the editors were given the option of using copy only or copy and miniature photographs of inside coverage.

A page from the old *Review* shows a generally gray front page, except for the splash of color provided by the nameplate.

The new design eliminates color and implements a magazine-cover effect with emphasis on people—in this case four young women from the community who received medals at a rowing competition. Notice the small "pReview" box. The nameplate is simple and provides a line of continuity.

Another front page from *Review* shows what the editors do when they wish to include copy. Notice the use of a photo for the "pReview" box.

The new editorial page emphasizes horizontal movement, art, and continuity through standing sigs.

### *Star-News* (North Syracuse, N.Y.)

The five-column *Star-News* also changed its design, although not as radically as *Review*. Although owned by the same company, Brown Newspapers, Inc., *Star-News* is more news-oriented, and the editors wanted to preserve a "newsy" look. The key element in redesigning this newspaper was to give the editors ways of organizing their content. For example, the newspaper was crowded with many short items, some of which had to go on page one. A new front-page section, "Top of the News," was designed to accommodate important but brief items. The entire newspaper is set in 9-point News, with 2 points of leading. Headlines are set in Mallard Light and Bold, with no italics.

Notice the old front page (marked with circles to indicate gray areas). The nameplate was too big and the page lacked graphic impact. The new front page uses a smaller but more distinctive nameplate. Notice "Top of the News," a regular feature placed anywhere on the page, depending on content.

### *Suffolk County News* (Long Island, N.Y.)

The editor and publisher of the *Suffolk County News* (opposite) wanted to continue the tradition of community-oriented journalism established by their newspaper in 1884, but they decided that it was time to give the newspaper a more contemporary look. They also wanted to maintain the graphic impact provided by photos, but at the same time retain at least three news items on the front page. The result was an attractive package of photos, copy, easy-to-read headlines, and graphic continuity.

## FORMAT

Today's community newspaper must establish its own identity through a specific format. Although most community newspapers are tabloids, there are variations in the number of columns and the design approaches used. The following newspapers illustrate various ways of reaching the reader graphically.

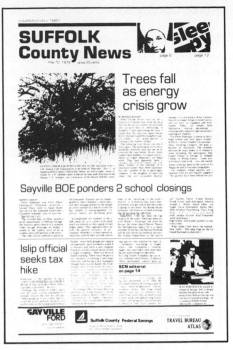

Compare the traditional front page of the *Suffolk County News* (left) and its new look on the right. The new typeface used for headlines is MicroStyle Light and Bold; notice how the nameplate has been modernized and also incorporates MicroStyle Bold into the design. In essence, this is a one-typeface newspaper for editorial content. The design is primarily horizontal. Notice that an inch of space at the bottom of the page has been devoted to advertising. The idea is to sell valuable ad space on the front page, but not for timely ads. Instead, the space is reserved for established businesses in the community, which buy the space for six-month periods at a time. Of course, the rate is much higher than for the same space inside the newspaper.

The *Suffolk County News* publishes a regional edition for residents west of its publication area. Notice how most of the design strategy here remains identical to that of the major publication, except for the impact of the word *west* set in Antique Olive and reversed for easy identification.

Notice how this county page from the *Suffolk County News* reflects the graphic continuity initiated on the nameplate. The bold line at the top indicates that this page is a different section. Horizontal movement prevails, as well as effective use of a headline on the side.

# North County News

Yorktowner Edition    February 14 - February 20, 1979    Volume 1 Number 44    20¢

Notice the simple nameplate and headlines in 48-point type to tell newsstand customers what's on the inside. The bottom of the page emphasizes a photograph and news story.

Notice how ads are perfectly blocked at the bottom of the page to create a structural design on an inside page based on one article.

## North County News (Yorktown, N.Y.)

Like many community newspapers, the *North County News* depends on newsstand sales for much of its business. The design of its front page accommodates impulse buyers by including four headlines above the fold, enticing readers to the inside stories.

Many community newspapers are developing special sections as part of their coverage. The *North County News* produces a well-designed section entitled, "North County Views," emphasizing features on travel, personality profiles, cooking tips, and a splendid two-page spread called "Around Town," with calendar information about gatherings and events, library news, the arts, theater, and music.

This sports page is typical of what a clean and attractive page can do to interest the reader. Notice the horizontal emphasis, effective placement of photos, and good use of white space.

This double truck emphasizes calendar items. Notice the effective use of wide columns, photographs, and breakers to create a pleasant design.

The front page of this section has a cover photograph and an index (bottom) to inside content.

## City/East (Rochester, N.Y.)

*City/East* is typical of the community newspaper that emphasizes a feature exclusively on its front page. Inside pages take care of news content. A highlight of this publication is its calendar pages, providing reader service through very detailed accounts of what is going on in the community.

Notice the four-column format, use of one feature story on the page, clean nameplate, and effective use of nameplate space for index.

The inside calendar page from *City/East* makes effective use of bold and medium type for contrast. Lines help divide content and guide readers through columns of information.

This front page has an illustration to entice readers to an inside page story emphasizing "a close encounter with spiritualism." Notice the use of art and type.

## The Examiner (Buffalo, N.Y.)

The newsmagazine format has been adopted by many community newspapers to emphasize color, illustrations, and/or a photograph on the front page, reserving inside pages for news. *The Examiner* (shown at right, top and bottom) uses such a format effectively.

Packaging their newspapers in a more attractive manner has become a challenge for many community newspaper editors. As staffs continue to make better use of electronic editing, more time becomes available for the designing aspects of production. The result should be easier-to-read and more-pleasant-to-look-at community newspapers everywhere.

This is how editors of the *Examiner* developed their cover story on an inside page, using an identical illustration to establish quick identification for the reader.

## 18
## special uses of the newspaper format

The newspaper format is familiar to most readers. It is also convenient, easy to handle, and when newsprint is used, economical. Thus the format is desirable for publication of house organs, newsletters, and even brochures.

Most of the newspapers used as illustrations in this chapter are variations of the tabloid format, and in many cases the front page resembles that of a weekly newspaper, with emphasis on copy and photos, a dominant nameplate, and sometimes (for newspapers with more than twelve pages) an index box.

The designer of a house organ or newsletter that appears every month with news of a specific industry, hospital, or plant will want to include copy on the front page but also to create graphic impact through photographs, preferably of the people most familiar to readers of the publication.

### AN ANALYSIS OF *TODAY*

*Today* is a four-column tabloid published for employees and retirees of Weyerhaeuser Company, with headquarters in Tacoma, Washington. Like many other house organs, *Today* carries mostly personality profiles of company personnel, speeches, long columns of brief news about people, committee reports, and business news in general.

When designer Frank Ariss, of Minneapolis, was hired to redesign *Today*, he found an unorganized publication that used five narrow columns, very small photographs, and long masses of gray matter.

Initially he encouraged the staff to switch to a four-column format, to increase the size of photographs and vary the sizes throughout the publication, to crop photographs more dramatically, and to use the front page economically by including an index at the top of the page. The result is evident in the following examples.

Before the redesign, the front page of *Today* used a five-column format, with small photographs spread all over. The nameplate was almost invisible, and the page had more emphasis below the fold than above.

Designer Frank Ariss conceived this new front page with four wider columns, a photographic index directly below the nameplate, and a full box at the top of the page which includes nameplate, folio lines, and index. Notice the masthead information on this front page.

An important consideration in redesigning *Today* was the change to Helvetica Medium as a primary typeface. Notice also that Ariss uses Helvetica for the nameplate and standing sigs, giving the publication its typographic continuity and order.

Ideally, the design of a company newspaper should combine attractive pages with sound journalistic practices. If it is going to look like a newspaper, then it should read like one.

Ariss designed a page of news based on a dominant story at the top, displayed horizontally. At the bottom of the page he allowed space for the inevitable two- and three-paragraph items that are an essential part of this type of publication.

Horizontal and vertical emphasis blend nicely in this news page. Notice the small headlines.

Personality profiles abound in industry newspapers. Unfortunately, they are usually difficult to read, especially when a question and answer format is followed. Ariss designed a special style for personality profiles, placing the question on the left and the answer spread horizontally on the right, with lines dividing the questions.

The most economical page in Ariss' design of *Today* is definitely the last, which includes the following sections: "Briefly," "Coming Up," "Next Issue," and "Continued" (for jumps).

Notice the dramatic cropping for the photograph at the top, effective placement of bold questions on the left, and answers on the right. White space provides relief for the reader.

## SPECIFICATIONS

The success of any design is ultimately based on how well it can be carried out from issue to issue. A graphic style sheet can help maintain continuity. The following specifications were provided by Ariss to the staff of *Today*:

Page size:   11 inches × 17 inches
Printing area size:   $9^{13}/_{16}$ inches × 15⅞ inches
Number of columns per page:   each column 14 picas wide with 1 pica separating columns
Column widths:   1 column equals 14 picas, 2 columns equal 29 picas
Full-column depth:   115 units deep (15⅞ inches)
Basic depth module:   10 points equals 1 unit
News text setting:   Helvetica regular 9 points on 10 points body justified to 14 picas width
Text character count:   42 characters per line (1 column wide), 290 characters per approximate inch (1 column wide)
Typewritten count:   1 page of copy 6½ inches wide × 20 elite lines deep equals approximately 4 inches of set type.
Paragraph breaks:   1 unit/no indent
Headline settings:   Helvetica Bold solid, flush left set at 12/18/24/36 points
Space between elements:   2 units

Bylines/credits: Helvetica Bold 9 points on 10 points, flush left

Photo captions: Helvetica Bold 9 points on 10 point body justified to 14 picas width

Head grid line position: All heads/first line/top of caps flush with top grid line

Text grid line position: All text/first line/base of "x" height flush with bottom grid line

Photo grid sizes: All photos determined in picas wide and units deep with inch measurements equivalent

## OTHER PUBLICATIONS

Not all house organs and newsletters use newsprint. Like some others, the *Reda News*, the monthly publication of TRW Pump Division of Bartlesville, Oklahoma, uses a glossy paper for its front and back pages and heavy colored paper stock for the inside pages.

The *Reda News* is designed as a tabloid newspaper. Its front page highlights inside content over the nameplate and includes a column of news briefs on the right. Headlines are bold and small, and body type is sans serif.

For inside pages, the *Reda News* uses large initial letters instead of headline breakers, as illustrated below:

Smaller sizes are functional for some house organs. The *Squealer*, a bimonthly newsletter published by the Colony Square Hotel of Atlanta, Georgia, is printed on a page 10½ inches deep by 8¼ inches wide.

Four pages long, the *Squealer* uses its front page for a single story and photograph. The nameplate includes the hotel's seal with readable type. Pages two and three are devoted to news and short items, and page four is a feature page.

Color, special photographic effects, and packaging can all be part of a newsletter's design. When the Liverpool (New York) Central School District decided to publish a newsletter to indicate what educational programs were available, it used such a combination of elements (next page, top left).

The front page of *School Bell* emphasizes color at top (for the nameplate and as tint on upper portion of the page). Notice how the background was dropped for the top photograph. The rest of the page conforms to packaging strategies for photographs.

The front page depends on the nameplate for impact. Notice the illustration at far left, showing continuity of the vertically placed nameplate on the double truck.

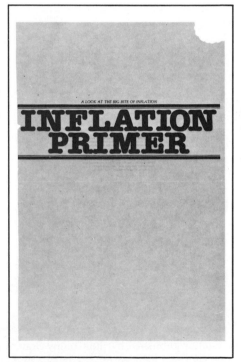

Notice the impact of reverse on this page, with the words "on the move" set in white type against a black background. The front page is dominated by a story of the company's growth. The nameplate is simple, packaged as part of the entire page.

The bite at the upper right-hand corner is no accident. The entire section borrows the design gimmick from a key word in its content, "the big bite of inflation."

Newsletters and in-house publications can afford to experiment with typography and design more freely than daily or weekly newspapers, mainly because there is more time between issues. Notice, for example, the issue of *Focus* (published for Anheuser-Busch St. Louis employees) shown at left. The nameplate is placed vertically, a practice that we have generally not recommended in this book. Here, however, the entire page is based on the nameplate as a Center of Visual Impact. The single news story on the page is set in ragged right style, the headline is small, and white space is used generously. Color also helps make this small page attractive.

When photographs are not available, type becomes a target spot on the page, as illustrated by the interesting treatment shown in the page opposite from *Western World*, the publication of AT&T Long Lines, San Francisco.

Creativity in designing a newsletter or house organ is always appreciated by readers. When the staff of the *Reda News* included a special section on what it described as "a look at the big bite of inflation: an inflation primer," it designed the twenty-page section complete with an actual bite on the upper right-hand corner.

The publications shown in this chapter combine the simplicity characteristic of well-designed newspapers with the creativity that attracts readers and sets publications apart.

## the minneapolis tribune: case study of a newspaper's redesign

To newspaper readers, Monday, April 5, 1971 was a typical news day, dominated by stories dealing with what a reporter described as the "long and melancholy drama of the Vietnam War."

To students of newspaper typography and design, however, that date has greater historical significance as the day when the *Minneapolis Tribune* staff accomplished a complete typographical redesign of the newspaper, breaking a 104-year tradition of narrow columns and static makeup.

To the editors and staff of the *Tribune*, particularly Bower Hawthorne, who was the vice-president and editor, and Wallace Allen, who was managing editor, April 5, 1971 marked the end of four years of discussing, planning, experimenting, and phasing in a new design.

The new design of the *Tribune* changed more than the look of a specific large daily. At a more significant level, it also accomplished the following:

1. It became a visual testimony of what attractive newspapers can do to keep and lure readers, while offering advertisers a more appealing vehicle for their products.
2. It established a working relationship between contemporary graphics and computer technology.
3. It demonstrated the importance of establishing corporate identity for newspapers.
4. It set the pace for greater visual awareness on the part of newspaper editors. The 1970s was a decade of progress for newspaper typography and design, and much of the credit must go to the *Tribune* for showing that a bold, precise, clean, and contemporary look was possible for newspapers.

## HISTORICAL PERSPECTIVE

Typographically, the *Tribune* followed the makeup trends of the times. In fact, the newspaper can hardly be described as an innovator in design between the period from 1867 to 1971. The first issue of what was then called the *Minneapolis Daily Tribune* was published May 25, 1867, and consisted of a nine-column format for its front page, three columns of which were used for advertising. By 1927 the newspaper's name had changed to the *Minneapolis Morning Tribune* and the format included eight columns. Banner headlines and photographs gave the front page a more interesting appearance. Column rules remained, as well as staggered headlines.

In 1969 the *Minneapolis Tribune* continued to use an eight-column format but dropped column rules, giving the page a more open appearance. Bolder headlines, photographs, boxes, and more white space made the front page look busy but appealing. Column rules were returned to the *Tribune's* front page in 1970, along with a more vertical emphasis. The presence of a well-designed "News Digest, Index, and Almanac" section horizontally placed at the bottom of the front page anticipated the promise of a more contemporary look.

An observer of the *Tribune's* design through the years would have found it difficult to predict that this newspaper would radically depart from traditional newspaper appearance—but then, as we shall see later in this chapter, such wasn't the intent of the editors when they first set out to change just the nameplate.

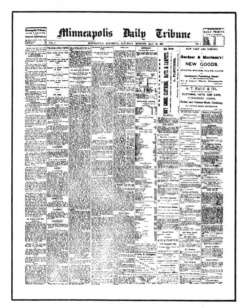

Pages representing a 103-year span in the history of the *Minneapolis Tribune* (above and right) illustrate the design trends of the times but did not indicate that this particular newspaper would depart so radically from its tradition.

## IN THE BEGINNING

January 3, 1967

Memorandum:

I talked for more than an hour today with Frank Ariss, a visiting professor of graphic and industrial design at the Minneapolis School of Art. . . .

Ariss is much interested in looking at the Tribune and wanted to know in some detail our thinking and philosophy about the paper.

He seemed to grasp at once what we are looking for—an updating and brightening without destroying the basic format or tradition.

He is going to give some thought to the nameplate design. . . .

Wally Allen

This memorandum from editor Allen set everything in motion at the *Tribune*, but it wasn't easy to convince everyone in authority at the newspaper. First, Allen's contacting of Frank Ariss, an Englishman with a flair for contemporary artistic design, was questionable. "What does he know?" many asked. Allen answered,

But that is precisely what we're trying to do, to hire help from somebody who would not be prejudiced by newspaper tradition, or affected by habit. Newspaper formats are tried and true—changes come about slowly. . . . It is a matter of following the "we've-always-done-it-that-way syndrome." So we asked, "Why do we have to do it that way?"

And they didn't. The editors of the *Tribune* gave Frank Ariss a free hand to experiment. At first, he was supposed to design a new nameplate for the newspaper, but he soon found out that he could not redesign the nameplate alone; the entire newspaper had to be redesigned if it was to be compatible with the nameplate. But more important, if the newspaper was going to be completely redesigned, the editors wanted it to be compatible with the new technology—cold type, electronic editing, pagination.

Ariss plunged into the redesign project full time, talking to editors, staff members, press room personnel, composing room people, and readers in the community. Allen said,

It became a case of our editors pulling Ariss back and of his pushing us forward. He wanted to get us into the 20th Century. So he pulled us forward, we pulled him back and ended up in the middle. Tradition can't be ignored and we wanted to make changes in the light of the still significant past.

But we knew the moment we started to effect design changes that design is extremely important to today's newspaper—newspapers simply can't continue to be dull.

Frank Ariss made sure that at least the *Minneapolis Tribune* would not look dull.


## ARISS: A DESIGNER LOOKS AT A NEWSPAPER

Ariss never went to journalism school, but he claims to have had a long love affair with newspapers. He sees newspapers as deserving of the same craftsmanship and corporate identity as other essential products in the business market. Creating a newspaper that illustrated precision through craftsmanship and that had a unique corporate identity became Ariss' primary concern when he began redesigning the *Tribune*.

Ariss says he fails to understand why so many American newspapers have survived without any drastic changes in their typography and design in the last hundred years. "Why should newspapers hide behind Victorian crinoline?" he asks.

Typographically, Ariss feels that too many American newspapers have been involved in an endless love affair with the Bodoni typeface, the use of which he condemns as an anachronism:

> Bodoni Bold is the beloved typeface of American newspapers. Some catalogs for old machines used Bodoni Bold, pages from very old books used Bodoni. It was around before George Washington was born, before the French Revolution took place or before Beethoven wrote his first symphony. Yet, many American newspapers used that very same typeface to tell readers that man had landed on the moon. It is likely that it will be used to announce the cure for cancer or other future developments.

Although many newspaper editors may respond to this statement by asking why they should change a good thing, Ariss doesn't think that Bodoni is a readable typeface, or at least not as readable as Helvetica, the typeface he used throughout the new *Tribune*. "Helvetica," Ariss says, "is a typeface of the twentieth century. It is readable, economical and represents today."

In his redesign of the *Tribune*, Ariss used Helvetica for the nameplate as well as for display. "There is nothing wrong with a nameplate that uses the same type as the rest of the publication."

By the time Ariss completed the design of the *Tribune* he had become an outspoken supporter of a new look for American newspapers, with some strong opinions on the subject:

1. Newspapers are not hurt by television but by their deplorable design.
2. Do away with Bodoni type—it doesn't fit into computer-style operations and sets the newspaper back a couple of centuries.
3. Don't use italics—they are difficult to handle and tough to read.
4. Use Helvetica or a sans serif typeface. Helvetica is larger, nicer and more economical, as well as easier on the eyes.
5. Promote the product—give it a sense of corporate identity.
6. Incorporate fewer—but more consistent—headline styles.
7. Departmentalize. Each section front page should be treated as the front page.
8. On ad positioning: block them.
9. Inside pages should be done with the same visual impact and clarity as page one.
10. On the new technology: it will force more readable design and will give designer greater freedom of experimentation with type.

More specific applications of Ariss' theories will become obvious as we analyze a step-by-step sequence of how the *Tribune* staff planned, executed, and implemented his design.


## THE REDESIGN


There were five major elements involved in the redesign of the *Tribune*.

1. A new nameplate and logotype were substituted for the nineteenth-century nameplate.

Before the redesign, the *Tribune* used a standard full-width nameplate, with Old English type for the name of the newspaper and a line of small all caps for the folio line and postal rate information.

Ariss created a three-dimensional shape for the new nameplate, emphasizing the

# The Minneapolis Tribune  TUESDAY

Vol. CIV—No. 184    Copyright 1970 Minneapolis Star and Tribune Company    MINNEAPOLIS, MINN., TUESDAY, NOVEMBER 24, 1970    ★    Price 10¢

This is the way the *Tribune*'s nameplate looked before redesign.

**Minneapolis Tribune**

| Monday<br>April 5<br>1971 | 3<br>Sections<br>15¢ Single copy | Volume CIV<br>Number 316<br><br>S.<br>Copyright<br>1971<br>Minneapolis Star and<br>Tribune Company |

The new logo used by the *Tribune* is a symbol of corporate identity that can be seen on the nameplate, through every inside section, and on the newspaper's vehicles, offices, and stationery.

word *Tribune* in Helvetica Bold and incorporating a logotype, which would be used throughout the newspaper as well as in editorial offices and on company vehicles, as a means of corporate identity.

The new symbol can be viewed in two perspectives—as an open newspaper in the hands of a reader or as a web of newsprint flying through a press. It can also be interpreted as a white checkmark on a black background. To readers of the *Tribune* is has become a familiar symbol, one that means the *Minneapolis Tribune* at a glance.

To avoid surprising the readers, editors phased in the new design, starting with the editorial page a month before the entire newspaper converted.

In designing the new nameplate Ariss repeated the three-dimensional concept. He used a thin line for the name of the newspaper but decided on a heavier line for folio lines, section headings, and other pertinent information. The same three-dimensional design is carried throughout the newspaper for section openers, for example, sports, business, and so on.

2. Helvetica is used for all headlines; Helvetica type (Helvetica Roman Medium) in sizes from 14-point to 72-point is followed consistently throughout.

No italics are used—instead, Helvetica Bold is used for contrast. The *Tribune* used Vogue and Futura before the redesign. Although Helvetica is used exclusively, editors retain freedom to use other typefaces for so-called "custom" layouts of special sections or to create a typographic mood. In terms of style, caps and lower case are used throughout, and headlines are flush left without exception.

The emphasis is on smaller-than-usual heads but also on more lines per headline. Four- and five-line headlines are common in the redesign, as well as uneven lines. Editor Allen admits that his headline writers are not slaves to fitting headline counts, although the *Tribune*'s current headline schedule reminds them to write headlines slightly short of the maximum count; multicolumn headlines should not have more than an inch of air at the right ends of lines.

3. Standardization of size of body type (9 point on 9½-point slug) and two pica widths (1 column and 2 column) eliminate what some editors refer to as "freak composition" (use of multipica or multicolumn measurements without any standardization). The only exception to this style is editorials, which are set 10 on 11 and 1½-column measure.

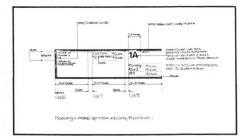

Notice the precision with which this sketch has been drawn, showing the number of points, picas, and spaces.

One of the interesting and most economical aspects of setting all body type in 9 point is that all type can be set by computer in one operation for each piece of copy, including byline, dateline, jumpline, and the spacing between paragraphs.

With the new style came practical changes in the way type was set. For example, hand-leading was eliminated. White space is left at the bottom of a column, if it turns out that way, instead of leading or using a filler.

Because Ariss conceived an all-flush-left newspaper, body copy is not indented and all other elements, such as bylines, photo credits, cutlines, and of course, headlines, are flush left.

4. A grid establishes a basis for computerized makeup. The grid includes precise vertical and horizontal measurement for every element on a page.

Here's how the grid works. The *Tribune* page is divided by an imaginary grid. Horizontally, it is divided into eight columns each 10.6 picas wide. Vertically, it is divided into 167 units, each 9½ points deep (the depth of the slug on which body type is set).

All elements on the page—logotypes, headlines, photographs—are made to a depth (in points) that is divisible by 9½. The page is made up on the grid. As the in-house style sheet for makeup personnel explains, the bottom of each line of type, the bottom of each photograph, etc., falls on one of the imaginary 9½-point unit lines.

Essentially, what the grid system does is to create very precise vertical and horizontal measurements for every element on a page, facilitating composition and giving the page designer a sense of organization from which to unify the visual contents.

5. Emphasis from left to right dominates.

Ariss conceived a front page which would display its most important story in the upper left-hand corner, prompting one of the *Tribune* editors to comment that "not only does the Tribune's new design reflect contemporary graphics, but a time-honored,

The *Tribune* adopted Helvetica Medium and Bold for its headlines. Part of the redesign included new headline schedules, as indicated by illustrations above.

The lead story appears on the upper left-hand section of this front page. Notice that other important stories appear directly below but also on the left-hand side of the page. At least one story on page one uses ragged right type, in this case a story at the bottom of the page.

The inside front section for local news follows the same principle. Notice the three-dimensional design for the columnist's standing sig and the display ads at the bottom.

venerable principle of journalism—dominant news on the right—has been eliminated.''

Ariss reasoned that it is natural to read horizontally from left to right, and so the most important news story is now on the left-hand side of the front page, a principle which is followed consistently throughout the inside section openers as well.

## TRIAL AND ERROR

Redesigning any newspaper involves various stages of experimentation. Initially, the designer and the editors discuss what they want the newspaper to be like. But they also want to arrive at a working design that will be economical, will be practical, and will endure beyond the fads of the day.

When Allen and Ariss first met to discuss the redesign of the *Tribune* they were concerned with change, but they wanted an intelligent and well-planned redesign that could be improved upon for a number of years.

One of Ariss' first prototypes (the term used to describe a practice run of a design style, usually set in type and pasted up and often printed) shows that some of his ideas remained in the final design. It also illustrates that his most daring design possibilities were too overpowering for acceptance by the *Tribune*'s editorial staff.

On the left is the front page of the *Tribune*, February 27, 1969, as it was published that day: eight columns, no column rules, a combination of Vogue and Futura headlines, and an old nameplate. At right, the prototype prepared by Ariss shows a larger CVI created by a photograph of a Vietnamese family escaping from an attacked village. The lead headline has moved to the left, and other stories are displayed under very small headlines. The nameplate has been switched to a sans serif typeface, but Ariss has already implemented a three-dimensional design for the nameplate and folio. More startling, however, is Ariss' dramatic concept for the index, in which he brings in his art background to the front page. This idea was apparently discarded in the final redesign.

It was back to the drawing board for Ariss, who conceived yet another prototype for the June 1, 1970, edition.

Here we have the same prototype, but revised, apparently at the request of the editors, who liked most of what they saw but who wanted Ariss to "lighten up" the index box with all the illustrations. But even after the illustrations were turned from black to gray, the idea was completely discarded as too overpowering for the front page.

This prototype brings Ariss and the *Tribune* closer to the final redesign. The lead story is still in the upper left position. The nameplate has been finalized, with the new logo now in position. The word *Minneapolis* is small, emphasizing *Tribune,* and *Minnesota* has been dropped from the nameplate. In this prototype Ariss is experimenting without the use of the three-dimensional nameplate design that would eventually be adopted. This page tends to be more gray than his previous prototypes, probably a reaction to the editors' dislike of his overpowering index in the earlier ones. The index at the bottom of the page is simple, elegant, and easy to read. It would remain as a feature of the new design. Notice the one- and two-column measurements as opposed to a standard six-column format.

## PHASING IN THE NEW DESIGN

Once the final prototype was accepted, reviewed, and ready for implementation, the next step was for the editors to decide how to put the design into operation.

The *Tribune* editors first set out to explain the redesign concept and to show sample pages to key personnel in production control, composing, advertising, circulation, promotion, and the news and editorial departments. All who saw the presentation expressed approval of the proposed new design, and there was an almost unanimous vote in favor of making the change "all at once."

Newspapers that undergo drastic graphic changes have the option of changing all at once, which is simple for news and composing departments and more advantageous for promotional purposes and advertising sales. However, many newspapers prefer to phase in the changes, to avoid taking the reader by surprise. Established newspapers, such as the *Tribune,* with no immediate danger of losing readers, prefer to phase in the change a bit at a time.

As one *Tribune* executive said, "The danger of an all-at-once change-over would be the unfavorable shock to readers. The presumed advantage of a phased change-over would be that changes could be made so gradually (except the change of nameplate) that readers would not be upset."

As expected, the *Tribune* editors decided to phase in the changes slowly, a process which required organization, a continuous schedule of communication among personnel, and a gradual development of production tasks leading to the target day, April 5, 1971, when there would be a new *Tribune*.

A series of memoranda from Allen to his staff tells the story of the many details that led to the final redesign. The editors decided to start changing the style of the newspaper from the back to the front. "We reached one point, in the middle of the phasing-in process, when the paper looked sort of confusing, with the women's pages in the new, but the rest of the newspaper in the old format. It was a necessary evil and we had to live with it," Allen said.

The phasing-in memos from Allen became a vital tool for all that had anything to do with the *Minneapolis Tribune* during the period from March 1 to April 5, 1971:

*Phasing-in Memo No. 1*

Next Monday, March 8, is the date for the first major changes in phasing in the *Tribune* redesign. We should do these things:

1. Set all type nut indent and drop column rules.
2. Start using more 2-column type throughout the paper.
3. Phase out the women's cover, making Page 1B the local page.
4. Editorial page should plan to go to its new format on this day.

*Phasing-in Memo No. 2*

The 6-column present local page will be dropped as such. Four columns of it or more will go into Page 2B. . . .

The Women's pages will appear near the middle of the second section. Advertising layout will try to provide a good newshole on the first page, on which we may put fashion layouts or whatever we may have. Women's section will be labeled as "Family." . . .

*Phasing-in Memo No. 3*

Next step: Sunday, March 14, we will go to 1 column nut and 2 column nut indent type on Page IC, dropping the six column format. We've asked for conversion of the ad on the page to fit the new measure.

*Phasing-in Memo No. 4*

This week we are phasing out, as completely as possible, Futura, condensed and italic headline type. We are also aiming for as close to 50-50 balance between one-column and two-column as is reasonable.

Next week we should use the newly designed logos on the Family section (old Women and Society), Home and Recreation Section, Arts Section and TV Week.

Next Monday we will use the new logo on the second section, business and sports covers daily.

Also Monday, go to new cutline style throughout the Tribune.

*Phasing-in Memo No. 5*

Monday March 29:
Drop the indent paragraph.
Use new style for spacing.
Use new byline style.
Use new dateline style.
Use new jumpline style.
Complete installation of all new standing heads.

Note: the newspaper is using two names for this phasing-in period. It is *The Minneapolis Tribune* old style and the *Minneapolis Tribune* new style.

*Phasing-in Memo No. 6*

Major changes for April 5:

Use new logo on Page 1A.
Use Helvetica type throughout the paper.
Complete transition to flush left style, with play on left covers.
Use new page folios.

Also, there is no rigid headline style. We should use the type as it is needed to tell the story. If three lines of 30-point in one column don't do it, then go to four or five, for instance.

*Phasing-in Memo No. 7 AND LAST*

Only one thing left to do: pick up the new logos on Page 1A, 1B and 1C this Sunday.

Eureka!

## APRIL 5, 1971

If there was any fanfare heralding implementation of a new look for the *Tribune,* it certainly was kept within the confines of the newspaper's plant at 425 Portland Avenue. The new *Tribune* emerged as a quiet but determined winner. On that particular

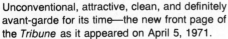

Unconventional, attractive, clean, and definitely avant-garde for its time—the new front page of the *Tribune* as it appeared on April 5, 1971.

A section opener on the first day of the new design displays a photo essay, a news analysis, and three vertical ads.

day, emphasis was heavier on copy than photos for page one, but the designers managed to incorporate special treatment for a feature story about the feelings of freshmen in college and for the bottom-of-the-page inside news digest, index, and almanac.

The front page of the *Tribune* would never again look dull. For all practical purposes it must have definitely looked avant-garde and out of step with its counterparts throughout the country.

## AUDIENCE REACTION

The ultimate test of a newspaper redesign is its acceptance by readers. In the case of the *Tribune,* in which the design and typographic changes had radically altered the way that newspaper had looked for many years, editors wanted to make sure that their readers appreciated and accepted the transformation.

By mid-June 1971, two months after the first redesigned edition was published, a survey of fifty *Minneapolis Tribune* readers gave strong hints that the Tribune audience was settling down with the modernized design and liking it. The survey showed that readers were less conscious of the redesign than they had been in an earlier sampling. There was a 13 percent gain in readers who said the changes had been an improvement.

> Readers voiced fewer objections to the type. More found the format easier to read. There was less objection to not being able to find items they want to read, greater appreciation of the cleaner style, fewer problems in identifying sections, and a decided swing toward preferring the new style.

If reader reaction to the redesign was favorable, that of newspaper professionals was above expectations. The *Tribune* won first place in the category of largest newspaper in the annual typography and art design contest sponsored by Inland Daily Press Association and Northwestern University's Medill School of Journalism, where the redesign was described as "the one significant change that's been made in newspaper design this past season."

The *Tribune's* design change was described as trend-setting and unique:

> Rather than with art or esthetics or through trickiness of design, addition of color, or simply a change of nameplate, the Minneapolis people designed their paper with rationale and logic. The design of the newspaper makes sense and can be explained easily, whereas the design of most newspapers is based primarily on tradition.

## THE REDESIGN EVOLVES

Newspaper designers know that a good style is one that can constantly evolve from within its framework—adapting to new technological advances and practical day-to-day production needs. Such has been the case in Minneapolis. Almost ten years after their redesign project, the newspaper's editors continue to experiment and to change.

Internal correspondence among editors shows the constant updating:

> We've done well in reducing our jumps. We've increased our story count and we've made a good stab at getting some lightness onto the page.
>
> But we need to do more.

Notice how the design has evolved, starting from the basic framework by Ariss. In this front page a photo creates a dominant CVI. The lead story continues to be on the left, but the columns are wider than in the original design. The bottom of the page is dominated by a feature, with ragged right type.

Photos dominate this local news page, but organization of content prevails through well-designed and uniform standing heads.

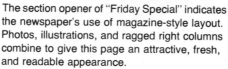

The section opener of "Friday Special" indicates the newspaper's use of magazine-style layout. Photos, illustrations, and ragged right columns combine to give this page an attractive, fresh, and readable appearance.

The basic design concept is carried throughout—including the newspaper's television supplement.

Lightness and brightness at the top of the page is still a problem. We need a story above the fold that will grab the reader right off the bat, but the ideal sort is the human interest reader.

And, again, consider the freshness of all the news as it develops during the night. Very often a local news story may be better for the page than an old and dull foreign story. . . .

The story of the *Tribune's* redesign is by no means typical. It involved a great deal more planning and experimenting than many newspapers have the resources or the time to accomplish. What is typical, however, is the editors' concern with upgrading the visual quality of their newspaper.

## TIPS FOR THE DO-IT-YOURSELF REDESIGNER

The word *redesign* sounds busy. It brings to mind great changes, difficult adjustments, radical departures from the comfortable routines we all establish. It is often better to think of *redesign* as a flexible term. In some newspapers, it means total and absolute change. In others, it means a slow process that begins with a new typeface or a redesigned nameplate and standing sigs.

Redesigning a newspaper may not require hiring an outside consultant. Many small newspapers have incorporated effective visual changes within their format by allowing their own staff to develop such changes. But whether the change involves a nameplate or an entire format, redesigning is not easy.

It involves trial and error, and the risk of displeasing some of the readership—and sometimes even the publisher of the newspaper.

The following criteria should help editors who may be thinking about the visual presentation of their newspapers:

1. Editors must be convinced that their newspaper needs a graphic uplift before beginning the redesign process.

2. Once the editors know that change is needed, they should also be willing to accept new ideas—even when those new ideas depart radically from "the way we've always done it."

3. Deciding on a new format should be part of a compromise between esthetics and practicality. If it looks good, but the staff will not be able to execute it easily from day to day or week to week, then it is not a practical format. Such considerations as available staff, time limitations, and equipment capability are most important.

4. A new format and design should be compatible with the lifestyle of the reader in the newspaper's community. What may work for a newspaper in northern Texas may prove disastrous in central New York, for example. In fact, a designer's top consideration should be to find ways in which her design reflects and extends the personality of a locale and its people.

5. The new format should be compatible with the new technological advances that are quickly spreading to every newsroom and affecting production.

6. Changes in format are likely to affect the placement and impact of advertisements. The advertising department must be made a part of the redesign project, and advertisers must be brought in before a new format is adopted.

7. Redesigning the newspaper is a good exercise in evaluating content, too. It is a good time to upgrade content, to make the newspaper relevant and contemporary in the way it reads as well as in the way it looks.

8. Consult many newspapers before arriving at a final prototype for your publication. See what other editors, preferably within your league, are doing. Borrow ideas, adapt them, and change them to suit your needs.

9. Dare to be different. Make your newspaper unique in its visual presentation, even if it means defying tradition.

10. Promote your redesign strategy. Prepare readers for the new look and advertise your newspaper.

Earlier in this chapter we mentioned the need for editors to become introspective about the visual quality of their newspaper. The material presented throughout this book has been aimed at stimulating such introspection and at offering sufficient practical applications of design theory to allow willing editors to advance from introspection to execution.

## 20
## design and the new technology

Chapter 2 of this book discussed three challenges facing newspaper editors in America. A fourth challenge should be added: adapting to the rapidly developing new technology of newspaper production and making every attempt to utilize the many technological developments of the last several years to their full potential.

Page design has directly or indirectly been affected by most, if not all, the changes brought about by automation of editorial and composition processes. The introduction of Video Display Terminals to American newsrooms revolutionized production because it made each reporter more aware of such tasks as typographic style, column width, leading, and all the various details that used to lie in the domain of makeup editors and typesetters. Today's reporter is his own typesetter, and for all practical purposes, develops a strong link with the page designer. But at the same time, everyone involved in newspaper production today has also embraced the field of computer science.

Jeffrey R. Parnau, in a *Folio* magazine article ("Printing: The new technology comes of age," February 1980), writes that the editor of the future will be useless without a healthy knowledge of computer programming. "The editor who is comfortable in front of a terminal will be far more valuable than the journalism graduate who skipped the electronics course," Parnau writes. "The successful publishing employee will have the equivalent of two professions."

It is difficult to separate cold type from the electronic revolution taking place in newspapers. For more than 150 years newspapers were produced with such mechanical devices as the linotype machine (see Chapter 5). With the emergence and widespread utilization of cold type and the elimination of hot type, newspaper editors had found a fast, efficient, and simple procedure for reproducing type, photographs, and illustrations. Anything that can be photographed can be easily and rapidly placed on the page. The design possibilities now are limitless, and typefaces in all styles are available. Moreover, it is just as easy to use many sizes and widths of type as only one or two. The word *art* has a different meaning—it no longer refers to photographs—and many newspapers hire art directors.

In the typical American newspaper, graphics-oriented editors work hand in hand with professionally trained designers as they conceive meaningful and attractive ways to present the news of the day. Computer-assisted production makes their work easier by allowing the positioning of copy and headlines to be totally planned and executed from the newsroom, avoiding much of the guessing and improvisation that traditionally has taken place in the "back shop" of the newspaper.

During the mid-1970s, at the height of the electronic revolution in the newsroom, Joseph M. Ungaro, vice-president and executive editor of the Westchester Rockland Newspapers, Inc., announced that the culminating point of this revolution would be what he described as pagination—the use of computerized full-page photocomposers or plate-making machinery to eliminate manual pasteup. Ungaro was managing editor of the *Evening Bulletin* in Providence, Rhode Island when he became involved in the research of pagination. The first research of this kind was carried out by Dr. Hans Andersin, of the University of Helsinki, Finland, while he was at Brown University.

Dr. Andersin's original research was based on the following criteria:

1. Pagination should be a by-product of the normal layout work of an editor.

2. The layout editor should have complete control over the appearance of the page except for the positioning of advertisements.

3. The number of pagination stations in the editorial department should be large enough to give each layout editor immediate access to his pages without having to line up for a station.

The computer layout system would be programmed to perform such functions as sizing, cropping and correcting photographs, writing and fitting headlines, considering various story arrangement alternatives, creating and keeping track of jumps, and trimming and editing text. In addition, it will be able to replace already-made-up stories with new ones for later editions.

This computer layout system is now in operation at several newspapers. It was developed by Hendrix Electronics of Manchester, New Hampshire, on specifications from the Gannett Westchester Rockland Newspapers, which introduced it in 1980. Through the following pages and illustrations, Joseph M. Ungaro describes his perception of the system, especially as it affects the work of newspaper designers.

## ANALYSIS OF A PAGINATION SYSTEM
### by Joseph M. Ungaro

The 1970s became the decade of the front end systems—computer-directed systems for the creation, storage, and manipulation of text. These systems used optical character readers or Video Display Terminals for input and retrieval of material from the computer and the editing of that text. During the 1970s, second- and third-generation typesetters were developed. The third-generation typesetters provided the ability to typeset a column of type in just one minute.

For the designer, this decade opened new doors of typesetting flexibility as well as greater control of the text.

The historic process of having a printer rekeyboard the creative work of reporters and editors was eliminated. The editor assumed total control of the text from creation to typesetting.

The editor now could call a story up on the Video Display Terminal screen, put in some typesetting commands, and compose the text. The computer would hyphenate and justify the text and return it to the screen, showing the editor how each line justified and the precise length of that story in that type size and width.

If not satisfied, the editor could change the codes and reset the type in seconds in a different size and width.

Indents, initial letters, wrap-arounds, and a host of other typographical devices became easy. The design flexibility introduced with cold type grew easier and the potential for more design innovation expanded. The editor and the designer moved closer to total control of the printed page.

## The Age of Pagination

The 1980s will bring that final step. The decade will be the age of pagination, the electronic camera and darkroom, and the laser platemaker.

The page designer and creator will be like the painter; he or she will execute the page totally.

Pagination is the art of layout of a page. In the computer age of the 1980s it will be done with Video Display Terminals that are interactive: one terminal—just like the ones used in the 1970s—and a second one that will reproduce the face of the layout sheet proportionally.

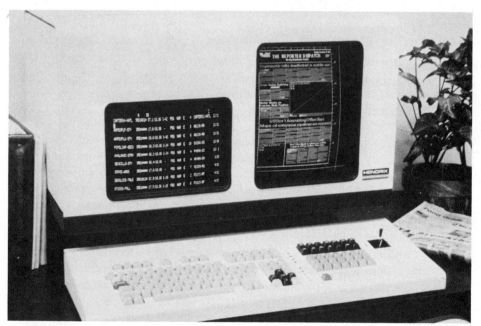

Double-screen Video Display Terminal, developed by Hendrix Electronics, shows news budget (left screen) and full-page layout.
(Courtesy of Hendrix Electronics, Manchester, New Hampshire.)

The concept of using the computer and Video Display Terminals has been under development since 1975. The Westchester Rockland Newspapers began working on the pagination concept at that time with Dr. Hans Andersin, who assisted with drafting specifications from which Hendrix developed the pagination system.

The concept gives the editor total control of the layout. Just as the painter works directly on canvas, the designer of the 1980s will work directly on the page.

## Total Control

The designer will no longer have to turn the layout over to a compositor to execute. This should provide new avenues of creativity, avenues which come at a time when newspapers face the challenge of attracting young readers who grew up as the children of the

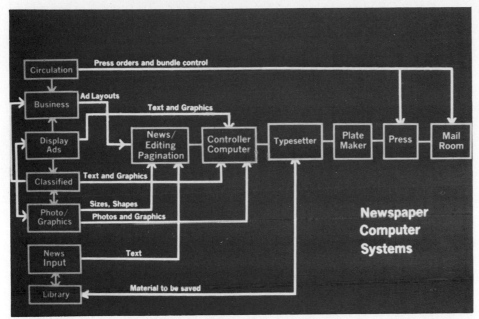

Chart displays how the computer layout system operates, providing for effective interplay of the various subsystems within the newspaper.

television age. Having grown up exposed to visuals, these young people have generally found the typography of newspapers too gray and too dull.

Pagination will be the tool of the 1980s to meet this challenge.

The interactive pagination system also will fill the role of the key element—in effect, the heart of the production system of the decade—pulling together all of the computer-directed subsystems of a total electronic newspaper.

The electronic newspaper of the 1980s will be a series of subsystems. On small papers, each function will have its own computer, and in some cases, backup computers.

For example, in a small paper one computer may serve the classified business office and circulation functions. But on a very large paper, two computers may be needed to serve the circulation department.

The subsystems and the functions they will provide are

● Circulation system: list of all subscribers, list of all nonsubscribers, all reader starts and stops, paid-in-advance or billing notices, all reader complaints on service, and demographics on the market; it produces manifests for each carrier each day, determines who gets what ad supplement, determines press order, and controls size of bundles in the mailing room route by route with direct links to the stacker.

● Business system: does payroll, does billing of all ads, pays all bills, provides daily layout of paper based on human intervention, provides all business records for advertising, circulation, and news.

● Display ad system: scans and displays ad graphics in position on tube; composes text of ads on tube; outputs text and graphics on photocomp for proofing, production, and storage; scans in all complete ads ready for use; creates classified display ads and sends them to classified system; sends an order information to business system.

● Classified system: inputs all liner ads, stores ads by publication date and category, sends billing information to business system, handles all legal ads and stores by publication day, organizes output and sends it in paginated form to controller computer at appropriate time.

● Photo and graphics system: receives all wirephotos; scans in local photos, art, logos; stores all photos and graphics; crops and enhances photos and graphics; tells appropriate system or controlling computer the sizes of photos and graphics for publication; outputs actual photos and graphics for pages to controlling computer; in future stores on disco photos and graphics needed for later use.

- News input system: receives reporters' input, wire input, copy from all non-premise remote systems; retrieves information from library; does preliminary editing of wire copy by news desk, and preliminary editing through city desk for local copy; outputs to news and editing pagination system.
- News and editing pagination: serves as hub of the electronic newspaper, receives page layouts from business office, receives copy from news input, receives photo and graphic sizes from photo and graphic system, lays out news text on pages, gives controller computer directions of preparing pages for plate maker.
- Controller computer: traffic cop for production of pages; organizes, schedules, and retrieves advertising editorial text and graphic material for output to laser plate maker; sends material after use to library for storage.
- Plate maker: using laser beams produces complete page to be placed on press manually; sends signals to press units for ink controls depending on density of photo for better reproduction.

The pagination system is at the center of the electronic newspaper because virtually every journalistic function is aimed at producing some part of the page.

Some examples: The display ad system must provide the pagination system with text for ads. The business system must tell it what ads must appear on what pages on what days. The input system must provide the text, the photo and graphics system, the pictures.

How will the interactive pagination system work?

The editor or designer sits at a work station (see illustration below) that has two terminals—one for editing and one for layout.

The editor calls up the page he or she is going to lay out. If it is an inside page, it would show the size and position of ads.

If it is an open page it would show no column grid. The editor would then tell the computer what column grid he or she wishes (that is, five column, six column, eight column, nine column, or any combination of widths that have been preprogrammed).

Then the editor calls up the directory of stories and pictures available for that page or section and begins to make selections and layout decisions.

The editor may select one story, give it a final editing, and write a headline. The headline is then composed by the computer. In seconds, the editor can see how it will fit. Thus the editor can keep changing the words until satisfied with the content and the fit.

The electronic age gives the editor great flexibility in headline sizes. In the era of the linotype, the headlines were generally in six-point increments (24, 30, 36, 42, 48, and so on). But with the computer the editor can just as easily have a 32- as well as a 37-point headline.

Then the editor begins the art of positioning the text.

Instead of estimating the length of the story and headline and dividing it by eight, for example, if the editor wants an eight-column square off, the editor types 5, 8, and hits a key called EXECUTE.

The computer then calculates the space needed for the headline and text, divides by eight, and shows boxes in proportion form on the layout screen.

If the editor does not like the look, he types ERASE and tries a different strategy.

If the editor wants to proceed, he types another command and the type flows into the box. It can't be read, but it does show the look of the page.

If the editor wants to read the text, he zooms in on a quarter of the page at a time.


## Other Computer Functions

Another approach is to design a page by drawing lines where the designer wishes the stories to begin and to end. Then the designer (editor) flows a story from the editing system into each box. If the story is too short, it shows how many lines too short. If too long, an arrow appears on the editing screen at the last line that fits.

The editor can have the computer perform many functions. By placing the terminal cursor at any point, it can create boxes or an irregular pattern for type.

The editor works back and forth between the editing screen and the layout screen to fit the page perfectly.

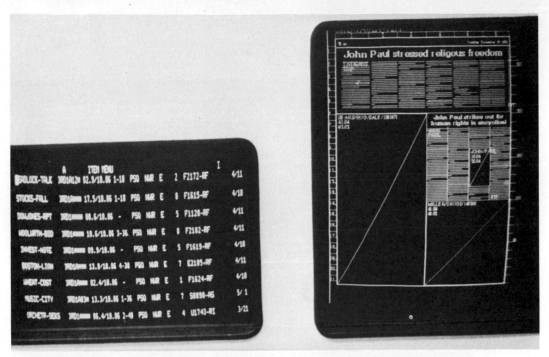

The editor (designer) calls the directory of stories (item menu on left of screen) and begins to make layout decisions through trial and error on the full-page screen (right). The computer calculates space needed for each story, headline, and photo and informs the editor of space availability.

In the 1970s the editor or designer created the page on a layout sheet, using as precise measurements as possible, set the type, and then went to the composing room to supervise the efforts of the compositor to make the type fit the created page design.

Under the pagination system, the editors use the computer to test the layout before the type is set and make sure everything fits as the designer wishes it to fit.

So the editor will have complete control of the page, leaving space for photos, graphic elements, and ads.

The display ads will come from the display ad system; the classified and legal ads, from that system.

The photo and graphics will come from another subsystem designed for that purpose. This system will include a very large computer (because pictures require more space to store than words) and Video Display Terminals with keyboards.

The photo editor will scan a photo into the system, then call it up on the screen, as illustrated below:

Then the photo editor will crop it to fit the space:

Then the photo will be enlarged:

The first photo and graphic system was installed by the Associated Press in the late 1970s. The illustrations in this chapter were taken from their system.

Widespread use of the photo and graphic systems is not expected until the midpoint of the 1980s because photo and graphic storage require much more computer space than words.

At some point late in the 1980s, the electronic camera will begin to be an important factor in newspaper operation.

**Electronic Camera**

An electronic camera—which takes a picture on a computer chip rather than film—has been developed for space photos by RCA and has been used experimentally by *National Geographic* magazine.

The electronic camera will require no flash bulbs because of extremely fast shutter speeds. It also will make possible the transmission of a photo over phone lines by a photographer to his computer. This will mean that just as the reporter transmits from a portable terminal in the field to his computer, so will a photographer transmit images.

**WHAT'S NEXT?**

Ungaro's detailed report on the new technology and its effects on newspaper design, as presented in this chapter, reveals the tremendous progress made by the newspaper industry toward full automation for all production. Ungaro feels that the next logical evolution in the 1980s in order to achieve total electronic systems will be the elimination of the typesetter.

The images for the page would be etched directly on a plate by a laser beam. This is likely to shorten the time span and eliminate some additional production steps.

Lasers are light beams used to scan images—photographs, pages, and other symbols—and to send the scanned results in digital form to cameras, to typesetting equipment, and to plate-making equipment (as described in this chapter).

Many newspapers use laser plate-making today; but they employ a pasteup of a page created through the traditional production steps. Ungaro feels that once the page can be created totally in the computer, typesetting will be obsolete. The computer will be able to send signals directly to the plate maker. "This is the reason pagination is the key to the total electronic newspaper of the future," Ungaro said.

If the pattern of electronic progression for the next ten years has any resemblance to that of the 1970s, then it is safe to assert that virtually every newspaper will use a computer to paginate by 1990.

In 1960 fewer than a dozen newspapers were using cold type. In 1980 every newspaper was on cold type. In 1970 less than half a dozen American newspapers and wire services were using Video Display Terminals. In 1980 virtually every one of the more than 1,700 dailies in the country had some form of computer front-end systems. Weeklies, too, had started to realize the benefits of computerized editing.

Of all the challenges facing newspaper editors, that involving adaptation of the new technological advances should become one of the most exciting. Ungaro sees pagination as a tool to provide the designer with the freedom and ability to control the layout of a page from concept to creation.

These advances will not affect the designer's creative process, which is likely to be enhanced as graphic journalists learn to understand the interface between technology and design.

Phillip Ritzenberg, assistant managing editor for design and production at the *New York Daily News,* emphasizes that the process that will not be programmed is the creative process.

> While our powerful text editing systems are helping us to get stories into type faster and helping make headlines fit, they cannot contribute to the well-crafted story or the headline that snares the reader's attention. The expanding new technology will take some of the drudge work out of producing a finished page, but it will not pick the stories and pictures and design an impelling page. The best we can hope for is to be able to put more time into the creative processes of news gathering, writing, editing and designing the newspaper of the 1980s.

## SELECTED READINGS

ARNOLD, EDMUND C. *Modern Newspaper Design*. New York: Harper & Row, 1969.

*The Changing Newspaper*. Associated Press Managing Editors Association, 1979.

CLICK, J. W., and GUIDO H. STEMPEL, III. "Reader Response to Modern and Traditional Front Page Make Up." American Newspaper Publishers Association *ANPA News Research Bulletin,* No. 4, June 4, 1974.

_____. "Reader Response to Front Pages with Four-Color Halftones." *Journalism Quarterly,* 53:736-738, 1976.

_____. "Rate of Adoption of Modern Format by Daily Newspapers." *ANPA News Research Bulletin,* No. 22, September 28, 1979.

*Computer-Assisted Layout of Newspapers*. Reston, Va.: ANPA, 1977.

CRAIG, JAMES. *Production for the Graphic Designer*. New York: Watson-Guptill Publications, 1974.

_____. *Phototypesetting: A Design Manual*. New York: Watson-Guptill Publications, 1978.

EVANS, HAROLD. *Newspaper Design*. New York: Holt, Rinehart and Winston, 1973.

GARCIA, MARIO R. "The Newspaper Editor as Graphic Strategist." *ANPA News Research Report,* No. 27, September 3, 1980.

HVISTENDAHL, J. K. and MARY R. KAHL. "Roman v. Sans Serif Body Type: Readability and Reader Preference." *ANPA News Research Bulletin,* No. 2, January 17, 1975.

NELSON, ROY PAUL. *Publication Design,* Second Edition. Dubuque, Iowa: William C. Brown Co., 1978.

*Newspaper Design*. Reston Va.: American Press Institute, 1978.

PRICE, HENRY T. "Front Page Design as Evaluated by the Newspaper Reader." *ANPA News Research Bulletin,* No. 7, June 28, 1973.

_____. "Some Possible Effects of Design on Readership." *ANPA News Research Bulletin,* No. 7, June 28, 1973.

*A Primer for the Newsroom on the New Technology*. Associated Press Managing Editors Association, n.d.

STONE, GERALD C., JOHN C. SCHWEITZER, and DAVID H. WEAVER. "Adoption of Modern Newspaper Design." *Journalism Quarterly,* 55:761-766, Winter 1978.

WEAVER, DENNIS, L. E. MULLINS, and MAXWELL E. McCOMBS. "Competing Daily Newspapers: A Comparison of Content and Format." *ANPA News Research Bulletin,* No. 8, December 31, 1974.

American Gothic

American Gothic

**American Gothic**

**American Gothic**

**American Gothic**

American Gothic

**American Gothic**

**American Gothic**

**American Gothic**

**American Gothic**

American Gothic

**American Gothic**

**American Gothic**

| Americana | Baskerville |
|-----------|-------------|
| Americana | **Baskerville** |
| **Americana** | **Baskerville** |
| **Americana** | **Baskerville** |
| **Americana** | **Baskerville** |
| **Americana** | *Baskerville* |
| **Americana** | **Baskerville** |
| **Americana** | **Baskerville** |
| Americana | Baskerville |
| Avant Garde | Bodoni |
| Avant Garde | **Bodoni** |
| Avant Garde | *Bodoni* |
| **Avant Garde** | **Bodoni** |
| **Avant Garde** | *Bodoni* |

appendix: a type sampler

*Bodoni*

**Bodoni**

Bookman

**Bookman**

*Bookman*

*Bookman*

Bookman

Bookman

*Bookman*

Bookman

Caslon

**Caslon Ad**

Caslon Antique

*Caslon Caps*

*Caslon Italic*

*Caslon Ultra*

**Caslon Ultra**

Caslon Ultra

Caslon Ultra

Caslon Ultra

Caslon Unique

Caslon Unique

Caslon Unique

Caslon Unique

**Caslon Unique**

**Caslon Unique**

Century Schoolbook          Compact

*Century Schoolbook*          **Compact**

**Century Schoolbook**          **Compact**

*Century Expanded*          **Compact**

**Century School**          Compact

**Century School**          **Compact**

Century School          **Compact**

**Century Shaded**          **Compact**

Cheltenham          Friz Quadrata

**Cheltenham**          **Friz Quadrata**

*Cheltenham*          **Friz Quadrata**

**Cheltenham x-23**          Garamond

**Cheltenham**          Garamond

**Cheltenham**          **Garamond**

**Garamond**

Garamond

Garamon

Garamon

Helvetica

Helvetica

Helvetica

Helvetica

Helvetica

Helvetica

Helvetica

Helvetica

Helvetica

**Helvetica**

Helvetica

**Helvetica**

**Helvetica**

Helvetica

**Helvetica**

**Helvetica**

**Helvetica**

**Helvetica**

Korinna

**Korinna**

**Korinna**

**Korinna**

Optima

Optima

**Optima**

**Optima**

**Optima**

*Optima*

Perpetua

Perpetua

Perpetua

**Perpetua**

**Perpetua**

**Perpetua**

Souvenir Gothic

Souvenir Gothic

**Souvenir Gothic**

**Souvenir Gothic**

Souvenir Gothic

Times Roman

**Times Roman**

**Times Roman**

Univers 45

Univers 55

**Univers 65**

**Univers 75**

Univers 53

**Univers 63**

Univers 63